Dark Mirror
The inner work of witchcraft

Yvonne Aburrow

By the same author

The Night Journey: Witchcraft as Transformation, Doreen Valiente Foundation in association with the Centre for Pagan Studies, 2020.

All acts of love and pleasure: inclusive Wicca, Avalonia Books, 2014.

Pagan Consent Culture: Building Communities of Empathy and Autonomy, co-edited with Christine Hoff-Kraemer, Asphodel Press, 2016.

The Endless Knot, Birdberry Books, 2012.

Many Names, Birdberry Books, 2012.

A Little Book of Serpents, Birdberry Books, 2012.

Dark Mirror: The inner work of witchcraft

First edition published by Birdberry Books, 2018.

Second edition revised and updated, 2020, published by The Centre for Pagan Studies in association with The Doreen Valiente Foundation.

Copyright © 2020 by Yvonne Aburrow
www.yvonneaburrow.com

Cover photo of a witch's mirror by Doreen Valiente. Star photo from Free Photos on Pixabay.

All rights reserved. No part of this publication may be reproduced, distributed, or transmitted in any form or by any means, including photocopying, recording, or other electronic or mechanical methods, without the prior written permission of the publisher, except in the case of brief quotations embodied in reviews and certain other non-commercial uses permitted by copyright law.

www.centre-for-pagan-studies.com

www.doreenvaliente.org

Praise for *Dark Mirror*

"*Dark Mirror* will make you think why as well as how you work your magic wherever you are on the rainbow of human experience. LGBTQIA+ needs, expectations and impressions have never been so well explored in all aspects of magical practice. This book is for absolutely everyone from those who have been leading a Pagan life for years as it reminds them and gives fresh options for doing things to the wonderful new generation of folk who are Witch curious. This is a very readable and reliable textbook for everyone to understand with ease."

> **- Geraldine Beskin,**
> **The Atlantis Bookshop, London, UK.**

"This is a book about transformation through ritual. Its scope is impressive and would be useful for both those new to practising contemporary Pagan witchcraft (or a similar path), and those who are more experienced practitioners. The discussion points, exercise, and further reading that conclude each chapter are useful and serve very well to support the chapter content."

> **- Julia Phillips,**
> **Postgraduate Researcher, University of Bristol, author of *Witches of Oz* and *Madeline Montalban, Magus of St Giles*.**

"Wicca meets critical theory in this transformative work, which updates Wiccan practices for the 21st century through radical inclusivity. Pushing well beyond "Wicca 101," this book gets at the heart of modern Pagan witchcraft and is recommended for both beginners and experienced practitioners."

> **Sabina Magliocco, Professor of Anthropology and Chair, Program in the Study of Religion, University of British Columbia, and author of *Witching Culture: Folklore and Neopaganism in America*.**

"Inviting us to examine many different aspects of Initiatory Wicca, this book is aimed at both initiates and non-initiates. It could certainly be used as the basis of a coven training programme but is also invaluable for the solo practitioner."

   - Morgana Sythove,
   Pagan Federation International
   https://silvercircle.org and https://wiccanrede.org

"Feeling the energy of the web of life is fundamental for anyone who wants to be a real witch. This book teaches how to do that. The web of life, of course, includes the world around us, the cycles of nature and our relationships with others. *Dark Mirror* moves on from explaining how to become more attuned to our own feelings, to ways of sensing the connection between ourselves and all of these seemingly external things."

   - Lucya Starza,
   www.badwitch.co.uk

"*Dark Mirror* is enchanting! It is a great learning tool for inclusive Wicca. I recommend it to all my students, and in fact, I am starting a book club teaching session with this book because the ideas presented are well thought out and researched. I especially love that each chapter ends with questions to be discussed, making it an easy reference tool to use when introducing someone to the Wiccan path. This book includes tables, and illustrations that help fill in the blanks and answers important questions. It allows students to think through the ideas presented and develop their own perspective on topics discussed. This book elevates Wicca to the next level, matching our modern perspective on humanity, where consent and equality become paramount values held up and venerated."

   - Lydia Knox,
   Gardnerian witch, artist, astrologer, medium, and empath. www.instagram.com/lydiaknoxart/

"In *Dark Mirror: The Inner Work of Witchcraft*, Yvonne Aburrow has managed to achieve what I assumed to be impossible. They wrote a book with value to both the novice and the seasoned witch alike. With a careful eye toward inclusivity and the politics of access, Aburrow offers an inside look at the Craft that is at once nuanced and historically accurate. They walk readers through important milestones such as picking a name while also showing them in vivid detail why these processes are magically and socially important. This book is a must read for anyone interested in Wicca, Paganism, or Western occultism in general. Aburrow's work reminds us to be critical of the legacies of power that haunt us all. If Aburrow is correct, and "the Pagan worldview has the potential to change the world," then Aburrow's work has the potential to transform Paganism into a more supportive and inclusive practice."

> **- Tim Landry,**
> **anthropologist and occultist.**

"*Dark Mirror* is an exploration of the 'inner work' of witchcraft, the internal processes which ritual sets in motion to initiate change and transformation, both within the ritualist and in the world around them. Over and beyond that central goal, though, the book is an outline of Aburrow's conception of Wicca as an inherently inclusive practice: anti-racist, queer-positive, sex-positive, and body-positive. The scope of what they cover is impressive, from basic techniques of ritual work to discussions of theological principles, all presented in a clear, pleasant writing voice reminiscent of Doreen Valiente, equal parts 'straightforward instruction' and 'chatting over tea and biscuits.' As an academically trained feminist nerd with a taste for systems analysis, this approach makes me positively giddy with delight."

> **- Misha Magdalene,**
> **author of *Outside the Charmed Circle: Exploring Gender & Sexuality in Magical Practice***

Dark Mirror
The inner work of witchcraft

Yvonne Aburrow

This book is dedicated to Leonora James

Dark Mirror

The sword-bridge is balanced between known and unknown.
We walk barefoot into the dark interior
on the slippery blade, between seen and unseen.
Deep waters below us, reflecting the moonlight,
Vast dark mirror of dreams, memories, reflections,
The alembic of change and of the inner work.
The witch works by starlight, navigates by instinct,
Across the inner seas, to find the hidden place
Where sweet waters and salt meet and mingle and merge.
Love is our compass, darkness our companion,
In the forgotten places and the endless woods
Where the Horned One and the Lady of the Moon
Call their hidden children to the Sabbat on the hill.

Yvonne Aburrow, 2016

*Photograph by Doreen Valiente of a witch mirror,
courtesy of the Doreen Valiente Foundation*

Foreword by Thista Minai 11

Introduction: the inner work 14

Part 1: Coming to the Circle............................ 23

1. The Pagan worldview 24

2. Creating sacred space............................... 34

3. Raising energy 45

4. Magical Names 57

5. Archetypes and the inner work 63

6. The Mysteries 80

7. Evocation and Invocation 87

8. Symbolism in Ritual................................. 99

9. Spell Work 122

10. Magical Tools....................................141

11. The Moon...153

Part 2: Embodied Spirituality.........................160

12. Relationships 161

13. Ritual nudity....................................194

14. The Erotic and Spirituality 205

15. The inner aspects of the festivals 222

16. Grounding and Centering 236

17. Making an Altar 238

18. The Fire and the Hearth 244

19. Food in ritual 251
20. Walking 261
21. Gardening 269
22. Spirits of the Land 274
23. Meditation, Visualisation, Contemplation, Prayer
.... 278
24. Creativity and Embodiment 292
25. Cultivating the virtues 316
26. Rites of passage 324
27. Inclusive Wicca 355
Conclusion 374
Further Reading 377
Thanks 385

Foreword by Thista Minai

A dark mirror is a tool that Witches use for scrying. Like so many terms in modern Witchcraft, "scrying" can mean many different things. Some people scry to learn the future, while others seek information about current events, places, or people. What separates scrying from other forms of divination is its overwhelming reliance on the person doing the scrying. Tools such as runes and Tarot cards present specific messages which are then open to interpretation by the diviner. Most scrying tools, by contrast, offer very little in terms of direction to the scryer. The crystal ball, for example, will always be the same sphere of crystal. What message appears within it must take shape in the scryer's mind. Thus, in the process of scrying a Witch will learn as much about themselves as they learn about whatever subject they are scrying on.

In my own training I learned the use of two different types of dark mirror. One was a flat piece of glass painted matte black on the back, and decorated with personalized sigils and symbols around the edge. Looking into this mirror, I could see a dark version of myself, and in meditation this became a shadow of my soul, daring me to acknowledge that which I would rather hide from knowing.

The other dark mirror was a concave piece of glass, again painted matte black on the back, but otherwise unadorned. This I was taught to use in a dimly lit room, for by tilting the mirror in just the right way, looking into it I would see nothingness. The mirror became an endless void, and with nothing left to distract my attention, I could finally hear what the shadows whispered to me.

Today's literary landscape for Witchcraft is a bit like the opposite of a dark mirror: rather than staring into a void, a seeker must wade through an endless tide of information. Within that tide will be the eddies of the misinformed, whirlpools of bigotry, and deceptively strong trendy currents. These are treacherous waters, but in that vast ocean of information seekers will find the primordial seas where magic's lightning can strike life into their hearts.

The key to that spark on the sea rests in how well a book challenges us to think about how and why we engage with Witchcraft, and how well we readers accept that challenge. In "Dark Mirror", Yvonne Aburrow has thrown down a metaphorical gauntlet, which we must eagerly pick up.

What does your Witchcraft mean to you? Is it radical? Political? Inclusive? Magical? Religious? Transformational? Earth-based? Whether or not you agree with Aburrow's interpretation of Witchcraft, asking yourself these questions is an essential process for every Witch. Aburrow's wild ride through a progressive, liberated, and inclusive form of Witchcraft will urge you to consider your own Craft, whether theirs resembles yours or not.

In this sense, Aburrow has chosen a perfect title for their book. I write this foreword not for those who will agree with Aburrow's perspective on Witchcraft, but for those who will not. Read anyway. Look into this dark mirror, and let it challenge your concept of self. Stare into the shadow of you that appears as you traverse its pages. Strip away preconception and listen in that void. Learn from the darkness of your reflection.

The legitimacy of Witchcraft as a modern-day religion rests not in pseudohistorical claims of an ancient legacy, but in *us*, the present-day practitioners, and how we craft our Craft. We must adapt and change along with the world we live in. We must grow to be better than our past.

Dare to peer into Aburrow's Dark Mirror. Hear a voice of radical inclusivity, and ask yourself: What kind of Witch do I want to be?

Thista Minai

August 2020

Thista Minai is the founder of Spectrum Gate Mysteries, and the author of *Casting a Queer Circle: Non-binary Witchcraft* and *Suffering for Spirit: Empowerment Through Ordeal*.

Photograph of Doreen Valiente's personal witch mirror, courtesy of the Doreen Valiente Foundation

Introduction: the inner work

The aim of this book is to introduce the concept of the inner work of ritual. When witches come together for ritual, we are not only performing the outward actions of ritual, such as lighting candles or reciting words. The words, symbols, and gestures are meant to create an inner process. I have observed that some witches spend a lot of time getting the words and gestures right, but do not focus on what is happening in the psyche of the practitioner. That inspired me to write this book. I wanted to explore the inner processes of ritual in a way that is inclusive of everyone (whether they are LGBTQIA+, disabled, or people of colour).

What is the inner work?

Inner work is a name commonly given to the inner processes that happen in ritual. It can also mean the transformation of the psyche that comes about through engaging in religious ritual. However, the best kind of inner work also has an effect outside the individual and outside the circle. When rituals are focused only on self-development, they tend to be a bit too introspective. Ritual is about creating and maintaining relationships and connections - between body, mind, and spirit, with the Earth, Nature, the land, the spirit world, the community, and friends. It is also about creating, maintaining, and restoring balance. It is about making meaning, telling our stories, and reclaiming our history from the oppressors. Witchcraft weaves a web of symbolism, story, mythology, meaning, community, and love to stand against the ennui and emptiness of relentless consumerism.

Witches create loosely held but welcoming community, a community that welcomes and celebrates diversity (of body shape, skin colour, physical ability, neurodivergence, sexual orientation, gender expression and identity, biology, cultural background, age, talkativeness or lack of it, and so on). Practising witchcraft can create a strong and authentic identity to resist the pressures of consumerism and commercialism and capitalism. Witches weave relationship with other beings: humans, animals, birds, spirits, and deities.

The inner work of ritual may be intrapersonal, interpersonal, restorative, or community-building. The kinds of relationships that ritual helps to maintain may be of various kinds - friendships, erotic relationships (including kinky ones), patron/client relationships. Inner work might be meditation, visualisation, prayer, magic, balancing archetypes within the psyche, lucid dreaming, healing, connecting with the body, or attuning to Nature.

There are many different techniques that we can use in the circle, but often they are seen as items on a magical checklist to be ticked off, as ends in themselves, whereas they can also be means to an end - the goal of enlightenment, the creation of meaning, or the restoration of harmony. The magical journey, known in alchemy as the Great Work, has the goal of restoring harmony to the world. Traditionally, the goal of witchcraft and shamanism is to maintain relationships and harmony with the spirit world, particularly land-spirits.

Ritual and the inner work

Ritual is a social activity, the creation of shared meaning. The inner work that we do in ritual helps us to connect with each other, with the gods, with Nature, and with the wider community. It helps to develop our empathy and compassion for all beings.

Ross Nichols once said, "ritual is poetry in the world of acts" - in other words, that it is the acting out of metaphor and imagery and myth. We do ritual not just for its own sake, but to create meaning and beauty and connection. But ritual is not merely the outward performance of the ceremony, or the actions or words that we present; it is also about the movement of energy among the participants and the shifting of patterns and processes in the psyche. That is the inner work of which ritual is the outer container.

I would argue that spirituality is not the same thing as the inner work. Spirituality is often done for its own sake, to 'be more spiritual', and often involves bypassing or ignoring real issues, denying strong emotions such as anger, and avoiding the real inner work.

The inner work is engaged upon to attain some other goal, such as being a more effective trade union caseworker, and sometimes happens anyway as a by-product of other activities. Doing the inner work of ritual will help you to become a more effective human being, a more effective activist; it is not about escaping from reality into some rose-tinted neverland. It will also make your rituals more enjoyable, as you will be able to engage in them more deeply, and (I hope) gain refreshment from them to do your work in the world.

Who is this book for?

Both beginners and more experienced witches can benefit from reading this book. Although the book starts from the basics of casting the circle and calling the quarters, it examines them from the perspective of the inner work and provides explanations of magical principles that include people of multiple genders and sexual orientations.

If you want to deepen your practice of witchcraft by understanding the inner processes that are meant to be triggered by the words, gestures, tools, and symbols that are used in witchcraft, then this book is for you.

The book is suitable for both initiates and non-initiates. It could be used as the basis of a coven training programme.

I hope that people from all witchcraft traditions will gain something from reading the book. Although my experience is Wiccan, and so I inevitably write from a Wiccan perspective, I am also a polytheist and a bisexual and genderqueer person, so I have some different ideas about the core ideas of Wicca and the magical concepts used in Wiccan rituals.

There is a difficulty with writing a book on Wicca or any tradition of witchcraft, that whatever you write, either non-initiated readers will think that what is presented in the book is the whole of witchcraft, or that initiated readers will think that the author believes that what is presented in the book is the whole of witchcraft. I have had conversations with people where they have read a book on Wicca by another author which made a specific claim, and the reader assumed that the assertion was true for the whole of Wicca. It did not describe the way that I operate, but I had some difficulty convincing the person of that – because the written word is often seen as authoritative.

Add to that the difficulty that you can find any number of people who assume that their version of Wicca or another form of witchcraft is definitive, and/or that everyone uses words derived from the Key of Solomon to consecrate the elements and call the quarters, and/or that everyone starts calling the quarters in the East, or assigns the four elements to the same cardinal directions. No, they do not.

Many books on Wicca claim that Wicca is duotheist (worshipping 'the God' and 'the Goddess'). In fact, Wiccans can be animist, pantheist, polytheist, duotheist, monist, or atheist. Some people even say "all of the above depending on the day" when you ask about their theology. So, books do not necessarily describe people's actual behaviour, values, and beliefs.

Add to that the fact that what is written down is only ever a description, a shadow, of the lived reality of ritual – and you come to realise that it is actually very difficult to write a book about witchcraft. It can only ever be a meta-description of the experience.

What is presented in this book is a set of spiritual and magical techniques and practises which would be of use to any practitioner of embodied spirituality, whatever type of witch they are. It is not a description of Wicca itself, or other traditions of witchcraft. These practices and ideas are widely used in various magical traditions and are not unique to any of them.

About me

I have been practising Paganism since 1985 and was initiated into Gardnerian Wicca in 1991. I got my second-degree initiation in 1996, and my third degree in 2014. I started my first coven in 2003, and have trained a dozen people in Wicca, each with their own unique perspectives. This book is the product of my experiences of ritual and training witches.

I started thinking about how to make Wiccan ritual more inclusive of LGBT+ people in 1995, as I am bisexual and have been genderqueer since before there was a word for it. I am still not sure if I am nonbinary or genderqueer or genderfluid (it depends on the day), but nonbinary is a good catch-all term.

I started thinking about how to make the Craft more inclusive of neurodivergent people in around 2003, when I was working with people with dyslexia. The product of both strands of thinking was my previous book on Wicca, *All Acts of Love and Pleasure: inclusive Wicca*.

It was quite a while before I realised that there were things about the Wiccan and wider Pagan communities that were excluding of people of colour – not least the way that deities tend to be represented as white-skinned.

From 2006 to 2008 I studied contemporary religions and spiritualities at Bath Spa University, and carried out research on queer spirituality, syncretism and dual-faith practice, and Pagan attitudes to science. The course also explored feminist spirituality, Paganism and the New Age, and the encounter between East and West.

My coven training methods have always focused on the inner work, but I am indebted to Geoffrey Samuel for the term 'inner work', as he chaired a strand entitled 'The Inner Work of Ritual' at a 2008 academic conference on ritual in Heidelberg, which I attended.

About this book

For me, the Dark Mirror is the surface of the unconscious beneath which we must descend to get in touch with the inner. I see a vast interior cave with an expanse of dark water, partially illuminated by the light of the Moon.

The first section of the book, *Coming to the circle*, looks at the inner work in the context of a ritual, and explores the inner aspects of what happens in a typical witchcraft ritual. The first chapter explores the Pagan worldview and how it is different from other ways of looking at the world; what is sacred to Pagans, and why. The first thing that happens in a witchcraft ritual is the process of creating sacred space, which is a protected space that symbolizes the sacred cosmos. Once the sacred circle has been created, we can raise energy within it. This might involve synergy, resonance, or polarity. The raising of energy is both intrapersonal and interpersonal. We tend to use magical names in circle, and these represent a different archetype or persona that we aspire towards; as such, they are an important aspect of the inner work. This leads on to looking at archetypes and how they impact on the inner work. One of the aims of witchcraft is an encounter with the Mysteries: the experience of the presence of the gods, and the joy that accompanies that experience. Gods and spirits can be encountered through the process of evocation and invocation. The other aspects of witchcraft rituals are the use of symbolism in ritual, the working of magic and spells, and the use of magical tools.

The second section of the book, *Embodied Spirituality*, explores the inner work in the context of the body, and how we relate to other people, both within and beyond the ritual circle, how we relate to Nature, to gods and spirits, to the seasons of the year, and to the land. The first chapter covers relationships and consent in Wicca, and how these might be managed in the context of Wiccan ritual and initiations; the second chapter looks at working skyclad, what it means and why we do it; the third chapter looks at the erotic and spirituality. The next chapter considers the inner aspects of the festivals, and how they relate to embodied spirituality. The following chapters deal with various embodied practices: grounding and centering, making an altar, the hearth as the focus of ritual and devotion, the place of food in ritual. Then we move out into Nature and look at labyrinths, meditative walking, pilgrimage, gardening, and spirits of the land. The closing chapters of this section deal with meditation, visualisation, and contemplation; poetry, storytelling, and reading; and the practice of cultivating the virtues.

Each chapter concludes with discussion points, exercises, and suggested further reading. I generally put the exercises at the end of the chapter because it is easier to find them again when you revisit the book later. Throughout the book, I have used the term 'inner work' interchangeably to mean both the inner processes that happen in ritual (such as visualisation, the movement of energies, invocation, and so on) and the process of transformation that happens in the psyche when we do meaningful ritual.

I hope that reading the book will encourage you to deepen and expand your Craft. I chose to practice witchcraft because I believe that the first step to changing the world is to change yourself, so I wanted a religion that would help me to function more effectively on all levels of reality: physical, spiritual, mental, and astral, and one that would acknowledge and celebrate all aspects of who I am - my gender, my sexuality, my body, and my mind. Your reasons for choosing witchcraft may be different, and are doubtless equally valid; if so, I hope you will still gain new insight from reading the book.

Part 1: Coming to the Circle

This section explores the inner work in the context of a typical witchcraft ritual: creating sacred space, raising energy within it, why we use magical names in circle, how we relate to archetypes and how they impact on the inner work. A ritual is an encounter with the Mysteries: the experience of the numinous.

1. The Pagan worldview

I believe that the Pagan worldview has the potential to transform the world. Many Pagans believe that Nature is in harmony with itself, and is a self-balancing system, so if we want humanity to survive and flourish, getting back into balance with Nature is the key to our survival and flourishing.

Pagans generally believe that the physical world is real, not illusory, and that the spirit world is immanent in, intertwined with, the physical. This is because we treasure physical existence and the pleasures of the flesh. Paganism is an embodied spirituality, and as such, physical existence matters.

Most Pagans, Heathens, polytheists, and animists believe that everywhere is sacred, but some places have a more numinous quality than others. I believe that places have more numinous qualities because they have been the focus of devotion towards, and conversation with, the genius loci, the spirit of place. The intensity of interaction with the spirit of place forms a nexus, or a greater weight of presence, in the place, and it becomes like a gravity well in the fabric of reality.

Einstein's Theory of Relativity pictures space-time as like a rubber sheet. Large objects such as stars and planets stretch the rubber sheet downwards, such that it makes it hard for an object to leave the space around a planet, because it becomes stuck in the gravity well around the object. I think of spirits of place in the same way: as being like a small planet in a gravity well.

The more conscious a place becomes, the 'weightier' it is, and so it attracts more devotion and more social interaction from people.

Spirits of place, and spirits of the land, are very important to Pagans. Most Pagans also care about the environment, ecosystems, trees, animals, birds, and flowers.

Responding joyfully to the sacredness and beauty of the physical world are a key aspect of Pagan values. This includes responding joyfully and gratefully to physical pleasures such as eating, drinking, consensual lovemaking, sacred sensual touch, and all the other wonders that being embodied brings.

Pagans' appreciation of being physically embodied means that our view of reincarnation is different as well - most Pagans look forward to being reincarnated, and some believe that it is our role to take care of the Earth and of sacred sites.

Things we care about

Pagans care about the same issues as many other groups – poverty, war, racism, homophobia, transphobia, the environment, saving indigenous lifeways, knowledge, and culture, women's rights, cruelty to animals, and so on. Like any other movement, there are many different opinions in the Pagan movement: some Pagans do not care about these things; some take a different view of them; and some care about them very much more than the average.

But there are some issues that are associated in people's minds with being Pagan, the two most obvious ones being environmentalism and feminism. Many people have claimed that Paganism is a Nature religion (and many others have claimed that it's not), and since Paganism and Nature-worship are synonymous in many people's minds, caring for the Earth seems like an obvious thing for Pagans to want to do. And since the Earth is often viewed as a goddess, or as the

Goddess, Paganism is an obvious choice for anyone who wonders why so many monotheists view their deity as exclusively male.

Environmentalism

Pagans care about the environment for many and varied reasons. Some people became Pagans because they care about the environment; others began to care more about the environment after becoming a Pagan. Either way, Pagans recognise that the Earth is our mother, and if we do not take care of her, we will all die, and so will many other species.

The causes of our current destructive course are many and complex. Some people blame capitalism; others blame consumerism; and others blame the dominionist views of conservative Christianity. I blame all three, and think they are historically interlinked.

Capitalism does not simply mean a market economy; it means the investment of surplus money in a business venture. This means that instead of being accountable to the whole community, a company becomes accountable to its shareholders, and shareholders generally want only one thing: a profit.

Consumerism is not simply wanting nice things; it is the view that only having nice things makes you happy, and the drive to acquire more and more nice things.

Dominionism is the view (a distortion of the book of Genesis) that God gave the Earth to humans for our use.

A major contrast with these views is deep ecology, which advocates the inherent worth of living beings regardless of their utility to human needs and argues that this requires a radical restructuring of modern human societies. This certainly chimes in well with the Pagan worldview, and I explored the ecological and embodied worldview in chapter 20 of my previous book, *All Acts of Love and Pleasure: inclusive Wicca* (published by Avalonia in 2014).

The language of ecology can be problematic, especially when it gets co-opted by business trying to preserve the status quo. Sustainability used to mean living in a way that prevents damage to the environment and loss of species habitat; now it has been co-opted to mean something like 'greenwashing' (paying lip-service to environmental concerns while actually continuing to act in a destructive way), or buying carbon credits and continuing to release carbon dioxide into the atmosphere. The "environment" implies something that surrounds us, but which we are not necessarily part of. We are part of the environment and of ecosystems; we are not separate from our habitat.

A group of Pagans (of which I was one) produced *A Pagan Community Statement on the Environment*,[1] which was translated into several different languages and reached around 5000 signatures. Whilst a statement will not fix things on its own, what it does is articulate the principles and practices which will help to fix things, and signing up to the statement means a commitment to its principles and to doing something for the planet.

Some people claiming to be adherents of deep ecology are also transphobic, homophobic, and racist, so be careful to examine the ideas of groups before supporting them.

---

[1] http://www.ecopagan.com/

Feminism

Some people became Pagans because they were feminists; others began to focus more on gender equality after becoming a Pagan. Either way, feminism is a natural bedfellow of Paganism, because most Pagan traditions worship a Goddess or goddesses, and value diversity and equality.

The roots of feminism lie in three simple premises:

- that women are equal to men,

- that women are not currently treated equally in society,

- and that we should do something about it.

However, as with any other philosophy, there is more than one flavour of feminism, because not all feminists necessarily agree on the correct tactics for getting rid of inequality, or indeed on who counts as a woman. I personally support trans-inclusive feminism.

Variants include: Amazon, Analytical, Anarchist, Atheist, Black, Chicana, Christian, Conservative, Cultural, Cyber, Difference, Eco, Equality, Equity, Fat, French, structuralist, Global, Individualist, Islamic, Jewish, Lesbian, Liberal, Lipstick, Marxist, Material, Maternal, Mormon, Neo, New, Postcolonial, Postmodern, Poststructural, Pro-life, Proto, Radical, Separatist, Sex-positive, Social, Socialist, Standpoint, Third world, Trans, Transnational, and Womanism.

Here are some of the ones that share concerns with Paganism:

According to Wikipedia,

> "Anarcha-feminism, also called anarchist feminism and anarcho-feminism, combines anarchism with feminism. It generally views patriarchy as a

manifestation of involuntary coercive hierarchy that should be replaced by decentralized free association. Anarcha-feminists believe that the struggle against patriarchy is an essential part of class struggle, and the anarchist struggle against the state."

Historically, anarchist feminists included those who advocated free love and campaigned against marital rape and the subjugation of women.

Black feminist theorists argue that sexism, class oppression, and racism are inextricably bound together. The way these relate to each other is called intersectionality, a theory which was developed by Kimberlé Crenshaw. The theory of intersectionality has been adopted by many other feminists and social theorists. Black feminism is sometimes referred to as womanism to distinguish it from feminism which fails to take racism into account.

According to Vandana Shiva, women have a special connection to the environment through our daily interactions. Eco-feminism considers our relationship with Nature, and the ecological knowledge and relationships developed by women over the centuries.

Again, caveat emptor, because there are feminists who are transphobic and essentialist in their views. Extreme transphobes peddle lies and hate about transgender people and endanger their lives by revealing their former identities.

Obviously, there are lots of other things that Pagans care about, but feminism and environmentalism are two areas that are fairly central to why so many people have joined the Pagan movement.

Pagan theology

Pagan theology is non-dogmatic, experiential, and descriptive. Usually people have an experience or perform a ritual, and then develop a theory to explain the experience. Quite often, Pagans will deny that this is theology – but to my mind, theology is any theory that seeks to explain the relationship of humans with the numinous.

The term theology was coined by the pagan philosopher Cicero in 49 CE, in his work of pagan apologetics, *De Natura Deorum* ('On the Nature of the Gods').

You are 'doing theology' whenever you explain how magic works, describe what you think a deity is, talk about the soul, or what happens after death. You are 'doing theology' when you wonder why bad things happen to good people.

Theology – and Pagan conversation in general – tends to confuse a lot of people because it involves specialised terminology. Here are some of the most common terms used in Pagan theology, with a short explanation.

Animism – the idea that everything (trees, rocks, animals, etc) has a spirit or a soul.

Apologetics – the process of explaining your religion to other people (not apologising for its existence!)

Dogma – theology codified as a compulsory set of beliefs, such as a creed.

Duotheism – the idea that there are two deities, a god and a goddess (sometimes expressed as "all the gods are one God, and all the goddesses are one Goddess").

Henotheism – the view that there may be many deities, but the henotheist worships only one of them.

Immanent – intertwined with or present in matter. Pagan deities, spirits of place, genii loci, land wights, etc are usually regarded as immanent.

Land wights (Landvættir) – a term used by Heathens to describe the powers and spirits of the land, who may protect whole countries, or smaller regions.

Monism – the idea that there is a single underlying unity of everything – spirit and matter are one substance.

Monotheism – the idea that there is only one deity, who is often, but not always, seen as transcendent.

Naturalism – the idea that there is nothing beyond Nature, and usually, no spirit(s) within Nature either.

Numinous – the power or presence or realisation of divinity; the experience of the supernatural or the preternatural.

Orthodoxy - a religion that emphasises that all its practitioners should believe the same set of ideas is orthodox.

Orthopraxy – a religion that emphasises that all its practitioners perform the same or similar rituals is orthopraxic.

Pantheism – the idea that deity (usually a single deity) is present in Nature, or in the universe.

Pantheon – a group of deities worshipped by a specific culture (e.g. the Greek pantheon, the Roman pantheon, the Norse pantheon, the Hindu pantheon).

Polytheism – the idea that there are many deities, with agency.

Prayer – having a conversation with, or communing wordlessly with, a deity or spirit.

Preternatural – a term suggested by Michael York to describe the experience of immanent spirits and deities. It can also mean 'strange and uncanny'.

Spirits of place – spirits of trees, rocks, and specific places, often guardians or protectors of the place (Latin: genii loci).

Supernatural – the idea that spirits and deities are transcendent and exist outside of nature.

Theology – a set of theories about the gods and our relationship with them (not necessarily dogmatic, as many different theologies can co-exist peacefully in non-dogmatic religions).

Transcendent – existing above or beyond something.

Epistemologically transcendent – the experience of something beyond the ego or larger than the individual, such as the sense of being swept away in a crowd.

Ontologically transcendent – existing beyond matter (usually referred to simply as 'transcendent').

Worship – A ritualised expression of respect and honour – offered to anything or anyone that you respect and honour.

Discussion

What do you think are the essential characteristics of a Pagan worldview?

What do you personally hold to be sacred?

What do you think is the goal of your personal spiritual path and/or the spiritual path of a witch?

How is witchcraft different from, or similar to, other Pagan religions?

Exercises

Draw a mind-map of what you think are the key ideas in your tradition.

Meditate on your path and its goals.

Meditate on that which you hold most sacred.

2. Creating sacred space

A sacred space is a space set apart, where we may encounter our deepest feelings about the world, the deities, spirits, and our relationship with them in a place of safety. Many Pagan traditions also work magic within their sacred space. Since we will encounter our deeper selves within our circle, it is important that we feel safe there. We strip away the mundane aspects of ourselves and show others our inmost selves.

Because Pagans create ritual in our own homes, or in the woods, or in spaces that may be used for other purposes, we re-dedicate the space each time a ritual is performed. This is both for the benefit of the participants, and to create the conditions necessary for the successful performance of the ritual.

Many religious traditions have some form of preliminary process for entering the ritual mode of awareness; they might start with a prayer, or asking the Divine to be present, or by lighting a candle to symbolise spirit.

Pagan creation of sacred space is often more elaborate, partly because the mode of ritual that is to be performed there is magical (wielding power) rather than liturgical (waiting for power to manifest), and therefore greater mental and magical preparation is required.

Very often, the sacred space is oriented towards a sacred representation of the cosmos. The creation of a Wiccan circle involves calling the four quarters, North, East, South, and West, and these are related to the four classical elements, Earth, Air, Fire, and Water. The four elements also correspond to seasons, colours, times of day, phases of human life, and psychological qualities.

The centre often represents spirit, and hence the central axis of the cosmos, which is traditionally seen as the means of access to the heavens, where deities dwell. In some cosmologies, the central axis is a mountain (Mount Olympus in Greek mythology, Mount Meru in Hindu[2], Buddhist, and Jain mythology). In other cosmologies, the cosmic axis is a tree (Yggdrasil in Norse mythology, Irminsul in Saxon mythology, a birch tree in Siberian mythology). The cosmic axis provides access to other worlds. In Norse mythology, the world tree, Yggdrasil, connects the underworlds (Niflheim and Helheim), the heavens (Asgard and Vanaheim), the world of the giants (Jotunheim), the world of fire (Muspelheim), the world of humans (Midgard), and the worlds of elves (Lightalfheim and Svartalfheim).

By creating a sacred space, we are orienting ourselves to these sacred cosmologies, and becoming a microcosm of them. By aligning ourselves with the cosmos, it is felt, we become one with it, and may wield its powers safely, and journey to other worlds within it.

In Wicca, the sacred circle is also regarded as a container for the power raised within it. The circle is regarded as a semi-permeable boundary. It is required to keep bad energies out, and to act as a container for good energy, until the power raised is sent out to do healing or other beneficial magic.

---

[2] Mount Meru, *Encyclopedia Britannica*
http://www.britannica.com/EBchecked/topic/376478/Mount-Meru

The shape of the ritual space is also important. The focus of the participants' attention in a circle is the centre of the space (once the quarters have been called and the sacred space has been aligned with the cosmos). People tend to gravitate towards standing in a circle, as they can make eye contact with each other, and read each other's body language. This is important for creating a sense of tribe or community and building trust.

In Quaker meetings, the participants sit in a circle or a square facing inwards, as they are trying to achieve a 'gathered silence' in which the numinous may make itself felt (and different Quakers will talk about the Inner Light, or the Spirit, or - if they are Christian Quakers - the presence of Christ). Once the gathered silence has deepened, the participants will begin to offer ministry - communication channelled not from the ego, but from the collective unconscious, which is connected to the divine.

In sacred buildings where the congregation sits in rows and faces the worship leader, there is less scope for eye-contact, and less opportunity for individuals to contribute, unless they are invited up to the lectern to speak, which some people find intimidating. This type of space can also be used to emphasise hierarchy, by demarcating areas which are only for the priesthood. However, you can get more people in the sacred space by arranging them in rows. They are also facing the altar, the pulpit, the iconostasis, the mihrab, the *Guru Granth Sahib*, or the *Sefer Torah*, depending on the religion, and all of these could be regarded as gateways to the divine realm [3]. In

---

[3] Irvine, Hanks, and Weddle. 2012 'Sacred Architecture: Archaeological and Anthropological Perspectives' pp.91-118 in

Orthodox Christianity, the iconostasis is not regarded as a barrier between the congregation and the inner sanctum, but the royal doors opening on the divine realm.

In a circle, however, the gateway to the numinous is wherever the attention of the group is focused at the time. If a magical practitioner is calling a quarter, they are opening a gate to the realm of the element associated with that quarter and direction. If a deity is being invoked, the gateway to the numinous becomes the person into whom the deity is being invoked.

When we consecrate something, we enter into a relationship with it, and dedicate it for ritual use. Once a stick has been consecrated, it is not just a stick, but a wand. Once a knife has been consecrated, it is not just a knife, but an athame or a burin. The same is true of sacred space - when it has been consecrated, it is not just somebody's living room, but a temple.

When ritual takes place outdoors, perhaps in a grove or a stone circle, the space is already sacred by virtue of the trees or the stones. It may have been used for ritual before. It is a good idea to ask the spirit of place for permission to do ritual there. It is also generally agreed that there is less need for elaborate consecration and purification.

To make a Wiccan circle sacred, it is first cleansed of all negativity by sweeping the circle, and then a boundary is created around it by focusing energy to form a circle. Next, the

---

Archaeology and Anthropology: Past, Present and Future. Association of Social Anthropologists monograph. http://nick-hanks.co.uk/research-projects/doorways-to-the-divine/

circle and the participants are blessed with symbols of the four elements (water, salt, incense, and flame). In outdoor rituals, some would say that water and salt and incense are unnecessary.

To make an object sacred, it is purified and blessed with symbols of the four elements, and often given a name. The blessings of the deities are asked for, so that the object may fulfil its new sacred purpose well.

If you are lucky enough to have a dedicated temple room, you can make it extra special by decorating it with pictures and symbols of your favourite deities, sacred places, and so on. You can also build altars for the seasonal festivals, for specific deities, or for the four elements. If these images are placed in the sacred direction with which they are associated (such as images of water deities in the west) then even more associations can be built up with the directions.

When Wiccans enter a sacred circle, we leave our personal baggage behind - but we do not leave our identities behind. When we enter the circle, we bring our whole selves into the presence of the deities - our identity, our gender, our sexual orientation, our politics, our concerns for the Earth. We leave behind petty worries so that we can focus on the magic and ritual - but we do not leave behind our core identity. Once we are in the sacred circle, we may set aside trivial concerns such as what we plan to have for dinner, what a colleague said to us last week, and so on - but we do not leave behind our core identity.

When calling to the quarter elementals and spirits, first make a connection with the beings of that element. Open your arms wide, as if you were opening a pair of doors, and imagine a thread of attention or energy reaching out from your heart to the horizon. Only when you feel that you have made contact with those energies should you start the actual words of the quarter call. It is also a good idea to invite the beings of the element politely to your circle - less of the peremptory summoning, more of the inviting, as you would with a friend. The elemental beings are powerful entities in their own right, not servants.

A Wiccan circle is a meeting point between the worlds, a place where we come into close contact with the realm of the unseen. It behoves us to enter it with honour and humility, mirth and reverence, strength and beauty, power and compassion within us.

How to call a quarter

There are many ways to call a quarter, but all of them have a common aim: to make a connection with the element.

What is a quarter?

The quarters are called 'quarters' because they divide the circle into four equal parts.

Before you start, what is your underlying theology of what you believe the beings associated with the four directions to be?

Are they an alchemical elemental (a gnome, sylph, undine, or salamander)?

Are they one of the classical four winds (Boreas, Zephyr, Notus, and Eurus)?

Do they have genders?

Do they have agency and personality?

What is the nature of their consciousness?

Where do they reside (the Otherworld, your subconscious, the surrounding natural world)?

Are you calling ancestors and/or the Mighty Dead instead of, or as well as, the four classical elements?

If you are a Druid, are you giving peace to the quarters? What does that mean to you?

All of these will affect how you call, and what words and gestures you use.

If you are calling one of the alchemical elementals or the classical four winds, use symbolism appropriate to them in your quarter call. For the four winds, use their names. If your quarters are a different group of named beings, address them by name too.

Do your quarters have gender? If not, then either address them as "powers of the [element]", or as "Lords and Ladies of the [element]". I prefer the former, as it acknowledges the existence of nonbinary genders.

Do your quarters have agency and a personality? If they do, it is probably a good idea to ask them politely to come to your circle, rather than summoning them peremptorily.

On a related note, there's no need to shout at the quarter; just project your voice so that the people behind you can hear your quarter call (this is necessary if you're facing towards the edge of the circle and away from the rest of the participants in the ritual).

What is the nature of an elemental spirit's consciousness? Can they pay attention to you and your circle alongside all the other tasks they have to do? Are they a multitude? Or do you just see them as archetypes?

Do you believe that there is a higher and lower aspect of the elemental being? If you do, then you may want to use something based on the Lesser Banishing Ritual of the Pentagram, which banishes the lower aspects before calling the higher aspects or angels of the elements. You can find various versions of this ritual online [4].

Where do they reside? This will affect how you imagine the elemental beings "arriving" in your circle. If they live in the nature around you, maybe they are just focusing part of their attention on your circle for a bit. If they are coming from the Otherworld, then you might visualize them coming to this plane of manifestation.

If you are just trying to make a connection with the physical elements, then it is a good idea to have a bowl of earth, a bowl of water, a candle, and some incense and/or feathers to represent each of the elements.

I envisage the Otherworld as being entangled with this world, so I tend to visualize the elemental coming through a sort of wormhole/stargate type thing.

If you are calling other beings (the ancestors or the Mighty Dead), where do you envisage them coming from? Do you call

---

[4] https://hermetictimes.org/2019/12/24/the-lesser-banishment-ritual-of-the-pentagram/

them by name? Again, it is best to avoid summoning them peremptorily or shouting at them.

If you are giving peace to the quarters, how far does it extend? How do you visualize sending out peace?

The actual call

The call itself consists of multiple parts:

The inner work; sending out the energy; contacting the entity; the gesture of calling; the verbal call.

The inner work consists of creating your inner process of yearning and calling to the element.

It is hard to do all these things at the same time, so it is a good idea to separate out the energetic process from the verbal call and the gesture.

Start by taking a moment to feel present and ready.

Then do the gesture that goes with the call (this could be drawing a pentagram in the air, opening out your hands as if you're flinging wide a pair of doors to let them in, or a dance that represents the movement of the element).

Take a moment to feel or send your sense of connection out towards the element and sense their presence.

After you have done that, speak the words of the evocation (the call to the quarter).

Remember that all this outward show is mostly for the benefit of the rest of the participants, so they know when you have finished speaking.

It is possible (and a good idea) to call the quarters silently and without words sometimes, so that you can practice doing the inner work and making the energetic connections.

Discussion

Examine the way you learnt to create sacred space.

What is the purpose and function of each part of the process?

Is it for preparing the participants or the space?

Is it for clearing away negativity, or for bringing in positive energy?

Do participants feel safe within the space?

Who creates the sacred space?

Does it get dismantled at the end of your ritual?

What theological or cosmological concepts underpin the way you create sacred space?

Does your sacred space align to your sacred cosmology?

What about how you close down sacred space? Do you uncast the circle **deosil** (clockwise, in the direction of the Sun's apparent rotation around the Earth) or **widdershins** (anticlockwise, in the opposite direction to the Sun's apparent path)? Why?

If you are in the southern hemisphere, is your deosil actually anticlockwise? What about the way you say farewell to the quarters? Are your closing words different depending on whether the ritual was primarily magical or celebratory?

Exercises

Experiment with different ways of creating sacred space.

Try moving the altar, or the focal point of your ritual - do you prefer it in the centre of the circle, or the North, or some other direction?

Try calling the quarters starting in a different direction. How do these changes affect the energy?

What is the simplest way to create sacred space? Can you pare down your circle opening to a very simple creation of sacred space?

Try setting up your ritual space completely silently, just focusing on the energies.

Try varying the way you close your circle - how does it affect the energies?

3. Raising energy

There are many ways of raising energy in the circle. When witches talk about raising energy, we mean creating a heightened sense of presence, movement, and power within the circle. It is hard to describe unless you have experienced it.

You can raise energy by dancing, drumming, chanting, making love, meditating, creating a gathered silence, using polarity, synergy, or resonance, focusing energy from the universe, and so on.

Robin Goodfellow (1629) [5]

Dancing, Drumming, and Chanting

There are several traditional witches' dances, which have been passed down among Wiccans, and maybe other witchcraft traditions too. Not all of them involve dancing in a circle.

---

[5] "Puck 1629" Licensed under Public Domain via Commons

One of my favourite lesser-known dances is described in *The Penguin Book of Witches*. It involves all facing outwards from the centre of the circle, linking arms, and dancing. I am not sure how well this would work, though.

Another dance that can raise energy without making you horribly dizzy is to link hands and rush inwards to the centre of the circle.

The point of dancing in a circle is to get the energy moving in a circle, and to raise a cone of power. You can also visualise the power moving in a circle, using everyday images, such as winding thread onto a bobbin, to help you.

Drumming can raise energy, create specific atmospheres, and set the tempo for dancing[6]. Shamanic practitioners use their drums as a horse to carry them to the other world on the rhythm of the drumbeats. Drumming rhythms can also be used for healing, and for meditations and visualisations[7].

One thing to be mindful of when using drumming is that not everyone has a sense of rhythm (I don't have one) and not everyone is physically able to dance - so if you are planning an extended drumming session in your ritual, warn everyone in advance - or restrict it to a shorter section of your ritual, so as to include everyone.

---

[6] Patti Wiginton (undated), Hosting a Drum Circle, http://paganwiccan.about.com/od/wiccanandpaganrituals/ht/DrumCircle.htm

[7] Sourcerer (undated), *Harnessing and Using the Energy Created by Drumming*, http://healing.about.com/od/drums/a/drum_meditate.htm

Chanting is also a useful tool in the ritual toolbox, and especially repetitive chanting, which helps to distract the chattering part of the mind (the bit of yourself that worries about what you are going to have for dinner, or starts thinking about what you are doing at work, or whatever else distracts you). Sometimes just chanting a single word, or the name of a favourite deity, can really get you into an altered state.

Repeating a word or phrase on the in-breath and out-breath is a meditative technique used in many different spiritual traditions.

Other, more complex chants and songs are also available, and they are a great way to raise energy. Rhythm and music stimulate the right hemisphere of the brain, the twilight consciousness, the poetic side of our natures, which is the aspect of the psyche that we use in witchcraft and magic.

Polarity, Resonance, and Synergy

Polarity is the idea that magical energy can be created by bringing together two things which are opposite in nature. In Wicca, many people take the view that the ultimate form of polarity is male interacting with female - or more subtly, yin interacting with yang. This surprises me greatly, as I would say that the ultimate polarity would be self and other, or something and nothing, or force and form, or spirit and matter. In my experience, we all contain many different energies, identities, and impulses within ourselves, and these can be used to generate magical energy even within our own psyche, and even more so when interacting with complementary energies, identities, and impulses in others.

The implication of this is that you can make polarity with any complementary opposite. In fact, at Witchfest [8] in 2015, I was talking about different opposites that you can use to make polarity, and I mentioned tea-drinkers versus coffee-drinkers; people who like Marmite and people who don't; cat-lovers versus dog-lovers; morning people versus night-owls. I had been planning to use morning people versus evening people to raise energy in the ritual, but the one that got the biggest reaction was Marmite. So when it came to the ritual, the people who like Marmite stood on one side of the room and thought about Marmite on hot buttered toast, and those who don't like Marmite thought about chocolate instead, as it seemed important to give them something nice to think about, instead of asking them to think about how much they hate Marmite. A few people changed sides when the other group decided to meditate on chocolate. This polarity created lots of energy.

The Marmite/chocolate polarity does not work so well outside of Britain (because other cultures have less experience of Marmite), so another polarity you could try is morning people and evening people. I did this with a group at a festival in Canada, and it worked very well. One group went off to enthuse about morning, and light, and whatever it is that morning people get excited about. Those of us who were night owls conjured up images of late-night conversation around the fire, stars and planets in the night sky, and the joys of sleeping in late. When we brought the two groups who were making morning and evening energy back together, there was a huge yin-yang symbol in the middle of the circle.

---

[8] An annual gathering for witches in England

Magical polarity can be created by any pair of things that are widely viewed as complementary opposites. Inner and outer, up and down, spirit and matter, lover and beloved, dark and light, masculine and feminine, camp and butch, air and earth, water and fire, monogamous and polyamorous, sexual and asexual, extrovert and introvert, and so on. And each pair of opposites is unique and cannot be mapped to other pairs of opposites.

You do not need to make explicit what aspect of the self you are using to make polarity. The aim of the exercises I have described above was to make people aware that polarity is not only made by bringing male and female together, but can be made by any pair of opposites.

I have begun to doubt that male and female are opposites at all; the qualities traditionally ascribed to masculine and feminine vary between cultures, and if male/female polarity were based purely on biology, then surely I could make polarity with any person who was assigned male at birth - but I don't find that to be the case, so something else must be happening.

Polarity exists on a spectrum, too. (It is not the same as duality, where two absolute qualities are viewed as opposites.) A person can be more yang than another person; but they can be yin in relation to a different person. People become a different polarity in relation to different people.

We need a more complex view of energy than a simple binary. Polarity is a spectrum and is not immutable; it can shift and change depending on your mood, on the situation, an on who or what you are interacting with. If you are heterosexual or bisexual, it is a lot easier to make erotic polarity with somebody of a different biological sex than it would be for someone who is not attracted to the other sex. That is not to say that it's impossible for a gay or lesbian person to make polarity with a person of the other sex, but it is much easier for them to make erotic polarity with someone of the sex or gender they are attracted to. Why? Because creating polarity has many components: the erotic, romantic, respect, friendship. It can be done without any erotic attraction, but the more of these elements are present, the easier it is to make a connection.

It is also important to recognise that polarity can be created without any erotic attraction to being present, as this is helpful for people on the asexual spectrum. You can make polarity between an extrovert and an introvert, or a morning person and an evening person.

So why would we restrict people to making polarity with only one of these possibilities (a male body plus a female body) when there are so many other possibilities available, and when so many people just don't fit into these categories? I personally do not experience male and female as being opposites at all.

As a society, we place undue emphasis on the sex that a person was assigned at birth, even though sex is assigned based on seven different biological characteristics, which can vary considerably.

Why would people hamstring LGBTQIA+ participants in ritual by preventing us from using the whole spectrum of polarities, energies, and connections available? And why privilege heterosexual polarity over all other forms of polarity? Why make magic and ritual much easier for heterosexual participants and place a barrier in the way of LGBTQIA+ participants? Same-sex magical partners also experience erotic polarity - but maybe it works differently, as Ed Gutierrez suggested [9]. He described a mirroring effect between two people who are similar, where energies are amplified between two people, like two mirrors facing one another.

I also described polarity in terms of mirrors, in a 1999 article entitled *Between Mirrors*. [10]

> As a child I was fascinated by the experience of standing between two mirrors, and looking at the room reflected in the mirror, reflected in the other mirror, and so on to infinity. I suggest that polarity is like this. ... where does female stop and male begin? The one is reflected in the other, to infinity. The black dot in the middle of the Yang half (and the white dot in the middle of the Yin half) can also be represented as another Yin Yang symbol, which also has its dots in each half, which are even smaller Yin Yang symbols, and so on into infinity.

Every time someone says that we must stand boy-girl-boy-girl in the circle, I feel that my bisexual and genderqueer identity

---

[9] Eddy Gutierrez (Hyperion), Episode 52 – *Polarity, Gender and Magic*: Hyperion answers a question submitted by Peter Paddon of *The Crooked Path* Podcast on Gender and Polarity in Magic. https://itunes.apple.com/us/podcast/the-unnamed-path/id214830491?mt=2

[10] Yvonne Aburrow (1999), <u>Between Mirrors</u>, *Queer Spirit*. http://pagantheologies.pbworks.com/w/page/25793251/Between%C2%A0Mirrors

is being erased and denied. It must feel even more erasing if you are gay or lesbian.

No one is saying that straight people must learn new ways of making polarity if they do not want to, but LGBTQIA+ people want to be able to make polarity in all the ways available to us. And we would like for our sexual orientations and genders not to confer second-class citizen status in the circle.

In many spiritual traditions, the goal is to transcend the gender binary and create a new synthesis of energies in the psyche. This synthesis is sometimes known as the Divine Androgyne, or the mystical marriage in the psyche.

As Lynna Landstreet so brilliantly put it, for her the ultimate polarity is not male and female, but the lightning striking the primordial waters and creating life. [11]

And the most inclusive way to express the concept of polarity is to talk about the lover and the beloved, or me and you, self and other. In the creation myth of the Feri and Reclaiming traditions, the first being becomes aware of Hirself, looks into the curved mirror of space, and forms a dyad of self and other, me and you. This too could be viewed as the ultimate polarity.

A friend of mine described polarity as 'the most overused word in Wicca'. There are, after all, other ways of making magic. There is also the synergy of all the energies in the circle coming together. Polarity is what happens when you work

---

[11] Lynna Landstreet (1993/1999), *Alternate Currents: Revisioning Polarity: Or, what's a nice dyke like you doing in a polarity-based tradition like this?* Copyright 1993 by Lynna Landstreet. Originally appeared in The Blade & Chalice, Spring 1993. Slightly revised in 1999. http://www.wildideas.net/temple/library/altcurrents.html

with a magical partner, to be sure, but often everyone in the circle works together to create energy. You can feel that this has happened when you feel connected to all the other people in the circle, and it feels as if you are in the midst of a warm glow and the energy is 'more than the sum of its parts'. Dancing in a circle, chanting, and all being focussed on the same thing (such as calling a quarter) can involve synergy - all the participants in the ritual working together as a harmonious whole.

Most of the time, we do not bother to analyse how we are making magic, or to explicitly work out where the polarity or resonance comes from. However, it can be a useful magical exercise to explicitly identify a particular polarity or resonance and work with it, to get people used to the idea that the source of your energy might be all sorts of things, not only being male or female.

What if your partner (magical and/or sexual partner) does not feel like an "opposite" for you at all? For example, if you are both femme-identified, or both introverts, or both morning people? Clearly in this instance, some other magical connection is at work, or perhaps just the simple and beautiful polarity of lover and beloved, constantly interchangeable between the two partners.

The other magical connection that is at work here could be the synergy of like with like, which was given the name resonance by Eddy Gutierrez of the Unnamed Path [12].

---

[12] Episode 61 – Resonance: A Gay Alternative to Polarity, https://itunes.apple.com/us/podcast/the-unnamed-path/id214830491?mt=2

In fact, if we look back to older occult ideas such as sympathetic magic, action at a distance, and so on, we can see that resonance is quite an ancient concept.

In sympathetic magic, the underlying idea is that if you act upon an object that is like the object you are trying to affect, the other object will be acted upon.

In the concept of action at a distance (which looks a lot like quantum entanglement), if you link two objects together, they will remain linked no matter how far apart they are moved. So, if you act on one of them, the other one is affected.

In the hermetic principle of correspondence[13] ("as above, so below"), there are hidden connections and similarities between similar things on different planes of existence.

The hermetic principle of vibration asserts that everything vibrates with energy; this principle supports the idea that if you bring two things into resonance with each other, you will amplify the vibration.

Whilst these are not the same concepts as resonance, they do bear some similarities, and serve to illuminate how resonance might work.

If two similar people work together to create magic, they can create resonance, where 'like vibrates with and amplifies like'.

---

[13] *The Kybalion: Hermetic Philosophy, by Three Initiates* (1912), http://www.sacred-texts.com/eso/kyb/kyb04.htm

Discussion

Have you experienced polarity, resonance, and synergy in your magical workings?

What pairs of similarities have you found that can create resonance?

What conditions are best for creating synergy in a group?

What pairs of differences have you found that can create polarity?

Do you experience a polarity with members of the other sex, or your own sex?

If you experience polarity with members of the other sex, do you think it is because you are different sexes, or for some other reason(s)?

If you experience polarity with members of your own sex, what differences can create that spark for you?

Is an erotic connection, or a potential erotic connection, required for you to be able to make polarity or resonance?

What methods of raising energy work best for you?

Exercises

Try creating polarity in a way other than the ones you normally use. Divide your working group into two groups such as extroverts and introverts, morning people and evening people, Marmite lovers and chocolate lovers, or tea drinkers and coffee drinkers. Get them to focus on the thing they love, and when both groups have reached some sort of crescendo, bring the two resulting blobs of energy together and observe the magical effect.

Try creating synergy with someone like you. Bring your energies together and perhaps hum together or brush each other's auras. Make balls of energies with your hands and bring them together into a single blob of energy.

Create a ball of energy and pass it around the circle. This is great fun and builds the group mind and the magical focus of the coven members. You can make a ball of energy by grounding and centering to focus energy in your belly, and then directing the energy you have made down your arms and out through your hands, then shaping and moulding it like Play-Doh / Plasticine.

Place a cauldron in the centre of the circle. All the members of the coven now focus their energy into the cauldron, visualising it swirling and growing in intensity.

Dance in a circle and visualise a cord of energy coming off each person, and winding onto a large bobbin in the middle of the circle.

4. Magical Names

Words and names have power. In many mythologies, the world came into being at the utterance of a specific word or sound. A magician who knows the true names of things has power over them. That is why, in *A Wizard of Earthsea* and *The Rule of Names* by Ursula Le Guin, everyone has a secret name, and a nickname by which they are usually known. Traditionally, Romani mothers give their children three names: a secret name whispered in the child's ear on giving birth, and again when the child becomes an adult; a name which they are known by among their own tribe; and a name for use among the *gadjo* (non-Romani) [14].

Why have a Pagan name?

Many people decide to have a Pagan name because they want to celebrate an aspect of Nature with their name. Hence people choose the names of plants, animals, or birds that they particularly like. Fortunately for me, the name Yvonne means 'Yewtree' anyway. My last name is probably derived from the Anglo-Saxon for fortified town *(burh)* but it may just possibly be derived from the Anglo-Saxon for burial mound *(beorh)*, though in that case my last name would probably be 'Berrow'.

There are many reasons why someone might want a Pagan name: to feel more in touch with a particular deity, animal, bird, or tree; to emphasise a quality that you possess, or to

---

[14] These practices are not known to all Romani, and are less widely practiced nowadays, according to a library of Romani culture at the University of Graz. Names of Roma. http://rombase.uni-graz.at/cgi-bin/art.cgi?src=data/ethn/topics/family-names.en.xml

which you aspire; to celebrate a connection with a particular animal, bird, plant, place, or being that you already feel.

Choosing your own name is a powerful magical act. Sometimes a name is suggested to you by others; if it feels right, go for it. Youi should have at least a couple of weeks to choose your witch-name; it is an important thing and you need to have time to mull it over. Sometimes the name only fits in a specific group or context. I am known by a nickname to a specific group of people, and it feels very odd indeed if anyone outside that group uses that nickname.

Using a pseudonym

When I wrote my first book [15], back in 1992, I considered using a pseudonym. Ironically enough, when it was published, some people apparently thought that Yvonne Aburrow was a pseudonym.

At that time, many Pagan authors used pseudonyms, because it was still legal to discriminate against Pagans at work in the UK, and everybody could still remember the 'Satanic Panic' in which fundamentalist Christians tried to convince social workers that there was an epidemic of Satanism in the UK, and that Pagans were Satanists.

Fortunately, the 2003 legislation on religious discrimination in the workplace [16] means that Pagans in the UK are protected by employment law. Pagans were explicitly mentioned in the

---

[15] Yvonne Aburrow (1992), *The Enchanted Forest: the magical lore of trees*, Capall Bann Publishing

[16] http://www.legislation.gov.uk/uksi/2003/1660/regulation/2/made

ACAS guidelines [17] on the Act, which have the same force as case law in the UK.

Employers should be aware that these Regulations extend beyond the more well-known religions and faiths to include beliefs such as Paganism and Humanism. The Regulations also cover those without religious or similar beliefs.

It is not necessarily the case that Pagans are protected by law from discrimination in the workplace in other countries, however. Some Pagans may still feel the need to use a pseudonym.

When creating a pseudonym, it is always a good idea not to use the pseudonym to claim a living ethnicity that you do not possess. Refrain from making up a fake Native American name, or a fake Celtic name. It is tacky, and it is cultural appropriation, and it is potentially fraudulent. It is okay to create a Latin pseudonym, because no current ethnic group uses Latin, so it is obviously not intended to be fraudulent.

Why have a magical name?

In initiatory Wicca, a witch-name or magical name is generally used only in circle, and known only to other initiates. The candidate for initiation is invited to choose a name prior to first-degree initiation.

When a witch is in circle, and using a witch-name, it feels as though we have stepped into our magical persona or power. Now we are ready to do magic and have entered sacred space

---

[17] http://www.acas.org.uk/media/pdf/f/l/religion_1.pdf

and sacred time. The magical name can reflect qualities we aspire to, or beings to whom we feel connected.

I read a book by Alan Richardson once, in which he suggests the following for "taking off" your mundane name and "putting on" your magical name in circle. What you do is intone your mundane name, knocking off one letter at a time, like this:

Y V O N N E

Y V O N N

Y V O N

Y V O

Y V

Y

Then build up your magical name one letter at a time. Imagine that my magical name was Yewtree:

Y

Y E

Y E W

Y E W T

Y E W T R

Y E W T R E

Y E W T R E E

Alternatively, you can just introduce yourself as your magical name once the circle is set up. Remember to reintroduce yourself as your mundane name at the end, to signal that you have re-entered the usual reality.

How to choose a name

Not many people know immediately what their magical name should be. I had been given a name as a sort of joke a couple of years before my initiation, and when I was invited to choose a name, that was the one that immediately came to mind. I considered a few others, but that name kept coming back to me, so I stuck with it. I have never regretted it.

That said, I would advise against just choosing the first name that comes to mind, or that sounds cool. And I would advise against using an internet name generator – fun though they are to play around with.

Some people get their names in a dream; others choose their names from mythology or from Nature. Using the name of a major deity is regarded as a bit hubristic, and somewhat risky in that you are taking on the whole archetype of that deity. Minor deities and spirits, human heroes, plants, birds, animals, and abstract qualities are generally regarded as a better source of names.

Meditate on what qualities or virtues you want to embody, or which you find yourself embodying a lot of the time, and think about what animal, bird, plant, or mythological person best represents that quality. That will probably be a good source of potential names.

Once you have found the right name, you will know, because it will just feel right.

Discussion

Is it appropriate to have a deity name as your magical name? What issues could this cause?

Do you feel people should be able to change their magical name if they have outgrown it? If so, when?

Should you choose your own magical name, or should it be suggested to you by someone else?

Should the coven name be kept private to the coven and those who visit the covenstead as guests?

Exercises

Create a ritual based on your magical name and present it to the rest of your coven as an esbat ritual.

Create a ritual based on the name of your coven, and use it to welcome new initiates, or new members, to the coven.

Create a ritual procedure for 'putting on' your witch name at the beginning of a ritual, and 'taking it off' at the end.

5. Archetypes and the inner work

The word archetype is derived from Greek, and the word literally means a 'primitive model'. It first appeared in English in the mid-16th century, derived via Latin from Greek *arkhetupon* meaning 'something moulded first as a model', from *arkhe-* 'primitive' + *tupos* 'a model'.

Contrast this with stereotype, which means a mass-produced image, and was introduced into English via printing, where it meant a solid block for printing an image. It was first used in the sense of 'over-simplified idea of the characteristics representative of a group of people' in 1922.

According to Jungian psychology, the psyche consists of the conscious mind and the unconscious mind. The unconscious is linked to the collective unconscious, in the same way that a well is fed by the water underground. Archetypes have their origin in the collective unconscious. They surface from the unconscious, sometimes as the Shadow, the Golden Shadow, the Anima, or Animus. The ego sits on top of the well of the unconscious like a lid of stone.

Archetypes and symbols

According to CG Jung, there are three levels of symbolism: personal, cultural, and universal.

Personal symbolism is the meaning that things have for you. A specific object, plant, tree, or symbol might have associations for you, because of an experience that you had relating to it, or because it reminds you of something. Personal symbolism does not necessarily have any meaning for anyone else unless they happen to share those associations or experiences. Personal symbolism can also form the basis of new and interesting metaphors and imagery in poems and stories.

Cultural symbolism is the set of symbolic associations something has within a culture. Different colours, animals, birds, and images mean different things in different cultures.

Universal symbolism is a symbolic association that appears to exist independently of culture, or that occurs in all cultures. Universal symbolism is generally derived from our perception of the world around us and how we relate to it. Mountains and trees generally symbolise the cosmic axis, though various mountains and trees have this role for different cultures. Examples of universal symbolism include archetypes such as the Great Mother, Water, the Shadow, the Hermit, the Wise Old Man, the Tower, the Tree of Life. Many of them are found in the Major Arcana of the Tarot.

According to these theories, archetypes exist on the level of universal symbolism. Archetypes are the images and ideas that underpin our imagery of deities. I am not suggesting that deities are only archetypes; rather that we relate to them on an archetypal level. Deities as we perceive them have been described as "possibly anthropomorphic interfaces of vast cosmic forces", and we often perceive them and experience them in and through the depths of the psyche, which is where archetypes can also be found.

Many mystics take the view that it is in the depths of the unconscious that we meet the Divine (and that has been my experience too). We enter the vast interior of the heart, and there we meet the realm of the gods, the Divine, the Goddess - however you conceive of the ultimate, the ground of all being.

Martin Laird[18] (a Christian mystic) calls it 'the silent land' and 'a sunlit absence'.

What is mysticism?

Common features of different descriptions of the mystical journey are the sense of descent into one's inner world, which is also connected with the vast interior space of the collective unconscious or the Divine; the realisation that one is inwardly connected with everyone else; the experience of encountering the Void (often including the setting aside of the ego); then entering into a larger consciousness (sometimes described as theosis). These experiences are probably more accessible if one takes the view that the Divine is accessible through inward contemplation; that the whole of reality is suffused with the Divine presence; that we ourselves carry sparks of the Divine. But sometimes people go through these processes of inner transformation in spite of having very different ideas of the nature of reality - which is what suggests to me that they are intrinsic to the functioning of the human psyche and its relationship to the universe.

An engaged mysticism is more interested in the practice of compassion than in achieving rarefied spiritual states. However, the two approaches go hand in hand – you cannot practice compassion unless you are also at peace with

---

[18] Martin Laird (2006), *Into the Silent Land: A Guide to the Christian Practice of Contemplation,* Oxford University Press.
https://books.google.co.uk/books?isbn=0199779430
 Martin Laird (2011), *A Sunlit Absence: Silence, Awareness, and Contemplation,* Oxford University Press.
https://books.google.co.uk/books?isbn=0195378725

yourself; and you cannot be at peace with yourself unless you practice compassion. You cannot separate the inner work from the outer work because your inner state and the outer world are intimately connected.

If we do not descend into our own depths and engage with the inner work, we are constantly confronted with the contents of the unconscious as they arise from the psyche in response to triggering events from the world around us, and so we find it difficult to be compassionate towards others, as we are too busy projecting our inner archetypes on them, and embroiling them in the dramas that we constantly replay in our minds. However, if we learn to recognise our projections and identifications, and if we allow this unconscious material into the light of consciousness, then we can control how we respond to other people and be compassionate towards them.

Perhaps the experience of constantly being bitten by the contents of the unconscious as they arise from the psyche is one of the ideas behind the Tarot card of the Fool, who represents the one who is about to embark on the spiritual journey. He is often depicted with a dog at his heels; sometimes the dog has even torn a chunk out of the seat of the Fool's trousers, exposing his bare behind.

The Fool Card from Jean Noblet's deck (1650).[19]

Projection and identification

We relate to other people on an archetypal level until we get to know them as individuals. Archetypes can overshadow our perception of a person, causing us to dislike them intensely, because we are projecting our Shadow onto them, or fall madly in love with them, because we are projecting our Anima or Animus (a possible term for a genderqueer, nonbinary, or gender-neutral inner archetype of a lover could be the Animex) onto them.

---

[19] Tarot of Marseille, by Jean Noblet and Jean-Claude Flornoy Own work. Licenced under CC BY 3.0 via Wikimedia Commons

Jung described many archetypal images, including the Fool, the Trickster, the Mothers, the Hermit, the Wizard, and so on; but he identified several that are often found within the psyche of the individual. These are the Shadow, which represents all the aspects of ourselves that we do not like, and which we have repressed; the Anima/Animus, which represents the other gender qualities that we find attractive; the Golden Shadow, which contains all the qualities we admire[20], but do not believe that we ourselves possess; the Inner Child, which is all the childlike and childish qualities we possess (play, innocence, petulance, and so on); and the Wise One, which is the wise and parental aspects of ourselves.

When we fall in love, we tend to project the Anima or Animus on them (with a certain amount of overlap with the Golden Shadow). Suddenly everything about the beloved is admirable, and we find ourselves almost seeing the world through their eyes.

When we take an instant dislike to someone, it is often because they are a good match for some shadow-aspect of ourselves that we have tried to deny and repress. The presence of the irritating quality in ourselves is reflected in them, and this pushes our buttons.

When we admire someone deeply, or recognise them as wise, it is often the case that we also possess the good qualities of the admired person, because we are projecting the Golden Shadow or the Wise One onto them.

---

[20] Thanks to Jim Blair for introducing me to the Golden Shadow concept.

When we find someone with whom we can be playful and light-hearted, we are letting our Inner Child out to play.

However, sometimes our projections of archetypes onto others are not a good fit, and we must withdraw them, and find out what the person is really like underneath. If you find yourself attributing motives and thoughts to others when you cannot possibly know whether they really have those motives and thoughts, you may be projecting an archetype. This applies to both negative and positive thoughts and motives that you believe they have - it might be believing that they return your love or believing that they are deliberately provoking or attacking you.

In Reclaiming witchcraft, they describe Talking Self and Younger Self. Talking Self is the bit of the psyche that tries to distract itself with chatter and can communicate verbally; Younger Self communicates through visual imagery.

Wiccan ritual involves a lot of work a lot with archetypes and the psyche, so projections and identifications and transference can occur. One of the prerequisites of inner work is an awareness of Jungian archetypes and how people project them on each other. It is possible to over-identify with an archetype. Because of this, it is a good idea not to always invoke the same deity, or the same type of deity, on the same person. For example, if someone feels very attracted to the Morrigan, and wants to aspect her a lot, they should also balance this with a different goddess such as Rhiannon or Blodeuwedd. If they always want to call the same quarter or avoid another quarter, ask them to reflect on why this is, and get them to call all the quarters, or a different one.

The aim of working with archetypes is to bring these unconscious structures into the conscious mind where you can work with them. Rather than being dominated or overshadowed by the archetypes, we bring them into the light of conscious awareness. Once there, we can see that they are not as mysterious and alluring as they seemed, and we cease to be ruled by our projections of archetypes onto others and move beyond simple identifications with them.

If we do not move beyond the archetypal level of existence, we find ourselves repeating the same patterns over and over again - the same type of job, the same type of lover, the same type of friends - until we recognise and identify the pattern and its source in some long-buried trauma, and stop recreating it in each new situation that we meet. Think of all the times you have repeated a pattern in your life. What did you do to escape from it? How did you break the cycle and move on? What patterns are you currently repeating?

Ritual roles and archetypes

Ritual roles are often allocated according to gender, but this does not need to be the case. Allocating roles by gender seems a lazy shorthand for the archetypes you want the ritual role to express. There are so many different archetypes, and not all of them are gender specific. How about if we allocated ritual roles according to the archetype they are intended to embody, or the skills that are needed for the task at hand?

In inclusive Wicca, we try to avoid allocating ritual roles by gender, but I had not thought very hard about how to allocate ritual roles until I read Thista Minai's excellent book, *Casting a Queer Circle*. Instead of focusing on who does what in circle, they have focused on what needs doing in a ritual, and what type of skills would be best to enable those tasks to be performed effectively. So, the roles in ritual are allotted to people with the skills that best fit those roles (instead of trying to match tasks to outdated ideas of gender). The role of Greeter reminded me of the coven role of Fetch or Summoner in some forms of witchcraft; the role of Guardian reminded me of the Tyler in Freemasonry.

Some of the skills that are necessary in ritual are:

- setting up the ritual equipment – altar, tools, candles, incense, props
- creating and holding safe space
- putting people at their ease
- leading guided visualisations
- extemporising and improvising
- reciting learnt words
- invocation (giving and receiving)
- evocation
- consecration
- spell work
- moving energy around

None of these seem particularly suited to one gender or another. In inclusive Wicca, a person of any gender may do these tasks. For example, casting the circle is not restricted only to priestesses, as it is in some circles.

Different people have different sets and combinations of skills, and just because a person has one skill, does not mean they necessarily have an apparently related skill. For example, I build websites, but I am not skilled at public relations or marketing.

Outside the circle, you need someone to organise the meetings, someone to write and plan rituals, and someone to organise the sharing of ritual texts, training materials, and so on.

For specific roles in a ritual drama, I usually let people pick the roles they want, though sometimes I do it at random, and sometimes it is necessary to cast people as the opposite of their normal inclinations (for example, if they always want roles associated with Water, get them to play a role associated with Fire) to balance things out.

Each role in a ritual drama is usually related to an archetype, such as the Trickster, the Wise Person, wildness, the planetary archetypes, the seasons, the four elements, a specific deity, or a specific quality. Sometimes you might pick the person who best embodies this quality; at other times you might get people to play a different archetype than the one they often express.

For other roles in ritual (consecrating, casting the circle, leading visualisations etc), I encourage all the participants to develop all the necessary skills. Obviously, everyone has an area where they are particularly comfortable and find certain things much easier than others; but it is also good to develop skills in other areas.

Some people do not like the very gendered terms 'priest' and 'priestess'. Different solutions have been offered to this problem. One is not using the words 'priest' and 'priestess' at all. The solution embraced by the Reclaiming Tradition is apparently that everyone is a priestess regardless of their gender. Another solution is to use the word 'priestex' or 'priestix' (although *-ix* is a feminine suffix in Latin).

Personally, I like the word priestess because it is unique to Pagan traditions. The word priest has been used by other religions, but priestess is ours, and it sounds all mysterious and full of numinosity to me; so that is why I am happy to apply it to myself, even though I am nonbinary. However, I refer to myself as a poet, not a poetess. Language is messy and fluid. If a word does not work for you, then use a different word.

Another great coven role that is gender-neutral is the coven fetch (traditionally, a messenger to other covens), and the summoner (this role is usually found in folkloric witchcraft covens).

The Myers-Briggs Type Indicator can be a useful tool for assigning people to ritual and coven roles, but it is good to take it with a pinch of salt. I usually come out as an ENFP on the test, but my results are borderline (51% extrovert and 49% introvert, for example). It is based on Jung's idea that people experience the world using four main psychological functions – sensation, intuition, feeling, and thinking – and that one of these four functions is dominant for a person most of the time. People who are predominantly thinking types have trouble accessing their feelings; people who are predominantly intuitive have trouble analysing things; and so on. You may need to take this into account when allocating ritual roles, if the role calls for a skill that the person struggles with.

The most important thing is that people should get to experiment with different roles and do not get saddled with the same or similar roles for a long time. Keep checking in with people that they are comfortable with the roles allocated and vary the method of allocating roles.

Exploring the psyche: exercises and visualisations

The Inner Child

Visualise a place where you liked to play as a child - a park, a meadow, a garden, the seaside. Take the time to recreate the image of yourself as a child and inhabit that smaller body and perspective nearer the ground. Remember the view of adults' legs as you walked through a crowd. But now you are alone in the place you liked to play, and you are free to run and jump and dance, climb trees, invent elaborate games, play hide and seek, whatever your favourite game was. Revel in a childlike sense of freedom and wonder. Explore the world around you with fresh eyes. Feel time slowing down, moving like a slow river. Those endless afternoons of childhood.

When you have finished exploring and playing, cup your hands over your eyes, then reopen them, and then take your hands away (this is a gentler way of opening your eyes after a visualisation).

The Shadow Exercise

Think of someone you know that you dislike, or possibly hate. Write down a description of that person. What is it about this individual's personality that you do not like? Be as specific as possible.

Then draw a box around what you have written, and at the top, write "MY SHADOW."

These characteristics will be the hidden and repressed aspects of yourself, that you dislike, fear, cannot accept, or hate. Maybe you really need to express or develop those aspects of yourself. Maybe you dislike those characteristics because they represent some quality you want but believe you cannot have.

The Golden Shadow Exercise

Think of someone you know that you admire, or even hero-worship. Write down a description of that person. What is it about this individual's personality that you admire? Be as specific as possible.

Then draw a box around what you have written, and at the top, write "MY GOLDEN SHADOW."

These characteristics will be the hidden and repressed aspects of yourself, that you admire, are in awe of, cannot accept, but do love. Maybe you really need to express or develop those aspects of yourself. Maybe you cannot believe that you possess those characteristics because they represent some quality you want but you are afraid of the potential change that owning that quality or acting upon it would bring.

The house with nine rooms

You are in a square white house with nine rooms. Wander from room to room. Note how you feel in each room. Is there another floor – above or below? What objects are in each room? How do the rooms relate to each other? The centre room may be a small courtyard with a pool and a tree.

Archetypes visualisation

It is twilight. You are standing in a sacred grove, trees all around you. Look at the trees and touch their bark. Feel the earth beneath your feet, the cool grasses brushing against you. Smell the breeze and listen to the wind rustling the leaves of the trees in your grove.

Now look beyond the grove to the landscape beyond. Ahead of you is a small hill. As you walk towards it, you see an opening in the side of the hill, with a low stone doorway – two uprights and a huge lintel. A small ochre-coloured stone stands outside, with three bands of red around it, and moss around its base. You may pour a libation here if you wish.

You stoop down to enter the doorway and find yourself in a tunnel which goes upwards into the hill. It is not too dark, as there seems to be a light source up ahead.

Eventually you emerge into a big open space, and as you stand blinking, your eyes adjusting to the light, you see that there are two people in the cave: an old person and a child. They are sitting by a fire, which reflects its warmth and light onto their faces.

Look at the old person: how are they dressed? Take their hand: how does it feel? Look into their eyes, listen to them, talk to them, give them a gift. Perhaps they will give you a gift.

Now the child: how is it dressed? What will it tell you? Talk with the child, look into its eyes. Maybe you exchange gifts.

And now, look into the fire, and notice how its dancing flames form shadows on the walls of the cave: hairy arms, hands, tongues, and beast shapes rise up and flicker on the walls of the cave. They are scary but you have the reassuring presence of the old person and the child.

And now you look again into the flames and see a person forming in the fire, beautiful and golden. The person rises out of the fire, the embodiment of your inner self. The person smiles at you. Gaze into their eyes, let your gaze caress them, but do not touch.

In turn, the firelight illuminates a deep pool at the back of the cave. Its dark waters are smooth and peaceful, rippling gently towards the shore, as the pool is fed by a spring.

You see that the moon has risen and is shining through a small opening in the roof of the cave and is reflected in the dark water. You can stoop down and drink the water. Feel the silver moonlight filling you.

Now it is time to go, and when you turn around, you see that the flames have died down to embers, the fire being has disappeared, and the old person and the child are two stalactites in the cave.

You turn and walk back down the passage, stoop low to go out of the entrance, and are back on the green slope of the hill. Ahead of you is your grove.

Walk back to the grove, greet the trees, and sit down once more on the earth. As you sit, close your eyes, and feel yourself gradually returning to this place and this time and this room.

The sea-cave

You are descending a slippery, dark, winding stair. Down into the earth and the darkness, down and down and down. The only sound is the far-off dripping of water, the only light is the faint glimmer of phosphorescence. Down and down you go into the earth, down into the cold and dark. At last you come to a great cavern, filled with dark water. Above you, you can hear waves booming on the cliffs, and you know that this deep cave must be connected to the sea. The dark water stretches away in front of you, very cold and very deep. It is entirely still, like a mirror, but every now and then a drop of water falls from the roof far above, and a circular ripple shines softly and dimly in the darkness, illuminated by some unknown light source. The water is dark as ink, and you feel afraid. Dive into the water.

[Long pause – can stop talking here if required and let people free-visualise before bringing them back out of the water and up the winding stair.]

You find that the water is cold but refreshing. As you become accustomed to it, you open your eyes and see that all is bright beneath the surface of the water – blue and silver and turquoise and green, and in some places all the colours of the rainbow woven together – the ocean of the streams of story – a many-coloured land beneath the wave. You swim on and on, and out of the winding tunnel that connects the cave to the ocean, and then play and tumble in the great rolling waves, riding the surf, letting the salt sea enfold you and caress you.

(You can meet a sea deity here, e.g. Njörð, Manannan.)

You become one with the sea, you are the water. As you are swept up on the crest of a wave, you are carried up into a cloud, then fall as rain in the mountains, run down into caves, then rise up into the world as a bubbling spring, and run gurgling and chuckling over the rocky stream bed and down to the sea again. Return to your body at this point. Return to the room and fully conscious awareness.

(Do not do the above until you are ready to dive into the subconscious.)

You can record these visualisations before doing them if you want to, but personally I prefer not to record visualisations, as for me, the tinny sound of the recording is off-putting. I made the imagery simple enough that you will probably be able to remember a rough outline of the visualisation.

Discussion

List symbols that have resonance for you. What do they represent for you?

Find images that represent the Animex, Animus, the Anima, and the Shadow for you. (NB – these may change over time)

Make a list of film or novel characters that represent different archetypes

List qualities that you admire, and people who possess these qualities. Can you recognise any of these qualities in yourself?

List traits that you dislike. Can you recognise any of these traits in yourself? Are you projecting them onto others?

List qualities that you find attractive. Can you recognise any of these traits in yourself?

6. The Mysteries

Wicca is often described as a mystery religion. What is meant by this is that it is an esoteric and initiatory tradition in which encounters with the divine realms cannot be fully described in words, only experienced: they are ineffable.

In ancient Greece, there was two classes of secrets in the mystery traditions: that which must not be spoken (*aporrheton*), and that which cannot be spoken (*arrheton*). [21]

Ultimately the word 'mystery' comes from the Greek verb *myein*, to close or to shut. This implies initiates keeping either their mouths or their eyes shut.

Aporrheton - that which must not be spoken

Things which must not be spoken about were the secrets of the tradition. They could be described in words, but it was not permitted to do so because the secrets were the techniques by which the mysteries could be accessed, and without proper preparation for an encounter with the mysteries, a person could be overwhelmed.

In contemporary mystery traditions such as Wicca and Feri and other witchcraft traditions, many of the rituals, symbolism, and techniques are secret for this very reason. It is difficult to write a book on the inner work of witchcraft and avoid writing about the secret techniques and symbols. Many people, on reading this book, will assume that what is described here is the totality of witchcraft. However, I have avoided revealing initiatory secrets. The techniques described

---

[21] Thanks to James Butler for introducing me to the concepts of *arrheton* and *aporrheton*.

in this book will form an excellent basis and on-going practical support for the work of initiatory witchcraft: but these are the techniques that are not secret. Many of these techniques are used in witchcraft rituals to prepare the participants for ritual. But this book will not tell you how to do an invocation of a deity, as that is something that can be an overwhelming experience, and requires proper preparation, which includes initiation into the mysteries.

The secrets of the tradition are the tapestry of symbols and meanings that are woven together to form a matrix in which to ground the experiences and encounters we have. One of the best reasons for keeping them secret is to prevent them being misappropriated by people who would use them out of context, denuding them of meaning and power by trying to use them in another paradigm where they do not fit.

Arrheton - that which cannot be spoken

Things which cannot be spoken are unutterable, ineffable, the mysteries. They cannot be described, only experienced directly. If you want to experience the mysteries, the presence of deities, the feeling of unity with all that is, then the best way to do that is to get initiated and join a mystery religion.

The experience of meeting a deity, or having a deity invoked into you, is profound and transformative - and it is different for everyone. If I described how it feels for me, then my description would act as a filter for your experience, as you might start looking to see how your experience matches mine, or differs from mine - and then you are observing yourself experiencing the experience, instead of experiencing it directly, and most importantly, as a fresh experience, unmediated by someone else's view of it.

Once you meet other people who have had the experience, it is possible to discuss it and gain some idea of how it feels for other people. Once you are at a certain level of understanding and shared symbolism, that makes it easier to communicate about these experiences, too.

Another profound and ineffable experience is the experience of being initiated - which is also different for everyone and should be unmediated by others' descriptions of it. The same applies to initiating someone and how that feels. It does feel like a big responsibility and a very important connection with your initiates. It is a sacred trust: a person is trusting you completely to provide with a transformative but safe experience.

Inner process of transformation

"Know thyself" said the inscription at Delphi, and initiation is a significant step – sometimes the first step – on a journey of self-knowledge. The inner self is often opaque to the conscious mind, and part of the spiritual journey is the process of bringing unconscious material into conscious awareness, the journey towards self-knowledge. Ultimately this is the discovery that you are unique and special - just like everyone else. It is a realisation of your powers and of your limitations. Both are equally shocking. It came as a shock to me to realise that I am a good leader.

Encounters with deities

When we encounter the divine in an initiatory experience, it can be because of an initiation ritual, or it can happen when the deities decide it will happen – it is not really under our conscious control. But the experience is one of great power and energy, of connectedness to all that is – perhaps a vision in which it is suddenly clear how everything fits together, or maybe a sense that everything is full of gods and illuminated from within.

An encounter with a deity can be a realisation of a vast awareness, or it can be a meeting with a deity of a specific place, such as a wood or a lake or a mountain. Either way, it is a revelation of something ancient and powerful, with a different mode of consciousness from ours. Their consciousness is non-local and potentially infinite, and possibly not temporally focused either; ours is finite and local and time specific.

Sometimes an encounter with a deity is a call to action. Deities are guardians of the land and the Earth and the seas, animals and birds and plants. They may call us to work towards social and environmental justice.

Experiencing group mind

Most magical groups seem to have had experiences of the group mind – knowing what is coming in a visualisation before the person leading it has said it; being able to sense where the other participants are in a visualisation; all turning up with the right food to make a feast; and so on.

The sense of a group mind develops gradually through working together, but if a new person joins, perhaps the jolt administered by the initiation ritual, and the shared experience of it, may be what inducts them into the group mind. Nevertheless, a new person joining a coven requires a readjustment of the group mind.

Online ritual

I have not done very much online ritual, but in my very limited experience it works best when you have already worked with the people in a physical space. It helps if you do the circle setup (sweeping and casting, calling the quarters) in each separate home, and then visualise your circles coming together on the astral plane. It is a good idea to have the same incense, cakes, and wine, and to all do physical activities at the same time as each other (such as making a talisman). If you are communicating via audio only, you can carry the phone around the circle with you; if you are using video, you can see each other but it seems more static. Chanting and singing are difficult because of the time lag on the audio channel, but you might be able to do some sort of call and response chanting. I find any sort of out-of-body magical work very disorienting, but working on the astral and doing hermetic exercises is apparently very effective.

To know, to will, to dare, to keep silent

These are known as the Four Powers of the Magus (*Noscere, Aude, Velle, Tacere* in Latin).

To know (*Noscere*) is associated with the element of Air. Knowledge of the hidden causes of events, and of the inner workings of the psyche, is necessary to know where best to intervene on a magical, spiritual, or physical level.

To dare (*Aude*) is associated with the element of Water. We dare to do things because of our emotional commitment to the outcome, and the emotions are associated with Water, because they ebb and flow, and are subject to change, like all things ruled by the Moon. Daring is needful for all actions where the outcome is uncertain.

To will (*Velle*) is associated with the element of Fire. The will is strong and energetic. The will is distinguished from merely wanting something. To will something is to focus on it, bringing your whole being into alignment with the desired goal. To do this, the goal has to be something that is aligned with one's True Will, which is in harmony with the flow of the universe.

To keep silent (*Tacere*) is associated with the element of Earth, because it is on the level of Earth that things are made manifest, and magical workings cannot be made manifest without silence. Most traditions agree that when you have done a magical working, you must keep silent about it for it to work. Even making a wish when you blow out the candles on your birthday cake is subject to this rule, that the wish will not come true if you tell anyone what it is. This is partly to let the magic work without further intervention or interference from your conscious mind. Silence and secrecy also hedge about the mysteries, in order to protect them from the profane (and to protect the unprepared form encountering their power unawares). Some magicians also regard the rule of silence as applying to other areas, such as the adage "if you can't say anything nice, don't say anything".

Discussion

Are the mysteries unique to each mystery religion, or do they represent the same underlying reality?

Can you access the mysteries without being initiated into a tradition?

Is secrecy necessary to protect the mysteries? If so, why?

Exercises

Meditate on the difference between that which must not be spoken and that which cannot be spoken.

Draw a mindmap of your concepts of secrecy, confidentiality, and the mysteries.

Meditate on the Witch's Pyramid - to know, to will, to dare, to keep silent. Why is it called a pyramid? Which quality is the apex?

Visualise the story of how the universe came into being as related by Victor Anderson: how the Star Goddess looked into the curved mirror of space, beheld herself, fell in love with the Other, and became two beings.

7. Evocation and Invocation

Evocation is the art of calling forth (from Latin *ex-*, meaning out of, plus *vocare*, to call). It is where the magician calls a quality or spirit out of their own depths, projecting all their desire for a specific magical outcome into the evoked quality or spirit. That is why the Western Mystery Tradition uses a magic circle, to ensure that the energy produced in this way can be contained. In certain types of Ceremonial Magic, the evoked spirit was regarded as untrustworthy, so the magician would call it into a separate container, known as the Triangle of Art. The magician may then direct this power to achieve some goal. Angels are referred to as being evoked [22] (though that is more usual in the practice of ceremonial magic).

Calling the elemental spirits of the four directions is also sometimes referred to as evocation. Given that they are qualities brought into the circle, calling the quarters might be better classified as a form of invocation.

A Jungian psychologist might say that what is evoked from the depths is an archetype. According to Jung, there are three types of symbols: personal symbols, culture-specific symbols, and universal symbols. Universal symbols are archetypes.

The collective unconscious is accessible via the personal unconscious, and so archetypes (universal symbols) can emerge from the depths of the psyche.

---

[22] Francis Barrett, F.R.C., *The Magus or Celestial Intelligencer*. [online] Available from: http://www.sacred-texts.com/grim/abr/abr005.htm

Invocation is the art of calling a being (usually a deity) into the magician's own body, so that the magician can be infused with the Divine energy of that deity. The aim of invocation is to achieve a sense of oneness with that deity, and experience reality as they experience it, non-local and infinite. There is also a benefit in this exchange of perspective for the deity, as they get to see the world from the finite and local viewpoint of a human. Human awareness is finite and local to one specific area of space-time, the here and now. Divine consciousness seems to be both spatially and temporally unfocused, and potentially infinite. Deities can benefit by accessing our local, temporal, and focussed consciousness, and we can benefit by accessing their atemporal, non-local and multiple perspective consciousness.

Wiccans have tended to only have a man invoking a goddess onto a woman, or a woman invoking a god into a man. However, many covens do have men invoking onto other men, women invoking onto other women, male deities being invoked into women, goddesses being invoked onto men, and genderqueer deities being invoked onto everyone. It is a good idea to experiment and see what works for you. As a nonbinary person, I find I can easily relate to deities with a different gender than mine. There is a range of energies from yin to yang, and if you are very feminine, having something very yang invoked onto you may not work for you (and vice versa). We do not all have to do all the experimental things, provided we acknowledge the possibility that what does not work for one person might work brilliantly for someone else.

The role of the invoker is often undervalued. But it is very important; otherwise the person being invoked on either has to say that they are not invoked (we have a convention that we will use the gesture of crossing the arms in the God position for this, though we have never had to use it). Or they need to fake being invoked (which seems like a bad idea to me). Or they need to use a previously prepared charge. Or they need to quickly invoke themselves. The invoker is very important. In classical Indian music, there are three movements of the raga, which is a piece of music that calls to a deity. The first movement is the expression of the performer's yearning for the deity; the second is the actual call to the deity; and the third is the celebration of their arrival. The Wiccan invocation – in both its verbal and nonverbal aspects – is rather like this. The invoker must want the deity to appear. Then they must call them; and then they must be pleased to see them. A successful invocation requires these emotional states to be present in the invoker, and preferably also verbally expressed in the text of the invocation, to get the coveners in the mood and participating in the act of invocation.

There are at least three processes of polarity happening in an invocation. The most obvious one is the polarity between the invoker (the one calling deity to come into the body of the other person) and the invokee (the person having the deity invoked into them). The invoker acts upon the psyche of the invokee, calling through them to the deity. The invoker is calling, and therefore active; invokees open themselves to the deity and make themselves receptive. In Wicca, the invoker and invokee would traditionally be of different genders, and the deity invoked would usually be of the same gender as the invokee; but in other witchcraft traditions, and in ceremonial magic, that is not necessarily the case. The next most obvious polarity is that between the invoker and the deity; the invoker must make a connection with the deity, to attract them. Finally, there is the polarity between the deity and the invokee; here the deity enters the invokee, who has made him- or herself receptive to the deity.

Different people experience being invoked upon differently. Some people find that it feels that the deity is occupying the same space; others feel completely intermingled with the deity; sometimes it feels as if the deity is standing right behind you; at other times it feels as if you are seeing through their eyes, but it is up to you to describe what they are showing you.

The goal of invocation (in my opinion) is not to lose the self in the deity, but to be fully present for the experience, and aware of the deity filling you and speaking through you. it is also to acquire the virtues of the deity (in the Pagan sense of the word 'virtue' meaning a quality or strength).

I regard invocation as one of the key practices of initiatory Wicca; it is not something that should be practiced by the uninitiated, as I believe that a Wiccan initiation prepares the psyche for the process of invocation. It is something that is also practiced in other initiatory traditions, of course, and their initiation rituals are doubtless also a suitable preparation for invocation.

David Wadsworth[23] describes the process of invocation as being similar to the four-stroke cycle in a motorbike engine –

---

[23] David Wadsworth (1987) <u>Wicca & The Art of Motorcycle Maintenance</u>, *Children of Sekhmet*, May 1988. [online] Available from: http://www.sacred-texts.com/bos/bos328.htm

suck (draw in energy), squeeze (compress it), bang (ignite it), blow (deliver the energy to the assembled company).

The deity being invoked represents force (pure energy), and the person being invoked upon represents form (a container for the energy). In Kabbalah, force (*Chokhmah*) is regarded as 'masculine', and form (*Binah*) as 'feminine'. Both are rooted in consciousness[24]. As the energy of the primordial lightning flash moves down the Kabbalistic Tree of Life (*Ets Chayyim*), however, the gender of the energy changes as it moves from one Sephiroth to another.

We can see from all this that polarity cannot be reduced to a binary gender model (male and female). It is much more complex than that and deserves a richer model of how it works.

In the process of invocation, a person of any gender can be the invoker or invokee. Heterocentric versions of Wicca only allow invocation where a man invokes a goddess onto a woman, or where a woman invokes a god onto a man. For some people, being invoked upon by a member of the other gender works better; but this is not true for everyone. Not everyone fits into the gender binary. It is also possible to invoke a deity (of any gender) onto yourself.

For a successful invocation to occur, the invokee must be in a suitably receptive state to receive the deity, and not be afraid of being possessed or afraid of the deity's energy; they must have confidence in the invoker and in themselves and know

---

[24] Colin Low (1991), <u>Notes on Kabbalah</u>. *Sacred texts.com* [online] Available from: http://www.sacred-texts.com/bos/bos072.htm

that they will be able to de-invoke the deity at the end of the process.

I was taught that learning to be invoked upon is a gradual process; the first few times, the deity only descends into the upper half of the body, and it takes time for them to descend further into the body.

My personal view is that delivering a Charge and then not allowing the deity to speak through you is rude to the deity being invoked. There is nothing wrong with delivering a Charge to get you in the flow, and then allowing the deity to speak through you, but if you just recite a pre-learnt Charge and then stop, it is hardly worth the deity bothering to turn up.

Levels of invocation in Wicca

Glamour

The first level is the light glamour (an aura of divinity) that occurs when doing cakes and wine. As the priest kneels before the priestess, he may lightly invoke the Goddess such that the priestess has an overlay of Goddess energy; or the Goddess energy may well up from within her. She is then empowered to bless the cakes and wine. However, there is usually no intention of fully invoking the Goddess here or channelling the Goddess's utterances. Similarly, the God may be lightly invoked on the priest in the blessing of the cakes and wine.

Drawing down the Moon

The second level occurs in the rite of Drawing Down the Moon. Here the Goddess energy is much stronger than in the blessing of cakes and wine, and it is specifically the Moon

Goddess being invoked, but again, we are just conveying Goddess energy to the other participants in the ritual, rather than channelling the Goddess's utterances. (Similarly, for the newer ritual of Drawing Down the Sun.) Some mythologies have Sun Goddesses and Moon Gods, so there is no need to restrict Drawing Down the Moon to priestesses or Drawing Down the Sun to priests.

Whispering in your ear

The third level doesn't have a name, but it feels as if the invoked deity is standing just behind you and whispering in your ear, and you are translating what they are saying for the benefit of the rest of the coven. You (the invokee) and the deity are both standing in the realm of the gods, but they are not fully in you. Sometimes the third level happens very briefly as a preparatory phase just before the fourth level.

Oil and water

The fourth level is where the deity is in you but not intermingled with your consciousness; it's more as if they're alongside you inside your body, and have just borrowed your voice to say what they have to say. This level is invocation proper; but it is like one of those executive toys with oil and water in a transparent chamber, where the oil and water can be shaken up but do not mix.

Wine and water

The fifth level is where the consciousness of the deity is intermingled or merged with your consciousness (this level is like the blending of wine and water). In this level of invocation, it is difficult to know where the deity ends and you begin. It feels to me as if they have descended into me through the top of my head, and I have opened to receive them. Other people have told me that it feels as if they have stepped in through their back (I have also experienced this feeling).

There are further levels of invocation, but they do not seem to be generally practiced in Wicca.

Trance possession

The sixth level is where your consciousness is entirely displaced, so that the deity has completely taken over and you do not remember anything about what happened during the period while the deity was present. I do not think this is a beneficial practice.

In his classic travelogue about the Caribbean, *The Travellers' Tree*, Patrick Leigh Fermor says that possessed practitioners retained an awareness of themselves, albeit dimmed; but more recent accounts by anthropologists and by practitioners themselves have stated that they did not recall anything that happened during the possession. Interestingly, practitioners are always "ridden" by the same lwa in Voudun. The lwa are said to enter the human body at the base of the skull.

In October 2008, I attended an academic conference in Heidelberg on the dynamics of ritual. There were five days of talks by anthropologists, theologians, psychologists, scholars of religion, sociologists and so on. Many of them were also practitioners of various paths. I attended a strand entitled "The Inner Work of Ritual" chaired by Geoffrey Samuel. One of the papers in this strand was by Angela Sumegi, an anthropologist who had compared shamanic possession with

Tantric Buddhist invocation [25]. The shamanic possession was like the experience of being ridden by the lwa in Voudun – the shaman left his body for the duration of the possession trance.

Entering the divine realm

In some esoteric Buddhist practices, the practitioner invokes a Buddha or a deity (such as Tara) and "ascends" to the realm of the deities (remember that up and down are just metaphors here). There, the practitioner merges his or her self with that of the deity, and then goes beyond the deity to the nameless divine ocean of bliss. [26] This practice solves two problems: the problem outlined at the beginning of the chapter about getting typecast or acquiring the characteristics of a particular type of deity; and it also means that we can go deeper and merge with the infinite without losing our awareness in the process.

How does evocation work?

The idea of evoking or calling the quarters is to make a connection with the spirits of that direction and primal element, in order to make the circle a microcosm of the cosmos (because "as above, so below") and create or restore cosmic harmony.

Many people focus entirely on the words and gestures used in calling the quarter, but the most important part of the process is establishing a connection with the energy. The easiest way

---

[25] Angela Sumegi (2008), "Being the Deity: The Inner Work of Buddhist and Shamanic Ritual." In: *Ritual Dynamics and the Science of Ritual*, vol IV, edited by Geoffrey Samuel. Wiesbaden: Harrassowitz Verlag.

[26] Geoffrey Samuel, personal conversation, 2008.

to do that is to visualise a gate opening to the realm of the element that you are calling. It is also a good idea to describe the symbolic characteristics and correspondences of the element, to remind yourself and all present who and what it is you are trying to connect with.

As it is often difficult to focus on several things at the same time, I always advise people to make the gesture of opening (or draw a pentagram, whichever you prefer), then focus on connecting with the energy, and then say the words of invocation and welcome.

How does invocation work?

Traditionally, invocation is seen as the process of inviting a deity or spirit into the body of the magician. As we have seen, what happens to the consciousness of the invoked-upon magician varies according to how intense the invocation is, or how deep it goes.

The aim of invocation in ritual magic is for the invokee to acquire the qualities associated with the deity. In a religious context, the aim is often for the worshippers to experience the joy of being in the presence of a deity, and sometimes to receive oracular messages from them. These aims are not in conflict with each other.

A question that we might ask about invocation is whether it is all happening internally, or whether there is an external consciousness really entering us. Patrick Leigh Fermor discusses the dynamics of possession by the lwa. He suggests that possession works by calling up some unconscious aspect of the self from the depths of the psyche and allowing it to take over from the ego for a while. He is sceptical of any external consciousness being involved. However, the idea of something arising out of the depths of the psyche is a useful one, as according to Jungian psychology, it is our subconscious that is connected to the collective unconscious, and according to many mystical traditions, it is through the depths of the psyche that we connect to the Divine.

It is also worth comparing the Wiccan practice of invocation with that outlined in Aleister Crowley's *Magick in Theory and Practice*. Crowley identifies three main methods of invoking deities. The first is devotion to the deity; the second is straightforward ceremonial invocation; and the third is to enact a drama of the deity's legend. He says that in invocation, the macrocosm floods the consciousness; whereas with evocation, the magician identifies with the macrocosm and creates a microcosm (the triangle into which the spirit is evoked).

Crowley outlines six phases of invocation, using the method where the magician identifies with the deity:

> The magician studies the symbolic form of the deity and builds up a mental picture, with as much care as the artist would bestow upon a model.
>
> The invocation begins with prayer to the deity, commemorating their physical attributes, but mindful of the symbolic meaning of these.
>
> The magician recites the deity's characteristic utterance
>
> The magician asserts the identity of his- or her- self with the deity.

The magician invokes the deity again, but this time it is as if the deity's will that he or she should manifest in the magician.

The magician becomes passive, and the deity speaks through the magician.

Discussion

What is the difference between invocation and evocation?

How does invocation feel to you?

How does evocation feel to you?

Where/how does the deity or spirit enter?

Has it benefited you?

Any issues with it?

Should you deliver a Charge, or allow the deity to speak through you, or both?

Exercises

Try invoking a goddess onto a man, and a god onto a woman.

Try having a woman invoke a deity onto another woman, or a man onto another man.

Try invoking a nonbinary deity onto a person of any gender.

Try to prolong an invocation as long as possible and ask the deity questions while they are with you.

8. Symbolism in Ritual

As described in chapter 5 (Archetypes and the inner work), according to CG Jung, there are three levels of symbolism: personal, cultural, and universal.

Personal symbolism is what things mean to you. So, depending on what part of England you live in, the symbolic colour of earth might be different for you. If you live in Devon, where the soil is red, due to the red sandstone geology, the symbolic colour of earth might be red for you; whereas if you live in the Cambridgeshire Fens, where earth is black, the symbolic colour of earth for you might be black. Personal symbolism may also vary depending on your experiences, your preferences, and your outlook on life. A specific tree might represent first love for you because you experienced your first kiss under it, for example. Or you might have a strong leaning towards the element of water, and therefore it might represent something specific for you.

Personal symbolic associations are not "wrong" or "incorrect" – but they do not necessarily have any meaning for anyone else unless they happen to share those associations. Poets and novelists often make use of personal symbolism to create new and interesting metaphors and imagery in their poems and stories.

Cultural symbolism is the set of symbolic associations something has within a culture. For example, in Europe, the colour black represents mourning; in other cultures, white is the colour of mourning. In China, the colour red is especially lucky; in English folklore, a bride should never wear either red or green, because those are the colours of the Fair Folk. In China, dragons are associated with water, live in lakes and wells, and bring rain; in Europe, dragons are fiery creatures that live under the earth. And so on.

Universal symbolism is a symbolic association that appears to exist independently of culture, or that occurs in all cultures. Universal symbolism is generally derived from our perception of the world around us and how we relate to it. For example, a hearth-fire, being generally a pleasurable thing, is good and associated with hospitality; and cold/wet/dark/outside, being generally not pleasurable, is bad.

The hearth fire: a universal symbol of warmth. [27]

When you are examining symbolism for use in ritual, it is a good idea to think about whether it is a personal symbol, only representing the thing symbolised for you and a small handful of others; a cultural symbol that is specific to a particular group of people; or a universal or very widespread symbol. It

---

[27] Pixabay. CC0 Public Domain

is of course fine to use a personal or cultural symbol in a ritual – but you may need to explain how you are using it, and what it means to you, or in the context of the culture or mythology you are drawing upon.

A related concept is that of Unverified Personal Gnosis (UPG) and Substantiated Personal Gnosis (SPG). An Unverified Personal Gnosis is an insight or revelation that you have received about the nature of a deity, or the nature of reality. It can be verified by checking it against experience, and/or other people's insights and revelations, and/or with reference to the lore of the culture you are working within. The Unverified Personal Gnosis (UPG) is similar to personal symbolism – it is not "wrong", but don't expect other people to agree with you unless it chimes with their experience, or with the cultural lore associated with the deity and/or pantheon you are working with.

Many people are dismissive of UPG, but there is no need to dismiss it as "incorrect" – you only need to say that it does not chime with your experience and move on. Many people are afraid that their personal symbolic associations with things are somehow wrong – but again, there is nothing wrong with creativity and personal symbolism, but your personal symbolism may not work for everyone. This is why, in my view, magic and the occult are an art and not a science.

Symbols and Sigils

When you are constructing a ritual, it is best to keep it simple, as most people can remember somewhere between three and seven symbols or ideas at a time (the optimum number is five). It also helps if the symbols or ideas are related to each other, and to the main theme of the ritual.

There are many symbols and sigils available to the witch. The pentagram is probably the best-known symbol of Wicca and other forms of witchcraft, but there is also the triple moon symbol, the sign for the Horned God, and many other sigils. Each planet has a kamea associated with it. All of these can be used to construct talismans and amulets, or as a focus for meditation and ritual.

The Pentagram

Each of the points of the pentagram represents one of the five elements (Earth, Air, Fire, Water, Spirit). It also represents the human body, as in the famous drawing by Cornelius Agrippa.

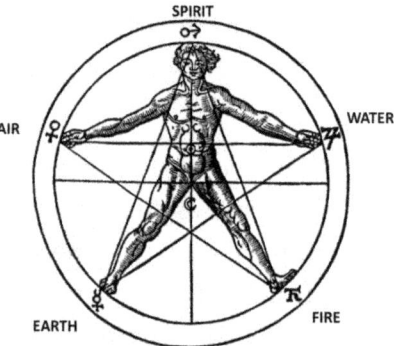

Many Wiccans use the pentagram at the quarters when summoning the elements. This is derived from the Lesser Banishing Ritual of the Pentagram, where it is used to banish the 'lower' aspect of the element. I have stopped doing this, as I do not believe in a higher or lower aspect of the elements - the shadow side of things is all

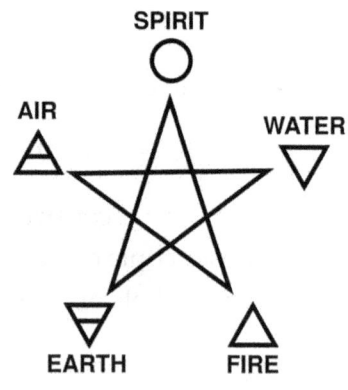

entangled with their bright side, and the one alchemically transforms the other. I do not "summon" the quarters, as it seems rather rude and peremptory. I invite them to come to the circle. Summoning and commanding spirits comes from a worldview that regards humans as the pinnacle of existence.

The pentacle can also represent the five stages of a human life: birth, initiation, consummation, repose, and death. These five stages were identified by both W B Yeats [28] and Robert Graves [29] as five faces of the Goddess.

Between birth and initiation, a person is in the repose of their parents' care. The journey from initiation to consummation is presided over by death (the death of the old way of life), and the journey from consummation to repose often includes a birth (the creation of a literal or symbolic child - a book, a work coming to fruition). As the person travels from the repose of old age to the gates of death, another initiation, into the mysteries of letting go, is required. The journey from death to new birth is presided over by both the consummation of encountering what is beyond death, and by the fact that a

---

[28] *The Living Stream*: Yeats Annual No. 18, edited by Warwick Gould. pp 114-115.
https://books.google.co.uk/books?id=hPTKdUNVXhcC
[29] Robert Graves, *The White Goddess*, p 398.
https://books.google.co.uk/books?id=XHwaVK17cf0C

consummation is required for there to be a birth. This pattern is worthy of considerable meditation and can form the basis of a ritual, especially if you mark out the pentagram and walk around it. [30]

The Pentagram is also known as the Endless Knot, because it can be drawn without taking your hand off the paper.

The Chinese elements can also be mapped onto a pentagram.[31] The "generative" cycle is indicated by pale grey arrows running clockwise on the outside of the circle. When shown in this order, they are known as the "mutual generation" (相生 xiāngshēng) sequence. In this sequence, wood feeds fire, fire generates earth in the form of ash, earth produces metal (because metal is found in the earth), metal enhances water (because water with minerals in it is more beneficial), and water nourishes wood.

The "destructive" or "conquering" cycle is represented by the arrows that form a pentagram inside the circle. This sequence is also known as "mutual overcoming" (相克 xiāngkè), where the order is Wood, Earth, Water, Fire, and Metal. In this sequence, wood parts earth (tree roots can break soil and rock), earth absorbs water, water extinguishes fire, fire melts metal, and metal chops wood. A huge system of correspondences branches out from these associations, including planets, deities, seasons, and times of day. This concept of the destructive cycle is particularly interesting because the number five also represents destruction and instability in the Tarot.

---

[30] This was a ritual devised by Sarah Fisher.
[31] https://en.wikipedia.org/wiki/Wu_Xing

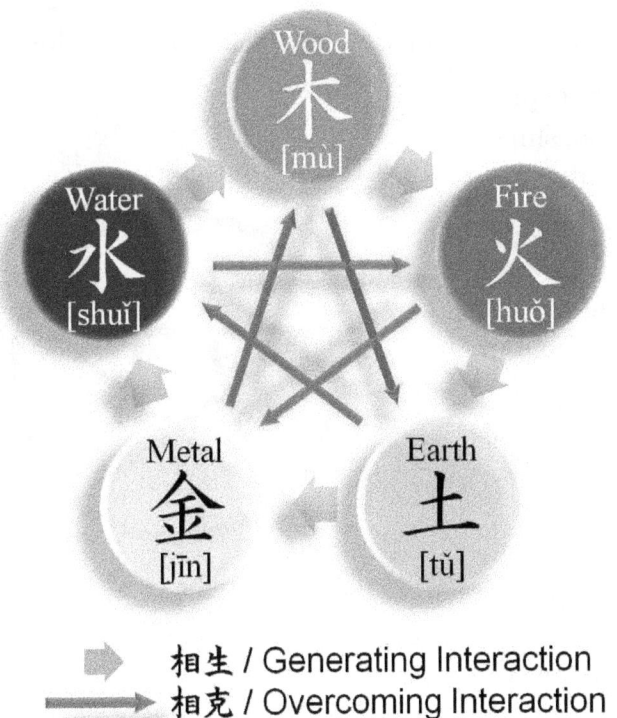

Five Chinese elements by Parnassus

The Iron Pentacle and the Pearl Pentacle

In the Feri tradition taught by Victor and Cora Anderson and its offshoots, there are two pentacles: the Iron Pentacle and the Pearl Pentacle[32]. The Iron Pentacle is a spiritual tool used to reclaim vital energies that are our birth-right as human beings, but which we have been taught to repress and feel shame

---

[32] I would like to thank Helix of Anderson Faery witchcraft for her help with the section on the Iron and Pearl Pentacles. For further resources on Anderson Faery witchcraft, see https://andersonfaery.org/

about. These energies are part of us and can be awakened more fully within us by running the Iron Pentacle Meditation.

The Iron Pentacle

The witch explores the relationships between the points by visualizing the pentacle on their body and following both the lines of the star (starting at Sex at the head and moving first to Pride on the right foot) and the circle (starting at Sex at the head and moving first to Self on the left hand). The points can also be contemplated as triangles (Sex - Passion - Pride for example). The circle represents the container of the energies, a boundary that is maintained by the witch themselves, not by others (to allow others to maintain it would be to give away your own power). [33]

Sex represents the creative power of the Universe, which includes both polarity and resonance. It represents the moment of orgasm when we open to the dance of matter and spirit, taking part in the constantly occurring cycle of creation and destruction. Enthusiastically and wholeheartedly

---

[33] T Thorn Coyle (2005), *Evolutionary Witchcraft*, Tarcher Perigee, page 116.

consensual sex is celebrated as the supreme expression of our humanity.

Pride means recognising our own worth and being able to live to the full without holding back, not comparing ourselves to others, and expressing our true nature. This pride is innocent and allows us to live in the moment. Think of a time when you were proud of something beautiful that you made or something excellent you did - that is the kind of pride that is meant here.

Self means being fully aware of our own potential and of our limitations, as well as how we relate to others and to the universe. Many spiritual traditions point out that if you do not love yourself, you cannot love others.

All these things together allow us to manifest Power - an outpouring of our own potential from the depths of our being. We project ourselves into the world, and this causes change, change in consciousness, change in the world. This is what is meant by power from within, which does not manipulate others, but acts co-operatively.

To experience Passion is to be open to the full range and depth of feelings, whether great happiness, deep sadness, ecstasy, or sorrow.

When all these points are in balance and working in harmony, the witch may attain to a state of joy and power, a state of being in our full human potential.

Each of the points of the Pearl Pentacle is another way of looking at the points of the Iron Pentacle, and a way of working with the raw power of the Iron Pentacle.

According to Helix, a Feri witch [34], Victor Anderson said that the Iron Pentacle and the Pearl Pentacle are two sides of a coin, or that Pearl is Iron played at a higher octave. The Reclaiming tradition (an offshoot of Feri), describes the Iron pentacle as expressing the energies of the individual self, and the Pearl as expressing how those energies manifest in relationships.

The Pearl Pentacle

When sex is shared between people, it flowers into love. This point is all about connection and erotic love, the generation of a current of life-force. The full energy of love is not available unless sexual energy is running freely.[35]

The expanded version of self is knowledge - not just the knowledge of the self, but the knowledge of all things, and of other people, who become mirrors for us, and we for them.

---

[34] Personal communication
[35] T Thorn Coyle, *Evolutionary Witchcraft*, page 158.

When we integrate all the experiences gained through passionate engagement with the world, we gain wisdom.

Law represents the natural order of things in the universe - where Pride is the expression of the true self of the individual, Law is the expression of the true self of the universe.

The point of Liberty (also known as Power and sometimes called Liberation) represents instinctual knowledge, standing in your own power, being free to explore and sense and enjoy.

Iron represents the strength of the energies embodied by the Iron Pentacle; it is associated with the element of Fire. The pearl represents the beauty that grows when we encounter irritants in life, rubbing up against other people and their quirks.

That is why one of the workings associated with the Pearl Pentacle in Reclaiming is the Oyster Trance, which involves a journey to the depths of the ocean to explore the existence of the oyster, and how a pearl begins to form when an irritant gets into the oyster's shell. First the oyster attempts to get rid of the irritant, but if this fails, the oyster produces layer upon layer of nacre to protect itself. Eventually the irritant is completely covered with nacre, forming a pearl. Similarly, humans can work with wounds and irritants in the psyche and transform them into pearls. [36]

If you decide to include the Iron and Pearl Pentacles in your practice, I highly recommend reading T Thorn Coyle's book *Evolutionary Witchcraft*, which explores them in much more

---

[36] George Franklin & Abel Gomez, "The Pentacle of Pearl", *Reclaiming Quarterly*, issue 103

depth and offers various meditations for working with them. They are part of Feri practice and taking them out of that context may mean that a certain amount of depth and nuance is lost.

The Inverted Pentagram

This symbol represents the descent of spirit into matter, and the need to face one's inner darkness [37]. It can also be a symbol of Baphomet, the androgynous goat-god. Baphomet was allegedly worshipped by the Templars and was enthusiastically embraced by French occultists in the nineteenth century, when Eliphas Lévi created his famous depiction.

My personal view is that witchcraft is all about the union of spirit with matter, rather than the separation of spirit and matter advocated by some Neo-Platonists, the Gnostics, and religions which were influenced by them.

The Hexagram

The hexagram represents the four elements working in harmony. Each of the sigils for the four elements is present within it. 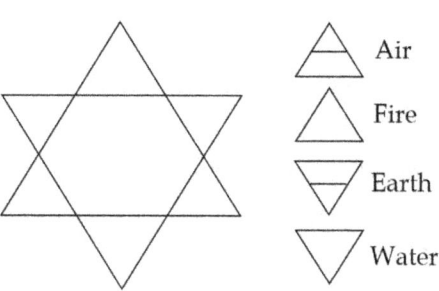 It is used in Freemasonry and witchcraft as well as in Judaism, where it is known as the Star of David. The points of the star and the centre represent the seven planets of

---

[37] Rob Purvis, *Symbolic Meaning of the Pentagram*, http://www.angelfire.com/id/robpurvis/pentagram.html

traditional astrology (Sun, Moon, Mercury, Venus, Mars, Saturn, Jupiter).

The Unicursal Hexagram

This symbol can be drawn as a single line without taking the pen off the paper and is important in Thelema. It represents the interweaving of the forces of the microcosm and the macrocosm.

The Triple Moon

The triple Moon symbol represents the waxing, full, and waning Moon. The Moon is very important to witches, as a symbol of intuition, the night, the Goddess, dreams, portents, the night journey, and the unconscious. The waxing Moon represents the Maiden aspect of the Triple Goddess; the full Moon represents the Mother; and the waning Moon represents the Crone.

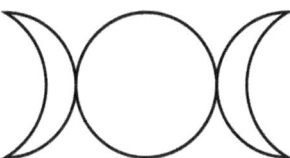

The Heart and Moon

I devised the heart and Moon symbol for inclusive Wicca in the summer of 2014. I was writing a poster for a LGBT+ ritual and wanted a symbol to represent inclusive practice. The symbol flowed through my arm and onto the paper, almost completely bypassing my conscious mind. On reflection, I see the heart as representing love in all its forms as the central mystery of Wicca. It also references the Sufi symbol of the winged heart. The heart replaces the full Moon in the triple Moon goddess symbol, and so represents the fulfilment of love. This includes erotic love in all its forms: same-sex love, opposite-sex love, monogamy, polyamory, kink, and all variations on consensual sexual relationships. It also includes the love of friends, the love of covens and tribes and groups, love among families (extended, biological, intentional, conventional, and unconventional).

The Horned God

The Horned God is represented by a circle with horns or antlers. The Horned God represents wildness, sexuality, and untamed Nature. He is the Lord of Animals, and in some traditions, the leader of the Wild Hunt. In folkloric witchcraft, he is the Devil - not the adversary figure of Christianity, but the god of the witches, rebelling against the cruelty and repression of the Church.

Hand Gestures

In India, hand gestures are known as mudras. Italian witchcraft is said to have included two gestures, one for the goddess and the other for the god, and some Wiccans also use these two gestures.

The goddess gesture (*mano fica*, or fig hand) requires making a fist and placing the thumb between the forefinger and middle finger. The thumb goes red and is somewhat reminiscent of a clitoris. It may have originated as a symbol for the yoni. It was also used to ward off the evil eye and is regarded as an obscene gesture in Slavic cultures and in Turkey. In ancient Rome, this gesture was made by the paterfamilias (the oldest living male of the household) as a warding-off gesture in the Lemuria ritual, the purpose of which was to ward off malevolent and fearful spirits of the dead.

The god gesture requires extending the little finger and the thumb to make horns; it is called the *mano cornuto* or horned hand. In India, this gesture is called Karana Mudra and is used to expel demons and remove obstacles such as sickness or negative thoughts. Similarly, in Italy, it is used to ward off bad luck, the evil eye, and illness.

The famous gesture made by Spock in Star Trek is a sacred Jewish gesture, which was used to bless the congregation of the synagogue.

Kameas

These are patterns made by drawing lines on a magic square. There are different magic squares for each of the seven classical planets. Each row and column of numbers adds up to the same number. Once you have constructed the magic square, you use the corresponding number of each letter of the planet's name to draw the planetary sigil on the square.[38] You can then charge the sigil magically to make a talisman.

---

[38] https://en.wikipedia.org/wiki/Magic_square
I would like to thank Darren Jones for his excellent workshop on Kameas in February 2015.

Mandalas

A mandala is a twofold meditation tool. The process of creating it is meditative, and it can be used as a focus for meditation once it has been created.

The idea of the mandala comes from Hindu and Buddhist tradition. The mandala is a diagram of the sacred cosmos. Tibetan Buddhist sand mandalas depict temples and palaces where specific Buddhas dwell, and pathways between them. A sand mandala is carefully and painstakingly constructed by pouring sand through special pointy tubes onto a surface, and after a certain amount of time, the sand is swept up and poured out as a blessing into a river, or given away to pilgrims.

Mandalas can also be drawn or painted. Carl Gustav Jung (the psychoanalyst) drew mandalas representing his inner states and encouraged his clients to do the same. Other Jungians also did this. Drawing a mandala can be a very satisfying experience – it does not have to be great art; it is the process of creating a picture of your inner world that is important. You can also make mandalas from seeds, pebbles, or shells.

Once you have created your mandala, you can use it as a focus for meditation, following the patterns you have created, or meditating on the meaning of the symbols within the mandala. In Buddhism, sand mandalas are deliberately made to be impermanent, and the sand is swept up and offered to a nearby river.

Runes and Bind-runes

Runes are a subject worthy of a whole book, so I recommend engaging with them properly before trying to work them into rituals. One way of beginning working with runes if you are unfamiliar with them is Katie Gerrard's technique, from her book *Odin's Gateways* [39], where you draw a rune as a gateway, chant its name, enter into the magical realm of that rune, and see what insights you get.

A runic alphabet is called a futhark (from the first six runes of the rune-stave), and there are at least four different futharks: the Elder Futhark, which has twenty-four runes; the Younger Futhark, which has sixteen; the Anglo-Saxon Futhark, which has twenty-nine runes; and the Northumbrian Futhark, which has thirty-three.

To make a bind-rune, you combine two or more runes together to make a sigil, and then empower it by chanting the runes that you have joined together. For example, you might combine Fehu (Feoh, wealth) with Wynn (joy) to represent bounty. When you create your bind-rune, you draw one rune on top of another (usually joining the verticals together).

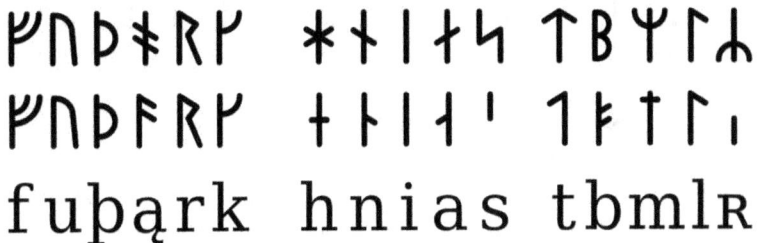

Two variations of the Younger Futhark

---

[39] Katie Gerrard (2009), *Odin's Gateways: A Practical Guide to the Wisdom of the Runes, Through Galdr, Sigils and Casting*, Avalonia Books.

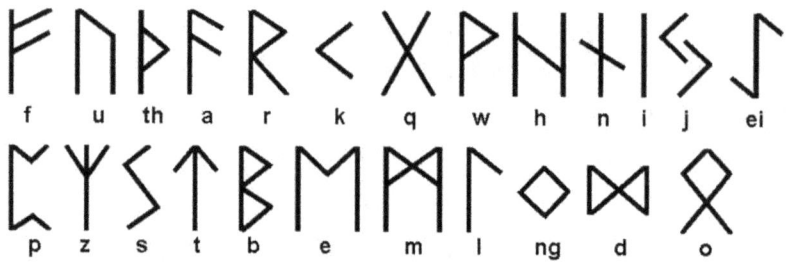

The Elder Futhark

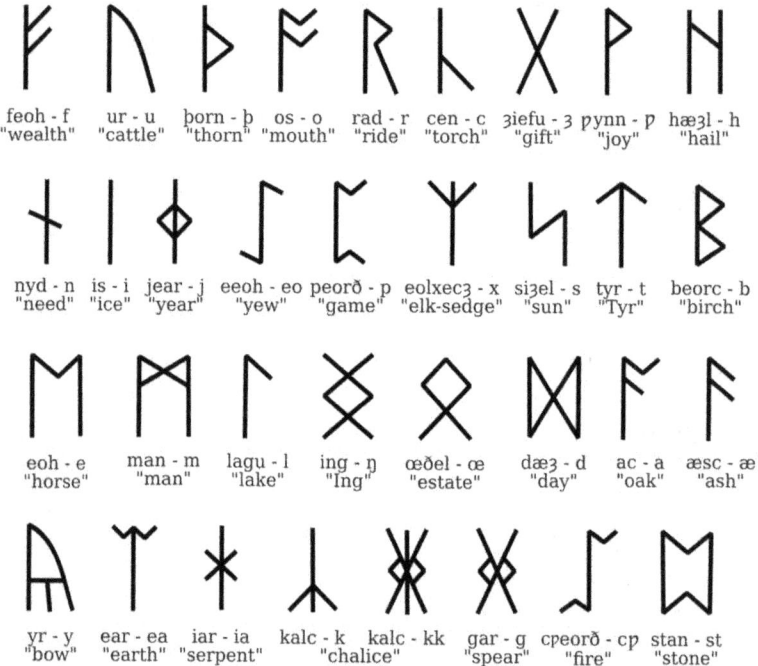

The Northumbrian Futhark

The Anglo-Saxon Futhark is generally held to stop at Ear (earth); the extra runes (Iar, Kalc, Cweorth, Stan, and Gar) were used in the Northumbrian Futhark.

Constructing a sigil

Austin Osman Spare devised a way of constructing a sigil to actualise magical intent. Say you want to increase mutual understanding among your friends or your coven. You would first write out the phrase MUTUAL UNDERSTANDING, and then delete any spaces and duplicate letters, so it becomes MUTALNDERSADIG. You then construct a sigil out of the remaining letters, by joining them together, rather like a bind-rune, but with more letters. The aim here is to impress the intent into your subconscious, whilst helping the conscious mind to forget what the aim was. The sigil on the right is constructed from the letters MUTALNDERSADIG (the only rules I followed in drawing it were that all the letters need to be touching or overlapping, and it must eventually cease to look like the thing it represents).

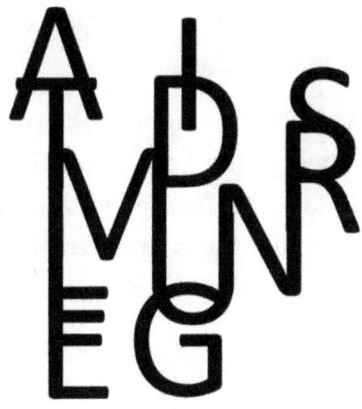

Sun wheel

An equal-armed cross in a circle may symbolise a number of things: the solstices and equinoxes on the Wheel of the Year; the four elements (Earth, Air, Fire, Water); the four phases of the Moon (waxing, full, waning, dark); the four seasons; the four tides of the year (resting, growing, reaping, sowing); the

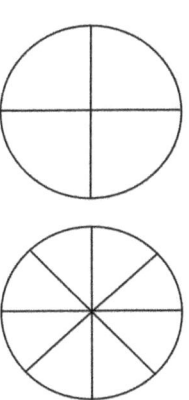

four ages of a human (infancy, youth, adulthood, old age); the four quarters of a magical circle - the origin of the phrase "squaring the circle".

A circle with eight spokes inside it usually represents the Wheel of the Year (Samhain, Yule, Imbolc, Spring Equinox, Beltane, Midsummer, Lammas, Autumn Equinox). It can also represent the eight tides of the day,[40] the eight winds, and other mystical qualities.

Tides of the day

Time	Old Welsh [41]	Anglo-Saxon [42]	Modern
04:30-07:30	Bore	Morgen	Morntide
07:30-10:30	Anterth	Daeg-mael	Undernoon
10:30-13:30	Nawn	Mid-daeg	Noontide
13:30-16:30	Echwydd	Ofanverth dagr	Undorne
16:30-19:30	Gwechwydd	Mid-aften	Eventide
19:30-22:30	Ucher	Ondverth nott	Night-tide
22:30-01:30	Dewaint	Mid-niht	Midnight
01:30-04:30	Pylgaint	Ofanverth nott	Uht

---

[40] Nigel Pennick (1989), *Practical Magic in the Northern Tradition*, Aquarian Press.
[41] http://trwelling.org/Tides%20of%20the%20Day.htm
[42] https://en.wikipedia.org/wiki/Tide_(time)

The eight winds

Wind	Direction	Virtue [43]
Solanus	East	Arousal, Awakening, Fertility, Vitality
Eurus	Southeast	Gentleness, Earning, Gain, Money
Auster	South	Sustenance
Africus	Southwest	Perceptivity
Favonius	West	Parenting, Joyousness, Spirit, Family, Children
Cautus	Northwest	Creativity, Teaching
Septentrio	North	Stasis, Healing, Regeneration
Aquilo	Northeast	Stillness, sleep, death

Symbols in ritual

Symbols can be used as the focus of a meditation which explores all the different facets and meanings of the symbol. If

---

[43] http://trwelling.org/Tides%20of%20the%20Day.htm

you decide to include this in a group ritual, it is a good idea to explain the symbol to participants as you go along. You can also use symbols for protection, either inscribed on a talisman or in the air, using energy. Symbols are often inscribed on magical tools, especially the athame, the pentacle, and the wand. But tools can themselves be symbols - for example, the athame can represent the element of Air. In fact, almost anything can be a symbol: a computer is a symbol of thought; a mill is a symbol of inner processes, churning and grinding the corn to transform it into bread. A spider is a symbol of industriousness; a web is a symbol of interconnectedness. Various flowers symbolise different qualities (rosemary for remembrance, a rose for love, poppies for the Corn King or for the Harvest Mother, and so on).

Symbols speak to the unconscious and the right side of the brain (the twilight side). They are an integral part of witchcraft.

Discussion

What symbols have meaning for you? Why?

What other connotations and meanings do your symbols have? Are they associated with any specific deity?

Exercises

Create a talisman with your personal sigil or symbol, and charge it with the appropriate energy, using planetary correspondences and energies.

Do the exercises associated with the Pearl Pentacle.

Meditate on Birth, Initiation, Consummation, Repose, Death, and Rebirth.

9. Spell Work

A cantrip, an incantation, an enchantment, a spell, a charm…. All these words imply chanting, rhythm, being ensorcelled through music and words. The magical arts were once known as Gramarye, and the book in which you wrote your spells was a grimoire. The magic that you wove was called a glamour. All three of these words are derived from grammar. These linked meanings come from a time when magical learning was not sharply distinguished from other sorts of learning, and all knowledge was deemed to be rather occult.

The creation of magic is a poetic function, along with the other twilight aspects of the mind: poetry, rhythm, intuition, perception of the shape of space, the qualities of silence, and other subtle energies.

The ancient druids who ululated and sang curses to put the fear of the gods into the Roman troops, or launched a satire against an unjust ruler, knew the power of the well-turned metre of a song or chant. The word charm comes from the Latin for a song (via the French word *charme*).

The traditional songs of many cultures carry magical and occult information, about water, trees, knives, the taboo against incest, the power of the white deer, the magic of the Fair Folk, and what to do if you accidentally get caught by La Belle Dame Sans Merci.

Many peoples believe that words carry the power to change reality, which is why they are so careful in their choice of words and names.

So, what is it in a spell that works the magic? Is it the impact of the words and rhythms on the unconscious mind, which then reaches down into the collective unconscious to work its effects? Is it the symbolic juxtaposition of things, working sympathetic magic? Or is it the magic of contagion? Or the sending of magical energy to bring about a particular result? Many theories have been put forward; and perhaps it is all these things, depending on where and how the leverage was applied.

If magic is a lever applied at just the right point, then much of the art involved is to locate the best point at which to apply the lever.

The Four Stages of a Spell

Like a four-stroke engine or the four stages of creation in the Kabbalah, a spell could be said to have four stages. The first stage is the gathering of the energy (suck); the second is concentrating it (squeeze); the third is manifesting it (bang); and the fourth is sending it (blow).

> Suck – Emanation (*Aziluth*) – Root
>
> Squeeze – Creation (*Beriah*) – Trunk
>
> Bang – Formation (*Yezirah*) – Branch
>
> Blow – Action (*Asiyyah*) – Fruit
> from *Wicca and the Art of Motorcycle Maintenance* by David Wadsworth [44]

Another advantage of David Wadsworth's excellent system is that "suck, squeeze, bang, blow" (the four stages of a four-

---

[44] http://www.sacred-texts.com/bos/bos328.htm

stroke engine) is a lot easier to remember than *Aziluth, Beriah, Yezirah, Asiyyah*.

For each stage in the creation of a spell, we need to consider the best metaphor for gathering, concentrating, storing, and sending the energy. For example, it might be the festival of the Autumn Equinox, and we want to help someone recover their creativity. Autumn Equinox is associated with the cider harvest, and the person likes cider. We decide to create a spell by visualising the apple harvest and a cider press, concentrating their creativity into a usable form. As the cider runs out into the pan, their creative juices start flowing. We can match the stages of our spell to David Wadsworth's system as follows:

Suck – picking the apples

Squeeze – crushing them in the cider press

Bang – turning the handle of the press to crush the apples

Blow – juices begin to flow

Imitative Magic

This is a spell or working where the practitioner performs an action which is like the desired outcome. For example, on New Year's morning (as soon after midnight as possible), I like to do a little sympathetic magic, as follows. Each person present has a ten-pound note, or a ten-dollar bill, and everyone stands in a circle. You then offer to pay the person to your left ten pounds, or dollars, to do something trivial like scratching your back. They do this, and then pay the next person ten pounds to do some equally light piece of work. Eventually everyone still has ten pounds (just not the same ten-pound note that they started with). The idea is that for the rest of the year, you will earn money just as easily as you did in the first five minutes.

James G Frazer, author of *The Golden Bough*, referred to this as Homeopathic or Imitative Magic (the Law of Similarity). In this view, like begets like; if you perform an action on an object which represents something, the thing represented will be affected accordingly, e.g. pouring water on the ground and shaking a rain-stick to obtain rain.

Sympathetic Magic

This is the idea that things that have once been connected can act on each other at a distance through an occult principle of sympathy, which means that they are still connected with each other. James Frazer referred to this as the Law of Sympathy (Sympathetic Magic). He thought that tribal peoples believed that anything ever connected with a person, such as hair or blood, could be manipulated to influence that person. Things act on each other at a distance through a secret sympathy. This is related to, but different from, the Law of Participation - the assumption that a thing can participate in or be part of two or more things at once.

We recall the concept of sympathetic magic every time we refer to a drink to cure a hangover as a 'hair of the dog'. In popular European folklore, it was believed that if a dog bit you, the bite would heal faster if you put one of its hairs in the wound. (The full expression is 'a hair of the dog that bit you'.) Similarly, the beers you consumed last night were the dog that bit you, and the beer to help you recover the next day was its hair. (Of course, the effect of feeling a bit better for having a drink after a night out on the town is probably because it tops up the alcohol in your system enough that you feel pleasantly drunk instead of hung over.)

Contagious Magic

This is the idea that the luck inherent in an object will rub off on you. Hence people acquire lucky objects (like a medallion of Saint Christopher or a four-leaf clover), or if we are of a magical persuasion, we make our own lucky objects in the form of a talisman, which will be imbued with luck or magical energy by inscribing it with occult sigils.

It is also a widespread belief that bad luck is contagious. That is why sailors were very superstitious about what or who they would allow on their boats.

James G Frazer, author of *The Golden Bough*, referred to this as Contagious magic (the Law of Contact): the use of a magically charged thing directly on the person or thing one desires to affect, e.g. talismans, charms, amulets.

A lucky charm[45] is any attractive object that carries happy memories - perhaps a gift from someone close to you, or something associated with luck.

An amulet is an object associated with a deity or holy person (a St Christopher medallion or a Thor's Hammer or a valknut [46]). It may also be an object believed to have specific properties, such as a crystal or a bezoar. Amulets were originally worn to protect the wearer from the evil eye. Knots

---

[45] Richard Webster, Amulets, Talismans, & Charms, *The Llewellyn Journal*, http://www.llewellyn.com/journal/article/583
[46] A valknut is a sigil made of three intertwined triangles and associated with Oðinn

are often used as amulets, as they are believed to distract and confuse spirits.

A talisman is an object that has been magically charged in a ritual, often at an astrologically significant time, and inscribed with an angelic or planetary sigil (a *kamea*).

Protection Magic

How to strengthen your aura

Ground and centre (see chapter 14: Grounding and centering). Draw in energy from the earth and sky, blend the two together in a spiral in your solar plexus, feel the energy spreading and filling your whole body and aura.

The thirteen openings of the body

Visualise white light sealing the 13 openings of the body – touch each one or seal it with consecrated water. The thirteen openings are your eyes, ears, nostrils, mouth, nipples, bellybutton, vagina, urethra, and anus (obviously men only have 12 openings). It is also a good idea to seal any scars with white light or consecrated water.

Skein of white light

Visualise a white thread of light winding around you like thread on a spindle, until you are completely cocooned in white light.

Threshold guardians

You can ask elemental spirits to guard your space – this is rather like calling the quarters but creating an impermeable sphere of light around you. You can also create threshold guardians as thought forms. Find a picture of a warrior and charge it up with power; place it near the entrance to your home. Any strong protective image will work.

Sealing the openings of the house

Draw pentagrams on each door, window, and mirror, and really focus on sealing them with light so that no harmful thing may enter.

Sphere of light

Create a sphere of light around yourself or your house. Relax and breathe deeply for a few moments and imagine a glow of bright white light deep in your belly; as you breathe the shimmering white bubble grows and grows, until it surrounds you entirely. Your body and your aura are now completely cocooned within this glimmering bubble. You can expand this out to protect the house but remember to draw energy from your surroundings to augment your own energy. You can now turn the bubble any colour you like. You could also call on a sacred guardian to protect you. This will anchor and strengthen the sphere.

Magical boundaries

Traditional protection spells and charms include sprite flails (made of bramble), wearing red thread around your wrist, sprigs of rowan carried in your pocket or placed over the door, witch bottles (a bottle full of pins or coloured threads), spirit traps, shoes in the wall, an egg or a knife buried at the threshold, runes and bind-runes, patterns to distract the spirits, amulets and charms, and protective sachets of herbs.[47]

Cord magic

The knotty spell can be used to bind the desired thing to your will, or to store energy in a cord for later release.[48] Tie the knots into the string or cord in the following order:

- 1 – 6 – 4 – 7 – 3 – 8 – 5 – 9 – 2 –

Then recite the rhyme:

> By knot of one, the spell's begun,
>
> By knot of two, it cometh true,
>
> By knot of three, thus shall it be,
>
> By knot of four, 'tis strengthened more,
>
> By knot of five, so may it thrive,
>
> By knot of six, the spell we fix,
>
> By knot of seven, the Stars of heaven,
>
> By knot of eight, the hand of Fate,
>
> By knot of nine, the thing is mine!

Apparently, this chant was written by Doreen Valiente.

---

[47] Nigel Pennick (1989), *Practical Magic in the Northern Tradition*, Aquarian Press.

[48] Pixie Zinzara (2014), *Historical Spells: Cords, Knots and Magic*. https://bytheknotofnine.wordpress.com/2014/02/04/historical-spells-cords-knots-and-magic/

Make sure that you focus on your intent each time you tie a knot in the cord.

Cord magic is all about binding and loosing. A knot binds things; undoing the knot loosens them. In a house where a woman is giving birth, all knots must be untied and all hair unbraided, otherwise it is believed that the birth will be difficult.

Handfasting is another example of cord magic, where the couple are bound together with cords to symbolise their union and the pledges made between them.

Many cultures believed that witches could control the wind by tying three knots into a cord or a handkerchief. If the knots were tied in the correct manner, the wind was tied up with them. In the Isle of Man and Cornwall, sailors used these cords. They believed that loosening one knot would bring a south-westerly wind, two knots a strong north wind, and three knots a tempest. In Scandinavian and Shetland Islands folklore, fishermen are said to be able to command the wind like this.

There was also a widespread belief that, when a woman was giving birth, all knots in the house must be loosened, in order to ease the passage of the child into the world.

Fith-fath (poppet)

The fith-fath or poppet is an example of sympathetic magic. The witch makes a doll to represent the person being worked on and may use some of their hair or fingernails to establish a link between them and the poppet. Sometimes the doll is given a rowan berry for a heart. As an object, the fith-fath or poppet is a neutral piece of magical technology: it may be used for good purposes such as healing, though there are many examples of it being used for harm. If you go to the Museum of Witchcraft and Magic in Cornwall, there are some truly alarming examples.

It is possible to use a poppet or fith-fath in a binding spell (though some would argue that this is functionally equivalent to cursing). You take the poppet and place it between two mirrors, and tell it that if the person it represents sends out either harm or good, then it will bounce back, so they would be better off sending out good. This is not to be used lightly: only for situations where the person you are binding has done something violent.

If you were thinking of using a poppet for cursing purposes, you would be ill-advised to do so, as you have thereby created a magical link between you and the person you have cursed.

Spoken Charms [49]

Spoken charms are usually rhythmic, rhyming, and alliterative. They presumably awaken the power of the twilight aspect of consciousness: the part of the mind that responds to rhyme and rhythm. When they are recited in a voice of power, they can be quite mesmerising. There is a wonderful example of this in the track *The Forming of Blodeuwedd* by Robin Williamson [50], on the album Songs of Love and Parting. Williamson recites the poem like an

---

[49] *Earth, Air, Fire and Water: Pre-Christian and Pagan Elements in British Songs Rhymes and Ballads* by Robin Skelton & Margaret Blackwood (Arkana, 1990); *Carmina Gadelica*, Alexander Carmichael (Florian Press); any book of Anglo-Saxon poetry

[50] http://www.last.fm/music/Robin+Williamson/The+Celtic+Bard/The+Forming+of+Blodeuwedd

incantation, so that you almost expect Blodeuwedd to manifest every time you play the track.

Witch bottles, Witch balls, and Spirit traps

According to traditional lore, spirits are easily distracted by patterns, threads, pins, mazes, sigils, and lines. The witch-bottle operates on this principle: you fill it with pins or short lengths of coloured thread and place it in a window or doorway. Any spirit will be distracted by the threads or pins and will not bother you. A spirit trap is where the pins or thorns or rosemary are intended to impale the spirit. A witch ball is just a glass sphere - sometimes with threads of glass within it, sometimes a fisherman's weight for a net - again to distract the spirits. Some older witch bottles used urine, hair, fingernails, and menstrual blood to create a magical link. These were buried underneath a hearth or threshold to protect a house.

Old Magic or New Magic?

We do not know everything about what people did in the past, so we have had to supplement with other techniques. Also, Wicca is not an ancient religion, but an outgrowth of many different strands of magic and spirituality coming together [51].

Even reconstructionist Pagan traditions have had to supplement the writings they have with a lot of personal gnosis (which starts out as unverified, but may become

---

[51] Ronald Hutton (1999), *Triumph of the Moon: the rise of modern Pagan witchcraft*. Oxford: OUP.

substantiated, either by matching it up with traditional lore, or by finding that the experience has been shared by others).

Some books of magic from the medieval period survive. Some 19th century handwritten books survive; they are not Books of Shadows in the modern sense. Avalonia Books are translating and publishing some of them. One very interesting book documenting 18th century fairy beliefs is *The Secret Commonwealth of Elves, Fauns and Fairies* by Robert Kirk [52]. Another very interesting book is by a Finnish traditional witch, Kati-Ma Koppana, and is called *Snake Fat and Knotted Threads*. It describes what survived of Finnish witchcraft. I also recommend *Practical Magic in the Northern Tradition* by Nigel Pennick.

The Pagan revival is a new thing building on old ideas. Paganism was wiped out in Europe by forced conversion and (in some areas) slaughter and persecution. However, many of its ideas, stories, and techniques survived - written down by Christian monks and antiquarians like Snorri Sturluson, or retained as folk customs and practices. The Christians who wrote down these ideas sometimes did so from second-hand hearsay, and sometimes tried to explain away Pagan deities as ancient kings and queens. Folk customs only began to be recorded systematically in the late nineteenth century, so in many cases, it is not clear how old they are, or how much they may have changed in the intervening centuries. The good news is that Pagan traditions are a human response to the land and its other-than-human inhabitants; even if all the books and stories disappeared, Paganism is inscribed in the

---

[52] Available from http://www.sacred-texts.com/neu/celt/sce/

land itself and our response to it, as John Male once said to me. That is why the old deities and the old customs would not, could not, lie down and die. People will always respond to the land in a magical and mystical way.

If you want old and traditional, start by researching the folk magic of your region: the seasonal festivals; the protective magic people did for their crops and livestock. If this information is not available from older people, it may have been collected by folklore collectors in the late 19th and early 20th centuries. But bear in mind that tradition is dynamic and fluid and always changing - it is not a fixed thing.

Older descriptions of magical techniques are not necessarily better than newer descriptions, and in any case, the newer books are generally based on older books, and draw upon them. The trick is to distinguish between fake and real. If it claims to be an old and unbroken tradition, it is very likely to be fake. If it has references to academic works, it is probably real. If it is realistic and moderate in its claims, it is probably real. If it claims to be the solution to all your problems - that sounds fake to me.

People assume that older traditions are better than newer ones, but this is not necessarily the case. Everything was new once. For me, the test of whether any traditional practice is any good is: does it work? does it help (in the long term as well as the short term)? Is it a coherent system? Does it both challenge and empower its participants? If you want to understand the underlying theory of magic, I recommend reading Isaac Bonewits' *The Laws of Magic*.[53]

---

[53] http://www.neopagan.net/AT_Laws.html

Magical techniques include visualisation, invocation, protection magic, cleansing, sigils, talismans, and divination. These techniques are very old and were used by most magical practitioners from ancient times to the present. They have been presented in new styles by several different writers; but they are essentially the same techniques. I once bought a book about witchcraft and magic in Russia, called *The Bath-house at Midnight*, thinking that Russian magic would be very exotic and different. I was disappointed to find that it drew on the same sources and almanacs as much of the folk magic of Western Europe.

Energy

How does magical energy work? There is an electromagnetic field around the Earth, and around anything through which electric current flows, including anything that is alive. If the energy that many Pagans talk about has a physical correlate, then it must be something to do with electromagnetism.

Scientists tell us that consciousness is an emergent property of complex systems. Humans are one such complex system. What if the Earth and its ecosystem was another such system? That would explain spirits of place. It has also been suggested that the universe itself is complex enough to give rise to mind.

Of course, all this is highly speculative and subjective. Scientists who are studying consciousness and complex systems have not reached any firm conclusions, it seems, but it is a very interesting area.

The trouble with a lot of Western thinking is that, since Descartes, we divide everything between spirit and matter. In Eastern thought, there is no such distinction. Spirit is a subtler form of matter; matter is a denser form of spirit. Eastern philosophy affirms that the distinction between matter and spirit is illusory - and once you get into subatomic physics, this insight is confirmed, as what seems solid contains a great deal of space.

Deities might be made of energy, or of consciousness. Even if they do not exist as objective phenomena, they certainly exist as subjective phenomena, as experiences or as archetypes. If I invoke the same deity, I will get a similar experience each time, which suggests that there is at least a symbol-complex or thought-form that answers to the name of that deity.

Finding the path of least resistance

When doing a magical working to bring about change in the world, your magic is much more likely to be effective if you choose the path of least resistance - a principle also known as "The gods help those who help themselves".

If your spell attempts to run counter to the laws of physics, for example, it will require a lot more magical energy to work than one that is in keeping with those laws.

If you do a spell to get pregnant, it helps if you are having sex with someone (otherwise the spell is likely to rebound and find the nearest fertile person to work on). If you do a spell to win the lottery, it is a good idea to buy a ticket. And so on.

What magic will do is shorten the odds against something happening and align your will with the desired outcome.

The Ethics of Magic

There are ethical considerations when using magic, just as there are with physical means of producing change. These are mainly around consent and minimising harm to others.

If you are sending healing to someone, it is a very good idea to get their consent first, and also to send energy in such a way that their body can decide where best to use it, rather than being too specific about what the energy is meant to do when it arrives[54].

If you do not have their consent, are doing a working with your group, and cannot contact them, one possible way round it is to 'park' the energy in orbit around them, and let them know it is available for their use if they wish it.

If you are working magic for some benefit to yourself, such as a new job or relationship, make sure that you are not violating another person's free will. It is best not to work for a specific job, or a relationship with a specific person, but to work for those things in general. You also need to work for the desired outcome in the physical realm; only using magic is disrespectful to the powers; and will probably not work anyway.

Another way of looking at it is that my rights end where yours begin, and that is why consent and boundaries are so important. Working magic is no exception - even if the magic you are working is beneficial. A specific magical working is

---

[54] This idea came from Simon Cox, a friend who was a member of the National Federation of Spiritual Healers.

different from merely wishing someone well or praying in a general sense for their well-being.

The Wiccan attitude to ethics is mainly based on the Wiccan Rede, "An it harm none, do what thou wilt". This is very similar to other versions of the Golden Rule found in other religions. However, it is significant that the Wiccan Rede is part of the first degree initiation. It was probably meant to show the new initiate that it is impossible to do anything without causing some harm, so it is necessary to carefully consider the consequences of one's actions[55].

The other famous (and often misquoted) "law" is generally referred to as the Law of Threefold Return. The actual text instructs the Wiccan initiate to return good threefold wherever they receive it.

In my opinion, the most important aspect of Wiccan ethics is the list of the eight virtues which occurs in *The Charge of the Goddess*. These are beauty and strength, power and compassion, mirth and reverence, honour and humility (see chapter 24, Cultivating the virtues). Each of these pairs of virtues points to the need for balance. Virtue ethics seem to have originated in ancient Greek philosophy, though whether Doreen Valiente was aware of this when writing *The Charge of the Goddess* is not known.

Ethics versus Morality

I have always felt that ethics are a bottom-up approach to behaviour, where your ethical choices spring from your ethos, whereas morality was a top-down approach, where morals

---

[55] From a conversation with Dee Weardale.

were arbitrarily imposed from above by a deity. (The dictionary definition of morals and ethics does not bear out this distinction, but I still find it useful.)

Some traditions may derive their ethics from the traditional body of lore of a culture. This wisdom from the past, embedded as it was in experience and an ethic of responsibility towards other beings, is an excellent source of ethical guidance. For example, the Irish triads and Scottish proverbs are full of wisdom.

My criterion for deciding whether anything is right or not is, "does it harm anyone?" Of course, it is impossible to completely avoid harm, but we can and should reduce the harm caused by our actions. I also draw on the Eight Wiccan Virtues as a guide to how to act.

Discussion

What are the key ethical principles of magic?

How does "An it harm none, do as ye will" work out in magical practice?

Does it matter how ancient a practice or technique is?

Exercises

Try out the various energetic protection techniques mentioned in this chapter: strengthening the aura, sealing the thirteen openings of the body, the skein of white light, setting up threshold guardians, sealing the openings of your house, creating a sphere of light, setting up magical boundaries.

Try some of the traditional protection techniques: cord magic, the fith-fath, spoken charms, witch bottles, witch balls, and spirit traps.

10. Magical Tools

Why does a witch need magical tools? Tools are part of a magical language of symbols and experiences and ideas that we all share. They are also useful. You do not need a knife and fork to eat your dinner, but it makes it a lot easier. You do not need an address book to write your friends' addresses in - but it makes it a lot easier to remember where they live and post them Yule cards. And you do not need a rite of passage to help you feel like an adult - but it makes it easier if a definite transition has been marked.

The purpose of a Book of Shadows is not to prescribe how you should do your rituals, but to record powerful rituals that you have done, and to transmit powerful rituals written by past Wiccans. Each witch's book should be unique to them, although it will also contain the rituals that have been passed down to them. A Book of Shadows is a magical tool for recording and transmitting good rituals.

What about tools such as wands, athames, swords, chalices, and so on? There are several reasons why they are helpful. I do think that a good witch should be able to do a spell or ritual without any tools in an emergency - but I still use tools when they are available.

Humans are tool-using animals. One of the things that helps us to think and solve problems is our tool-using propensities. Look at other animals who use tools. We tend to think they are cleverer than animals who do not use tools, because they can manipulate more of their environment.

According to *Tool Use in Animals: Cognition and Ecology*, animals use tools. Capuchin monkeys and chimpanzees crack open nuts with stones, and chimpanzees have been using tools for four to five thousand years. Corvids (the crow family) also use tools. [56]

Think about how we use physical tools such as screwdrivers, hammers, brooms, milk-frothers, egg-stiffeners, paint-stirrers, and so on, and how difficult life would be without those tools. Consider how chimpanzees have been seen getting ants out of anthills with a straw, or cracking nuts open with a rock. Frequently, tool use involves remembering that you saw a useful-looking rock, or a hollow blade of grass, going to fetch it, and bringing it to where the food is. Tool use involves the use of cognitive skills such as memory, comparison, and visualisation.

My partner Bob pointed out that it is much is easier to do a task (magical or mundane) without a tool when you have learnt to do it with a tool.

Tools are levers for affecting the world. You cannot tighten a screw without a screwdriver. You need a wooden spoon to stir a pan of soup or stew, otherwise you would burn your fingers. You can cast a magical circle without a sword or a wand - but it feels like a better and more magical circle when it has been cast with the appropriate tool. The subtle energies involved in magic are affected by physical tools in much the same way as denser matter is affected by tools (stirring, cutting, and so on).

---

[56] *Tool Use in Animals: Cognition and Ecology*
http://www.cambridge.org/gb/academic/subjects/life-sciences/biological-anthropology-and-primatology/tool-use-animals-cognition-and-ecology

Magic is not all in the mind - the body is part of it too. Doing magic is a physical process as well as a mental or 'astral' one. The conceptual separation of mind and body, spirit and matter, is a Western phenomenon which has been a disaster for our civilisation in so many ways, involving the denigration of sexuality and sensuality, the denial of the pleasures of the flesh, a dysfunctional relationship with food, and behaving as if the Earth, the other animals, birds, and plants with whom we share it are expendable 'resources'. Using magical tools helps to remind us that magic is an embodied spirituality, and to involve our bodies in the process of creating magical energy. Indeed, some of the tools used in Wicca have specific uses for enhancing the sense of being in the body.

Tools are powerful symbols. Much of magic and ritual is about engaging with and awakening the poetic and symbolic aspects of the mind (the "right-brain" functions). The use of tools as symbols speaks to these aspects of the mind (sometimes referred to as "Younger Self"). Tools are part of a complex set of magical associations involving directions, elements, planets, deities, trees, and so on, all of which speak to the poetic, mystical, and symbolic side of our natures. They are part of a poetic language of witchcraft. The process of getting into the twilight consciousness required for ritual is assisted and enhanced by using familiar words, tools, imagery, and physical movements, evoking muscle memory and awareness of space.

So, maybe you do not need tools, but why would you want to do without them?

The Witch's Tools

When gathering your tools, it is much better to make or find your own tools when the time is right, or when the right material comes to your hand. Some of my most powerful tools and implements are ones I have found in the woods and fields. I have cleaned them up and enhanced their natural interest very slightly. I see them as friends and allies. Tools that I have bought take much longer to 'bed in'.

In folkloric witchcraft, the stang is a very important tool. It is also an altar. The stang is a forked stick and was traditionally made of ash; some are made of hazel[57]. The Norse World Tree, Yggdrasil, is an ash tree, and the stang may represent the World Tree or Axis Mundi. The stang is adorned with crossed arrows, the weapon of the Hunter, the Horned Gods of the woods; these may also represent the crossroads of Hecate. The stang is sometimes decorated with a wreath of seasonal flowers, for the circle of the year and for the Goddess.

Both Wiccans and folkloric witches use the cup or chalice, but in folkloric Craft, it is part of the coven regalia. The cup is a feminine symbol and represents the source of all life, the vulva, or indeed any receptive and generative vessel. It can also represent the primordial waters. In inclusive Wicca, when consecrating the wine, we like to emphasise that we are celebrating all acts of love and pleasure, so we sometimes start the consecration of the wine by saying "as the lightning struck the primordial waters, bringing forth life, so the athame touches the wine". This is inspired by the writings of Lynna Landstreet, who identifies the lightning striking the

---

[57] https://downstrodden.wordpress.com/2012/05/05/implements-of-arte-part-i-the-stang/

primordial waters as the primary polarity.⁵⁸ Then we say, "as the athame is to the lover, so the cup is to the beloved".

Another way to consecrate the wine is to pour one cup of wine into another, and then repeat this around the circle, saying "I fill your cup with love". This was inspired by the Temperance card in the Tarot. (It helps if both cups are the same size.)

For me, the cauldron is one of the quintessential symbols of witchcraft. It can be used as a container for energy - each member of the coven focuses their energy into the cauldron, and it may then be used for healing or other magic. In Irish legend, the cauldron was a vessel of healing and transformation. In folkloric Craft, the cauldron represents the Goddess of the Craft.

Just as I started typing the paragraph about the cauldron, my cat Morrissey came and jumped on my lap, as if to remind me that familiars are also very important. Here is a picture of him sitting in my cauldron - not posed, he just jumped into it one day.

---

[58] Lynna Landstreet (1993/1999), *Alternate Currents: Revisioning Polarity: Or, what's a nice dyke like you doing in a polarity-based tradition like this?* Copyright 1993 by Lynna Landstreet. Originally appeared in The Blade & Chalice, Spring 1993. Slightly revised in 1999. http://www.wildideas.net/temple/library/altcurrents.html

My cat Bean sitting on my besom, hoping it will fly.

The broomstick is another traditionally witchy tool; it is also an item of coven regalia in the Cochrane Tradition. As well as being a representation of a horse which can carry the witch to other realms (perhaps by applying flying ointment to the handle before mounting it naked), the broom also symbolises the union of masculine and feminine, as the end of the handle is traditionally carved as a phallus, and the bristles represent the lady-garden. The handle is often made of ash (again to symbolise the World Tree), the bristles of hazel (a tree of wisdom), and the bindings of willow (associated with the Moon).

Isobel Gowdie, a Scottish witch put on trial in 1662, mentioned the use of the broomstick[59]. Her confessions were voluntary and not induced by torture, go into much more detail than others, and sound more genuine. She used the following rhyme in her practice:

> "Horse and hattock, Horse and go,
> Horse and Pellatis, Ho Ho!"

She believed that she was then able to fly by mounting a broomstick, and said,

> "Then they would put a strae [straw] between their legs, cry -- "Horse and hattock in the Devil's name!" and flee awa owre [away over] the muirs [moors] and fells."

In folkloric witchcraft, a skull may also be part of the coven regalia and used for oracular purposes. It may also become a

---

[59] Sarah Lawless (2013), *Horse and Hattock: The Origin of the Witch's Chant*, http://sarahannelawless.com/wp-content/uploads/2013/04/Horse_and_Hattock.pdf

spirit-house for an ancestor or spirit-guardian of the coven. Nowadays this is usually an animal skull.

The eight working tools of Wicca are the athame (black-handled knife), the boline or burin (white-handled knife), the sword, the wand, the pentacle, the censer of incense, the scourge, and the cords. It has often been remarked that there are a lot of pointy things in this list, possibly because Gerald Gardner was really fascinated by knives (fascinated enough to write a treatise on the Malay Kris).

People have also wondered why the cup and cauldron were not on the list. It is interesting to compare with the Cochrane Tradition, where they are part of the coven regalia.

The athame represents the witch's will and is used to direct magical energy and cast circles. The use of a black-handled knife comes from The Key of Solomon. Traditionally, the Wiccan athame has sigils etched on the handle, but I never did this to mine, as I prefer the feel of it without them.

No-one is quite sure of the etymology of the word athame, and there is not even a consensus on how to pronounce it (in our house we occasionally sing a little ditty which goes 'I say uh-THAY-mee and you say uh-THAH-may'). It seems that early Wiccans pronounced it 'uh-THAIM' as Philip Heselton's excellent biography of Gerald Gardner describes how a reporter mis-spelled it as "thaim". He had presumably heard the witches saying 'uh-THAIM' and though that an athame was 'a thaim'.

The burin or boline is a white-handled knife used for cutting herbs, etching sigils into wax (such as a wax pentacle or a candle) and is supposed to be used only for magical work.

The sword represents the will of the coven, and whoever holds it is wielding the will of the coven. It is often associated with Joan of Arc, who girded on a sword and became a warrior, and was later executed for witchcraft. The charges against her included dressing as a man, and she had a same-sex lover.

The wand is a very ancient magical tool, and I have several wands which I use for different purposes depending on the wood, the shape, and when and why the wand was made. Wands often represent a phallus or a sceptre, and are used for workings involving the Fair Folk, who do not like iron or steel. It may be used for consecration, and represents the lance, one of the sacred weapons associated with the mysteries of the grail.

The pentacle is used to reflect energy, to amplify it, and earth it. It traditionally has symbols etched on it. Some covens make a pentacle from a wax tablet, in honour of the idea that during times of persecution, witches' tools would need to be ordinary objects around the house, and easily transformed into something else. Others use a metal such as brass, bronze or copper.

The censer of incense is like an alchemical furnace. The incense is an offering to the gods, and a symbol of the transformative power of fire.

The cords are used to restrict blood flow and to create a light trance. This must be done carefully and not too tightly, with quick-release knots. They can also be used to make a pentagram on the pentacle. Some people use the cords as a belt in ritual.

The scourge is a widely misunderstood tool. It represents the flail that threshes the husks from the grain, an image we see in depictions of Osiris as a grain or fertility god. The scourge is not used for power and domination in the Craft, and its use should always be mutual and accompanied by a kiss.

Other things that are used in ritual and magic include a bell, for signalling the beginning and end of rituals, and also for clearing the space to create a sacred atmosphere; a mirror or a bowl of water for scrying, an altar with deity statues, candles (often black, white, and red), and seasonal objects such as corn dollies at Lammas, and Brighid's crosses at Imbolc. When preparing for ritual, it is a good idea to make a checklist of all the things you need, so that you won't find yourself running out to the kitchen for a bowl of water or some salt at the relevant point in the ritual.

There are a lot of lists of eight things in Wicca: eight Wiccan Virtues, eight working tools, eight festivals, and eight ways of working magic [60]. We could combine some of these for some interesting potential correspondences (and if this set of correspondences does not work for you, make your own, because this is somewhat conjectural anyway).

---

[60] http://afwcraft.blogspot.co.uk/2011/06/eight-ways-of-making-magic.html

Festival	Tool	Virtue	Magical pathway
Yule	Censer	Mirth	Incense, Drugs, Wine, etc.
Imbolc	Wand	Reverence	Projection of the Astral Body, or Trance
Spring Equinox	Burin	Strength	Chants, Spells, Invocations.
Beltane	Cords	Beauty	Dancing
Midsummer	Sword	Honour	The Great Rite
Lammas	Scourge (flail)	Humility	Use of the Cords
Autumn Equinox	Pentacle	Power	Meditation or concentration
Samhain	Athame	Compassion	The Scourge

An interesting series of rituals and meditations could be constructed using these correspondences to meditate on the qualities of the tool, the festival, the virtue, and the means of working magic.

Exercises

As part of the preparation for second degree initiation, I usually invite coven members to meditate on and research the magical tools. They should reflect on how they are used in magical work, their symbolism, history, and correspondences. Ideally the covener should write an essay (or make an audio recording of their reflections if they are dyslexic). They might also write some poems about the tools or create artwork around their symbolism. It is also meaningful and pleasing to make your own tools if you can. I made my own stang and my own wand.

11. The Moon

For as long as I can remember, the Moon has seemed like a source of mystery and magic. I have always had a bit of a thing about the Moon, and everything associated with the lunar side of life: poetry, intuition, silver, water, dreams, and stars. I always assumed that cats were lunar symbols until I discovered that dogs are lunar, and cats are solar. But I still prefer cats. The Moon represents the twilight half of consciousness (memories, dreams, intuition, rhythm). And of course, witches have always been associated with the Moon, and with a whole cohort of animals and birds who are also associated with the Moon, especially hares, bats, and owls.

The Moon in Poetry

The silvery light of the Moon transforms the landscape into a mysterious deep twilight blue. The moon-path (the reflection of the Moon on the sea) may lead to mysterious other realms. It certainly did for Lucius Apuleius when the great goddess Isis appeared to him as the full Moon over the sea, and transformed him back into a human being, releasing him from the enchantment that had turned him into an ass. [61]

> "Behold Lucius I am come, thy weeping and prayers have moved me to succour thee. I am she that is the natural mother of all things, mistress and governess of all the elements, the initial progeny of worlds, chief of powers divine, Queen of heaven, the principal of the Gods celestial, the light of the goddesses: at my will the planets of the air, the wholesome winds of the Seas, and the silences of hell

[61] https://legacy.fordham.edu/halsall/ancient/lucius-assa.asp

be disposed; my name, my divinity is adored throughout all the world in divers manners, in variable customs and in many names, for the Phrygians call me Pessinunctia, the mother of the Gods: the Athenians call me Cecropian Artemis: the Cyprians, Paphian Aphrodite: the Candians, Dictynna: the Sicilians , Stygian Proserpine: and the Eleusinians call me Mother of the Corn. Some call me Juno, others Bellona of the Battles, and still others Hecate. Principally the Ethiopians which dwell in the Orient, and the Egyptians which are excellent in all kind of ancient doctrine, and by their proper ceremonies accustomed to worship me, do call me Queen Isis."

This theme was picked up by Dion Fortune in her wonderful book, *The Sea Priestess*. Both Wilfred, the protagonist of *The Sea Priestess*, and his young bride at the end of the book, are awakened spiritually by communing with the Moon.

There is a great poem by Sylvia Plath, *The Moon and the Yew Tree* [62], which describes the contrast between the Moon, who is "bald and wild" and "terribly upset", and Mary, who is "sweet". I rather suspect that Sylvia Plath's poetry is a contributory factor in my being a Pagan and a Wiccan. She also wrote a wonderful poem about the Horned God, called *Faun*[63], which also evokes the Moon.

In times past, the moonlight was needed because of a lack of streetlights, and the Lunar Society (Erasmus Darwin, Watt, Bolton, Wedgwood, Priestley, etc) met on full moon nights to be able to travel at night. The *Carmina Gadelica* praises the

---

[62] You can hear Sylvia Plath reading the poem at https://www.youtube.com/watch?v=GNhzsoFOw14
[63] http://www.internal.org/Sylvia_Plath/Faun

Moon as 'the glorious lamp of the poor', and there are four prayers to the Moon[64] in the collection, which was gathered in the Highlands and Islands of Scotland by folklorist Alexander Carmichael in the late 19th century.

There are many Moon deities, both male and female. In Wicca, we tend to regard the Moon as female and the Sun as male; in Heathenry, the Sun is female and the Moon is male. Many other cultures have a male Moon deity too - Chandra in India, Shin in Mesopotamia, Tsukuyomi in Japan. There are also many Moon goddesses: the Greek goddesses Phoebe, Artemis, Selene, and Hecate; and the Chinese goddess Chang'e. Some of these deities are associated with witches.

In ancient times, people would kiss their hand to the New Moon. (This is mentioned in the Hebrew Bible[65], Job 31: 26-28.) The Moon was believed to govern growth and fertility, so that planting should always be done at the New Moon, so that the plant would grow with the waxing Moon. Many plants are associated with the Moon, especially white flowers that give off a scent at night, and ones that are traditionally used in witchcraft.

For me, the Moon is the source and origin of witchcraft: the lunar energy, the mysterious qualities of the Moon, and the association with the night, wildness, freedom, spirituality, and sexuality. Poets and mystics of all religions have praised the beauty of the Moon - especially the Sufis, who also have a mystical relationship with the night.

---

[64] http://www.gaolnaofa.org/rituals/prayers-to-the-moon/
[65] I never refer to this book as the "Old Testament". It is a book in its own right, written by the Jewish people.

The phases of the Moon are also important. The Moon rules the tides of the sea; but she is also believed to rule the tides of the mind. Magic for increase should always be done on the waxing Moon; magic for decrease, on the waning Moon.

The Moon rules the twilight side of life, the wild, the uncanny, the preternatural. Civilisation tries to ignore the Moon, because she is the liberator of the oppressed and shines her light into the nooks and crannies, revealing the deeds that are done by night. But the Moon always returns with her messages from the subconscious, from the endless sea of dreams.

Menstruation

The monthly cycle of fertility is also associated with the Moon, and some people menstruate in synch with the Moon. The month was divided into weeks to represent the phases of the goddess Ishtar's menses, and the day of rest was originally invented so as not to disturb her when she was menstruating.

The Moon itself represents inconstancy, changeability, growth, illusion, water, dreams, night, the subconscious, reflected light, receptivity, Yin. It is sometimes associated with fire – it was believed in some traditions that when a piece of wood burned, it was the energy of the moonlight being released. Hares were believed to be an omen of fire, and witches were often believed to shapeshift into hares. And of course, the Moon is associated with witches and magic.

Moon symbols

Animals: Dog, hare, rabbit, lobster, crab, snake (it sheds its skin so is cyclical); all horned animals, e.g. Bull, cow, stag (horns represent crescent moon).

Aspen, Alder, and **Elder** trees are sacred to the Moon. The aspen trembles, rather like moonlight reflected in water. Alder trees grow beside water. Elder trees are associated with the triple goddess of the Moon, because they have white blossoms, red unripe berries, and black ripe berries.

Bat: A creature associated with darkness, the Moon, and the feminine.

Circle: Before this became a symbol of the Sun, it was a symbol of the Moon. The stone circles on the Orkney Islands of Scotland are still called Temples of the Moon.

Crystal, especially quartz: This stone represents the full moon and its divinatory powers.

Garden Grotto: The moon goddess or god was often worshipped in a grotto or garden and contained either a Moon tree (e.g. an Olive), sacred stone, a spring or all three.

Moonstone: A whitish, cloudy form of feldspar gemstone that is said to cure nervousness and bring good luck to its owner.

Owl: The owl is a symbol of the Moon, wisdom, and sacred lunar mysteries.

Willow: A moon tree sacred to such Dark Moon deities as Hecate, Circe, and Persephone.

The Babylonian Moon Tree and the Tree of Life

There was a strong link between the image of the tree and the figure of the woman. Both were linked with the moon, and mysterious power. Poles, paintings, and sculptures were created to represent the tree - these representations often included crescent shapes to depict the Moon, circles to represent women and magic, and a leaf for growth.

The Babylonian creation myth says that the tree of life was to be found at the heart of a garden paradise. They believed that the first Babylonian Dynasty dates from the year that the gods made the garden. The tree of life is often associated with the primordial sweet waters - the Apsu.

In this ancient Near East religion, the king is closely associated with the Tree of Life and bears a branch from the tree of life as his sceptre. This tie between the king and the tree allows the king power over life and death. There are many references to the king summoning up the dead.

English Pagan Moon Names

Ice Moon - Silver	Lightning Moon - Silver
Snow Moon - Pink	Harvest Moon - Gold
Death Moon - Black	Hunting Moon - Orange
Awakening Moon - Blue	Blood Moon - Red
Grass Moon - Light Green	Tree Moon - Brown
Planting Moon - Dark Green	Long Moon - Purple
Rose Moon - Pink	

Blue Moon – there are 13 moons in a year, and a blue moon is when there are two full moons in a month.

Discussion

What do you associate with the Moon? (jot down your ideas on a piece of paper)

Does the waxing and waning of the Moon affect you?

Do you associate the Moon with gods or goddesses, or both?

Exercises

Meditate on the Moon at the different phases.

Let moonlight fall on a bowl of water. Drink the water in a sacred manner and feel yourself filled with moonlight.

Create a Moon garden with herbs and flowers sacred to the Moon.

Part 2: Embodied Spirituality

This section explores the inner work in the context of the body, and how we relate to other people, both within and beyond the ritual circle, how we relate to Nature, to gods and spirits, to the seasons of the year, and to the land.

12. Relationships

Relationships are the pivotal point where the inner work connects with the outer work - both in ritual, and in life in general. It is in working with a group that we "rub off the sharp corners" of our personalities, learning to play well with others. We also make ourselves vulnerable and open, which means that we need to take care of each other.

Body, Mind, and Spirit

The relationship of body, mind, and spirit is complex. The Egyptians identified thirteen different parts of the soul. Other cultures identify three parts. Based on the views of Victor Anderson, Starhawk wrote that people have three levels of awareness:

> "Talking Self", the conscious mind;
>
> "Younger Self", the unconscious and instinctual mind
>
> "Deep Self", the numinous aspect of the psyche, which can connect with the Divine.

In her book *The Spiral Dance*, Starhawk says that the purpose of witchcraft is to enable communication between these aspects of the self, and this is achieved by doing ritual. Having these aspects in balance seems like an excellent goal for ritual. These three selves are also explored in T Thorn Coyle's book, *Evolutionary Witchcraft*. The three 'selves' of the Feri and Reclaiming traditions also correspond closely to the tripartite Jewish concept of the soul.

> The **Nefesh** is the animal and instinctual part of the soul. It is connected with instincts and physical cravings. It is said to enter the physical body at birth. It

is the source of a person's physical and psychological nature.

The **Ruach** is the middle soul, or spirit, and contains the virtues and the ability to distinguish between good and evil. It equates to the psyche or ego-personality.

The **Neshamah** is the higher soul or Higher Self. In the Zohar, it is said that Nefesh disintegrates after death, and Ruach is sent to an intermediate zone where it is subject to purification and enters a "temporary paradise", while Neshamah returns to the source, the world of Platonic ideas, where it enjoys "the kiss of the beloved". Supposedly after resurrection, Ruach and Neshamah, soul and spirit re-unite in a permanently transmuted state of being.[66]

The Ruach and the Neshamah are not present at birth but are slowly created over time; their development depends on the actions and beliefs of the individual. They are said to only fully exist in people awakened spiritually.

Friendships

Friendships are structured by ritual (birthday parties and dinner parties, keeping in touch by phone and email) and gift exchange (birthday and Yule gifts, thank you gifts for house-sitting or pet-sitting, and so on). The first time you meet someone, and you make a connection with them, perhaps exchange contact details, you will probably arrange to meet again in a neutral space like a pub. It is only later that things will escalate to inviting each other round for dinner, telling

---

[66] Wikipedia

each other more about other areas of your life, introducing each other to other friends, and so on. Social media has added a different dimension to all this of course, as you can now be online friends with someone before you have physically met them. Social media has probably also altered the level of personal disclosure that people are comfortable with, too.

Friends are wonderful people, but it is interesting to note that there is a certain level of intimacy we reach with friends, beyond which it becomes difficult to maintain the equilibrium of the friendship. Many years ago, a close friend and I spent nearly every day together, and it got a bit too much. We had to pull apart for a bit. We are still friends, though, so it worked. People do not generally go into the level of detail with their friends that they would go into with a therapist. There is a good reason for this: friends are not objective; therapists try to be, and therapists do not know their clients outside of the one-to-one therapeutic relationship.

Friendships generally aren't expressed through erotic contact (except in the case of "friends with benefits"), so this is another boundary that tends to be maintained between friends, and it is often awkward to renegotiate a friendship as an intimate relationship.

There are two reasons for the rituals and protocols of friendship: one is maintaining the connection; the other is maintaining the distance. There are also steps in the process: first you meet on neutral ground, then you meet at each other's homes, and so on. There is usually a sense of reciprocity; not as an exact balance, but an awareness that if your friend helps you move to a new house, that means you would help them move house, or take them out to dinner. If a friend listens to your relationship problems, then it is generally expected that you would do the same for them.

The amazing thing about friendships is that they can start at any level - an instant sense of having known the person before or knowing that you would like them. Sometimes friendships build more slowly than that, and perhaps the ones you need to work at are deeper in the end; but that sense of instant recognition is very powerful.

Friendships contribute to the inner work, partly through the alchemy of social interaction, and working at being sociable, but also because our friends reflect back to us a facet of ourselves, or complement something that may be missing from our perspective on the world, or from our psychological makeup. But the most important thing about friends, it seems to me, is that they love you as you are. Friends that you have had for decades, who have seen you through life's ups and downs, are particularly special. Like Lucy and the Sea Girl[67], you looked at each other and recognised a friend, and that was it. Time, distance, neglect, bad behaviour, and so on may erode or erase that feeling, but it was probably there at some point in the friendship, even if it took time to grow.

Familiars

Many witches enjoy the companionship of an animal such as a cat or dog. Some have more unusual companion animals. During the witch persecutions, people with companion animals were looked upon with suspicion. Names such as Pyewacket and Grimalkin were recorded as names of witches'

---

[67] C.S Lewis, *Voyage of the Dawn Treader*

familiars; they are accordingly popular with contemporary witches.

The experience of being loved and trusted by a companion animal is a beautiful thing. Stroking a cat or dog has been shown to bring down blood pressure and ease stress. Many older people benefit from having a companion animal.

Cats and dogs sometimes seem aware of spirits and energies - such as when a cat sits and stares out of a window into the darkness, even though there is apparently nothing there.

In ancient Egypt, cats were worshipped as deities. Both cats and cat-lovers tend to feel this was entirely appropriate, and that the practice of cat-worship should be restored.

Spouses, Lovers, Paramours, Metamours

The key to any good relationship is communication and cooperation. Regardless of whether it is monogamous or polyamorous, communicating about what your boundaries are, what is happening in your life, how you feel, and so on, is going to be a good thing. However, endless conversations about the relationship itself, and the dynamics of it, can be very unhelpful for some people. It is often better to focus on doing something together, rather than on the quality of the relationship.

I regard being monogamous and polyamorous as like sexual orientations. I always assumed that I was polyamorous and then discovered otherwise. I tried and failed to be polyamorous. I am monogamous, and it is nothing to do with jealousy and everything to do with love. Friends who are polyamorous report that they have always felt that way. I have always thought that I would be polyamorous, but in practice I have mostly been monogamous, and I have enjoyed it more than polyamory, when I was with the right person.

I fully support the efforts of polyamorous people to get their relationships recognised and to get the security of a contract, up to and including marriage, if that is what they want to do. (Some opponents of polyamory have argued that this will open the door to unequal relationships – but a monogamous relationship does not guarantee equality, sadly.) I also fully support the right of polyamorous people not to get married, if that is what they choose.

Obviously, the issue is clouded by the fact that monogamy is assumed as a cultural default, so people rarely need to come out as monogamous. Most people must discover they are polyamorous and then work out how to make it work. I am sure there are many people who are naturally inclined toward polyamory who are trying awkwardly to fit in the cultural mould of monogamy. However, as someone who assumed from the outset that I was polyamorous, but then discovered that I am monogamous, I am convinced that a person's orientation towards poly or mono exists at a deeper level of the psyche than mere choice, and is a sexual/romantic orientation in the same way as one's preference for different-sex or same-sex partners, or both.

Whether you are polyamorous or monogamous, however, clear communication about the boundaries of your relationships, and how you relate to your partner(s), is the key to success. There are some excellent blogs, workshops, and books on how to improve communication in relationships, whether it is with spouses, lovers, paramours (people you are having a sexual relationship with), or metamours (sexual partners of your paramours).

The element of erotic connection in a relationship brings in a whole new set of dynamics and ethics. Morning Glory Zell's foundational essay[68], *A Bouquet of Lovers: Strategies for Responsible Open Relationships* (1990), sets out some of the boundaries to be negotiated. The first thing she sets out is the requirement for complete openness and honesty, together with the full consent of all parties to participating in a polyamorous lifestyle. It also sets out how to deal with jealousy, introduces the concept of primary and secondary partners (not embraced by all polyamorous people, but still a helpful concept), and discusses the use of a 'condom commitment cadre' to prevent the spread of venereal disease. This is a system where the members of the cadre are all tested and disease-free and commit to using a condom with anyone outside the group.

Since Zell's essay, many others have written articles and books on how to manage polyamory successfully.

Monogamous people can also learn from these efforts, because we also need to manage jealous feelings around our partner's ex-partners, friends whom we might see as potential partners, and so on. Jealousy is mostly a destructive and negative emotion, which needs to be kept in check, especially when it turns into its evil twin, possessiveness. If you trust your

---

[68] Morning Glory Zell (1990), *A Bouquet of Lovers: Strategies for Responsible Open Relationships*, http://www.patheos.com/Resources/Additional-Resources/Bouquet-of-Lovers

partner, have good communication with them, and have good self-esteem, why would you constantly live in fear that they are going to run off with someone else?

Successful relationships have good communication, trust, openness, and a desire for the wellbeing of your partner.

Community

In terms of age and class and education, Pagans are not particularly diverse, though our diversity is increasing. This is probably because Paganisms have not been around all that long. Many Pagans worry that the Pagan community is uniquely fractured, troubled, and generally argumentative. In my experience, this is normal. Most communities have conflict. What is great about the Pagan community is that we mostly try not to impose restrictive norms on our fellow Pagans.

Pagans are more focussed on individual friendships and networks of friendships than on gathering in community. In a crisis, Pagan friends will rally round. I have seen this time and again, where someone will have a problem, and Pagans will offer support.

It would be good if Pagans focussed more on shared values instead of differing beliefs. This varies from one Pagan group to the next, but as it is becoming more apparent that there is conflict whenever someone suggests inclusiveness towards LGBTQIA+ people, people of colour, and disabled people, Pagan groups are beginning to organise themselves by values rather than beliefs.

Wiccans have always been focussed on our practice and the mysteries rather than theological belief, but this can vary.

Groups

People join magical groups (covens, groves, clans, hearths) because they want someone to celebrate festivals with, and to learn from and bounce ideas off. Personally I love having a magical group, because it gives me the opportunity to do ritual with other people, to exchange ideas, and to have conversations about stuff that never normally gets talked about, and to experience those moments when all the energies of the group flow together and become more than the sum of their parts.

Groups can be wonderful if you find the right people to celebrate with; they can also be a bit dysfunctional. The trick is to go about the process of finding a group with your eyes open. If you experience warning signs and feel that the group you are considering joining does not fit your needs, proceed with caution. Finding the right group for your needs can be tricky. Most people are either incredibly cautious about approaching groups, or touchingly enthusiastic and hence vulnerable.

It is all too tempting to assume that the group you have found was somehow meant for you, and to ignore the warning signs - but sometimes that is not the way life works, and it is just a really excellent idea to run a mile. If the group that you are considering joining tries to tell you that they are the One True Way and that all the other groups have it wrong - run away. Even if the group doesn't exhibit the classic warning signs, but their approach and philosophy is just not a good fit with yours, then maybe they are not the right group for you, and you are not the right new member for them.

I often come across people who say that they do not want to join a group for various reasons. Some of them have had a bad experience of being in a group that has put them off. That is understandable, but not every group is the same. I had a couple of bad experiences, but that did not put me off groups completely – it just made me more cautious. Others say that they need to do more work on themselves before joining a group. My answer to that one would be that a group is a great place to work on yourself, because social interaction with others is where personal change and growth usually happens. Another reason for not wanting to join a group that I have come across is being an introvert. That seems like a valid reason. But joining a group does not necessarily mean you have to reveal your deepest secrets or spend vast amounts of time with others; it does mean engaging with them on a quest for meaning and connection.

When you are approaching a group, ask lots of questions.

- Does the group have ground rules?
- How often do they meet?
- Do they expect you to copy out rituals by hand?
- What is their attitude to disagreement - theological or magical or political? Are they prepared to learn from other people?
- How do they feel about members being involved with other traditions?
- Do they value previous experience?
- Do they value creativity and extemporisation, or do they prefer more formal rituals?
- Can you meet the existing members?
- Is there a training process prior to initiation?

- Can you attend an open ritual before deciding whether to embark on the training?
- Do they work skyclad?
- Do they have initiations? How far into the training do these happen?

You should also ask yourself a similar set of questions.

- Do you want a group that has ground-rules?
- How far are you prepared to travel for meetings?
- How many meetings per year are you willing to commit to?
- Do you want to copy out rituals by hand?
- How do you feel about people with different opinions from yours? Are you prepared to be challenged in your thinking?
- Do you have the time and energy to be involved with more than one tradition?
- What skills and experiences can you bring to the group?
- What style of ritual do you prefer?
- Are you prepared to put in the effort of engaging with the training process and learning new things?
- Are you comfortable with the idea of working skyclad?
- Are you comfortable with the idea of initiation?

The answers to these questions will vary from one individual to another, and from one group to another. Hopefully, you can find a group whose answers to the questions are a reasonably close match with your answers.

How to Spot an Unethical Group

I would strongly advise against joining any group that exhibits any of the following behaviours:

- Charges money for training or initiation. [69]
- Claims that sexual intercourse is required as part of any ritual or initiation (it can be part of the third-degree initiation, but it is optional). It is never part of the first- or second-degree initiation.
- Claims that sexual intercourse is acceptable between a senior member of the coven (i.e. high priestess or high priest) and a junior member of the coven (i.e. dedicant, neophyte, or initiate).
- Dismisses large swathes of legitimate members of the Craft as "not proper witches".
- Tries to limit social contact between coveners outside of meetings.
- Tries to limit your social contact with other Wiccans.
- Tries to tell you not to read certain books.
- Peremptorily dismisses any concerns you have about something that makes you uncomfortable, e.g. by calling you a prude.
- Tries to prevent you from reading widely and critically about Wicca. [70]

---

[69] It is ethical to ask members to contribute to costs for incense, candles, and photocopying/printing. It is usual to ask members to bring food to share.

[70] It is ethical to advise members not to read chapters in books which reveal details of initiations, as most people want the content of initiations to be a surprise.

- Dismisses and belittles anyone who disagrees with them.
- Has members who strike you as unduly dominated by the leaders.
- Works entirely from one specific set of teachings; does not allow deviation from those principles or allow people to question them.
- Makes it difficult to leave the group and claims you will not find another group if you do leave.
- Refuses to provide verification that they are what they say they are; cannot seem to keep their story straight.

Attitudes to Money

Contemporary Paganism - like much of the rest of the world - has a deeply conflicted attitude to money. Money is probably even harder to talk about than sex and death. People tend to think it is a deeply unspiritual topic. It probably is - but we still need to talk about it. Money can also make relationships difficult, especially if the people in the relationship have different attitudes to expenditure, lending and borrowing, savings, and so on.

Whenever the subject of Pagans and money comes up, there arises the vexed question of what spiritual services to charge for. The ethics of charging money for spirituality-related events is always tricky. On the one hand, there are those who argue that if they expend energy, they should be paid for it, and on the other hand, there are those who argue that money is the kiss of death to spirituality.

To think about this issue a little more clearly, let's go back to a time before money, and look at how money was probably invented.

The Tribe - communal effort

Let us imagine that I am the village spirit-worker. It is my job to find herds for the tribe to hunt, and to talk with the ancestors and the spirits to find out useful knowledge, and to heal ailments suffered by the tribe. I contribute my knowledge and skills to the tribe in order that the people may survive and flourish. The hunters contribute their hunting skills and bring back food. Various other members of the tribe cure leather, sew it together to make clothes, make tools and weapons and cooking pots, knap flint, and gather herbs. Everyone contributes, and everyone gets their share. And everyone knows that "what goes around comes around". No-one keeps count of who owes what to whom, because everyone pulls together for the survival of the whole group.

The Village - barter

In later centuries, a hierarchical view develops, and some people are considered more worthy of food and resources. Now, the tribe has settled in one place, and owns separate houses and separate cooking pots and separate hearths. A barter system develops, in which I exchange my work for food, clothes, and medicine.

The City and money

After a while, people start to think that it is a bit inconvenient to exchange work for things. What if you need me to help with your harvest, but you can only offer me a couple of chickens in exchange, but I do not want any more chickens right now? Then it is easier to say, well I will give you this lump of gold, and you can exchange it for whatever you want later. In addition, villages have got larger and become cities, in which the inhabitants do not know everyone else in the town. Tribal links are weakened, perhaps dissolved. Family links and alliances become more important - and it is only in family settings that people do not count the cost. Though perhaps guilds provide a kind of replacement for the tribe. And that, I would suggest, is how money was invented.

The Celts started to use coins from the 5th to 1st centuries BCE, and minted coins based on Greek designs (they needed money for trade with the Greeks). The ancient Greeks began to use coins in about 700 BCE. The Romans began using coins in the third century BCE.

At various points in our lives, we return to one or other of these means of exchange. During a harvest, or when someone moves to a new house, or at a Pagan camp, we return to communal effort mode. It feels idyllic, partly because we have lost our need to 'count the cost' in the knowledge that we are all mucking in together, and that the whole will be greater than the sum of the parts.

Sometimes, when money runs short, we return to barter mode. There are community credit schemes where you can exchange piano lessons for bread-making or baby-sitting for bicycle repair.

A Pagan Camp in Communal Effort Mode

If you go to a Pagan event with a large number of people, and a significant number (say, more than half) of them are offering workshops, helping out with the fire-pit, organising the technical aspects, and generally contributing to the community, then you know that you won't have to do more than your fair share, and you will get to benefit from other people's workshops, and at this type of event, you probably don't expect to get paid for your one- or two-hour long workshop, because you will attend at least ten other really good workshops given by other people, and you know that if you attend the same event in the future, you will benefit from the workshops there too. This type of event becomes like a mutually supportive tribe – what goes around comes around – no need to pay speakers.

A Pagan Camp in City Mode

If, on the other hand, you go to a different type of Pagan event, where less than half of the participants are offering workshops, and the workshop leaders are contributing more than a couple of hours of their time each, and are not getting a comparable benefit from attending other people's workshops (perhaps because the speakers have considerably more knowledge than most of the other attendees, or because it is a day or weekend event, and so there is no time for them to attend other people's workshops) – then it is a really good idea to factor in paying the speakers.

And it is really important to note that in both these examples, the speakers get paid – it is just that in the first example they are paid 'in kind' through receiving the benefit of workshops from other people; and in the second example, they get paid with money.

An Exchange of Energy

The giving of money in exchange for something does not create relationship, it ends it. If I pay in full for a service or a commodity, my obligation is discharged, and that ends the relationship. If I pay for a massage, a Tarot reading, or a workshop, that is because the masseur, Tarot reader, or workshop leader is not going to receive from me (at some unspecified future date) a massage, a Tarot reading, or a workshop. The relationship is ended by the payment. This is, I think, why Wiccans believe strongly that we should not charge trainees for training. Members of a coven are in a relationship, and payment for training would end that relationship. What you gain in return for teaching is an opportunity to formulate, clarify, and refine your own views in the process of transmitting them to others. You can also learn from your trainees. And in due course, you will have a coven to work with who can write rituals for you to take part in. All members of a coven are expected to contribute food for the feast and candles and incense for rituals, and help with the washing-up, however.

Note that I am not saying that charging money for services such as Tarot reading, or even rituals like a handfasting, is a bad thing. All services create some obligation. If I invite you to my ritual, you will probably feel obliged to invite me to yours. If someone gives you training in Wicca, you should feel obliged to turn up on time, make an effort to absorb what they try to teach you, and at some point in the future, to reciprocate by creating awesome rituals that they can enjoy, and to 'pay it forward' by training others in Wicca.

Paying money for services rendered just ends the obligation. That can help to make things simpler; sometimes we do not want to enter into relationship with a person who has done something for us, because they are not part of our social group, or because - for one reason or another - we will not see them again, so we discharge the obligation by paying them in full.

However, we do end up having a sort of relationship with people we pay money to - you go to a particular shop because the staff are friendly, or because the shopkeeper is nice; you go to the same hairdresser because you have become one of their clients, and you develop customer loyalty.

The barter and exchange model, and the communal effort model, both create a web of obligation and relationship. That is great – but there can be a shadow side to that, just as money has its shadow side. One can end up so obligated to others that they have power over you in some way, for example.

And then there's capitalism

Of course, all of this gets much more complex and layered by the introduction of capitalism. Once capitalism rears its ugly head, you get third parties who want to make money by brokering the services offered by others, and as Rhyd Wildermuth[71] has pointed out, it has even infected hitherto communal exchanges like offering acquaintances a bed for the night.

The introduction of capitalism means that people can buy the services of one person, and sell them at an inflated price to

---

[71] Rhyd Wildermuth (2015), "Putting Out". *Gods & Radicals.* http://godsandradicals.org/2015/06/19/putting-out/

someone else, and that a third party can invest in the whole enterprise, and expect to get a profit in return for their investment, despite not having done any actual work.

And then, even paying your workers comes to seem like a bad idea to some capitalists, so they go and kidnap a large population from somewhere else, treat them as property, and make them work for nothing. And that is how colonialism and slavery were invented.

Money is a form of energy

So, whilst the abstract nature of money is partly what made capitalism possible, it is also a useful marker for indicating that you are owed a certain amount of goods or services from the communal pool.

Of course, it might be wonderful to move towards a tribal model where everyone gets what they need - but that would entail a considerable loss of individuality, and I am willing to bet that even the most ardent advocate of communal living is not quite ready to go there yet. And we do not have the kind of society that makes that kind of community possible for more than a short space of time, though we can pioneer it as a model.

I think it would be very difficult not to reinvent money, even if we succeeded in re-establishing a tribal / communal model, because there would still be a need for long-distance trade with strangers who would be outside the pool of communal effort, which means you need non-perishable tokens of exchange (otherwise known as money).

Nor do I think it is realistic to ask people to offer workshops entirely for nothing - you either get paid in kind, or with money, or you operate on a pay-it-forward model. Yes, I train people in Wicca for the good of the tribe, and I don't expect money in return, but I do expect commitment and effort on the part of trainees, and one day, I can relax and let them run a ritual for me to participate in. What goes around comes around.

Wicca and Consent

The circle is a space where you can commune with the universe, develop the self, engage in sacred play, and honour the divine with each other. There is freedom from unnecessary social constraint. We celebrate the beauty of the night and the human body, and the firelight flickering on naked flesh. The leaping fire and candle flames are symbolic of life and passion. We feel that we are journeying together to other worlds, communing with the ancestors, the land, and the spirits of the land, walking with gods and goddesses.

Wicca, like other esoteric and ecstatic religious practices, has counter-cultural aspects. How do we negotiate consent around these? How do we ground our understanding of consent in the ethics of Wicca? How do we practice consent in the circle and in the coven? What are the points in Wiccan liturgy where consent is sought from the participants? And how does Wiccan mythology and theology support consensual practices?

The Ethics of Wicca

If you ask most people what the ethics of Wicca are, they will tell you about the Wiccan Rede, "An it harm none, do what thou wilt" (If it harms no-one, do your true will). They may also mention that the Rede is akin to the Golden Rule which appears in every religious tradition, with slight variations. Some have criticised the Wiccan Rede, pointing out that nearly every action results in some harm to another being. But hardly anyone has noticed that if you turn the Rede around, what it is implying is that since it is impossible not to do harm, it is also impossible to do whatever you want. The ethical implication is that we should think before we act and consider the possible outcomes of every action. The Rede also implies that even the smallest action can have consequences. To do something to someone else without their consent, however overtly friendly, or apparently trivial the offence may be, can harm that person by violating their autonomy and integrity.

In another important piece of Wiccan liturgy, *The Charge of the Goddess*, the listener is enjoined to cultivate eight virtues: beauty and strength, power and compassion, honour and humility, mirth and reverence. Brought together in balance, these virtues require the practitioners of Wicca to act with integrity. Those with strength should use it gracefully. With power comes the responsibility to act compassionately. Guarding your own honour should always be paired with having the humility to know when you have done something wrong. Laughter should not violate another person's boundaries (by laughing at something they feel vulnerable about, for example).

Another key point in *The Charge of the Goddess* is the statement that "all acts of love and pleasure are My rituals" (the rituals of the Goddess). For something to be an act of love and pleasure, it must be pleasurable for all parties involved. Consent is a prerequisite for pleasure, and a pre-requisite for trust and co-operation in any situation. Consent should be informed, given freely, and genuine. Informed consent means that the person knows enough about the activity to understand what they are choosing. Freely given means they are not under any form of coercion or compulsion. Genuine means that the activity is what they truly want to do of their own free will.

The Charge also states that "ye shall be free from slavery", which suggests that Wiccans should be autonomous and not enslaved by anyone or anything, and nor should we enslave others. That implies that we should be able to give our informed consent without feeling pressured into doing so, and that we should wait for informed, genuine, and freely given consent from others before acting in ways that affect them directly.

Further, the Charge states that the Goddess does not demand sacrifice, and that the love of the Goddess is poured out upon the Earth. This suggests that a loving and generous Goddess would not demand that we consent to things that will hurt us beyond what we can bear. I think the text is referring to literal sacrifice, and I interpret it as an injunction against the sacrifice of living beings. Elsewhere in Wiccan liturgy, we are told "To suffer is to learn" but this suffering is never interpreted as a sacrifice. We are also asked if we are willing to suffer to learn, which is an important moment of giving consent.

Consent in the Circle and the Coven

During the initiation ceremony, the candidate states that they are taking the oath, and by implication, undergoing the initiation, of their own free will and accord. As the contents of the initiation ceremony are secret, the candidate cannot specifically consent to them in advance, so they are given several opportunities in the ritual to call the whole thing off.

It is of course possible for a curious candidate to find the text of the initiation ceremony easily on the internet, but most people choose not to, preferring it to be a surprise.

There are a few counter-cultural aspects of the initiation ceremony which some candidates might find difficult (nudity, binding, and scourging). These are viewed as a test of the candidate's resolve to become a witch, as well as being potentially transformative. It must be noted, however, that by the time the initiation ceremony begins, a considerable amount of effort has been expended to set up the ritual, so it is possible that the candidate will feel pressured to continue even if they are uncomfortable. Therefore, I strongly recommend discussing the countercultural aspects in advance. You do not have to reveal specific aspects of the initiation ritual, or in what order these elements appear, but you do need to explicitly discuss each element, find out what the candidate's comfort level is in relation to it, establish how the candidate would express reluctance or discomfort whilst in an altered state in the middle of the ritual, and find out how the candidate would want you to respond if their consent changes.

Many people find ritual nudity uncomfortable, especially in front of people they do not know very well. Most covens maintain a high level of trust between the participants because they get to know each other very well through months and years of working together. But when there is a guest in the circle, some people may feel uncomfortable with being naked in front of the guest. However, sometimes practices that are intended to make people more comfortable can make them less comfortable. For example, I once worked with a group who had the women go into one room to undress and the men go into another. This separation of the sexes made me uncomfortable because it implied that there was something sexual about ritual nudity. As I have attended naturist events, where a sexual response to nudity is discouraged, I am able to dissociate nudity from the sexual. There are many activities which people do naked, or semi-naked, which are not sexual, such as sleeping, swimming, having a bath, and so on. A healthy consent culture ought to include the ability for anyone to walk around naked unmolested. Taking one's clothes off should not be automatically interpreted as a signal of sexual availability or consent to sexual touch.

During Wiccan initiation, the candidate is prepared for initiation by binding them. This is done to partially restrict blood flow and create an altered state, as well as to create a feeling of vulnerability and receptivity on the part of the candidate. Again, the candidate is given the opportunity to call a halt to the ritual.

The practice of scourging is also difficult for many people, as they tend to see it as "mortification of the flesh" or as a "punishment". In fact, it is a way of stimulating the production of endorphins, which can lead to ecstatic altered states, and is usually performed lightly. But again, there needs to be discussion around how people consent to this practice, and what its function in ritual is. Once people understand more about its symbolism, the biochemistry involved, and its function in ritual, they are usually much happier about it being a part of Wiccan ritual.

Some Wiccan covens do not explain to the candidate in advance that scourging is involved in the initiation ceremony, or discuss their reaction to it in advance, so although the ritual has built-in moments of asking for the candidate's consent, the candidate may be unsure of what they are actually consenting to, so their consent cannot be said to be fully informed.

Many people have argued that the element of surprise is a very important part of the initiation ceremony, and I am inclined to agree. So how could a coven go about preparing a candidate for initiation without losing the element of surprise? Instead of throwing candidates for initiation into the deep end, it would be better to discuss the more controversial elements (the oath, nudity, binding, and scourging) of the ceremony with them beforehand, without necessarily telling them the structure of the ritual. It could be argued that the power of the initiation ritual lies in the way it is structured, as well as its content.

I would be inclined to discuss ritual nudity, binding, and scourging, and their meaning, symbolism, and psychological effects, with a candidate before the initiation. However, I would also want to stress that no amount of discussion can convey how the experience feels. I think it is important for the candidate to understand the meaning of the practices, as they can be so easily misunderstood.

By the time the initiation happens, there should be enough trust between the initiator and the candidate that the candidate can consent to being surprised by what happens during the ritual.

The oath is there to create trust and confidentiality, and I devote a lot of time to discussing what it means both before and after initiation. I think it is also a very good idea to let people read and meditate on the oaths in advance. This is partly because I believe that the oaths create a block in the psyche, and partly because I wonder if people can genuinely assent to the oath when they are hearing it for the first time and repeating it by rote. We swear these oaths before the gods and our Craft siblings: it would therefore be a good idea for candidates to know what they mean, and what exactly they are being asked to keep secret.

Scourging should be viewed as a transformative shamanic practice, and not as punishment or "hazing". Binding is, in effect, a trust exercise, and is also used to affect blood flow and alter perception. Ritual nudity is also about trust; it symbolizes a primordial state of innocence and wildness.

After Initiation

Once the person is initiated into Wicca, however, something that I find troubling is that they are assumed to have consented to all the other things that happen in circle, such as ritual kissing (for example, it is customary to kiss other coven members on the lips to welcome them into the circle). I am not alone in finding these assumptions problematic. One Wiccan initiate commented that they would find these aspects of Wicca difficult in a non-ritual context, but as they were happening in a sacred context, they were happy with them. Another Wiccan initiate seemed to be uncomfortable kissing other coven members on the lips, despite the sacred context.

I think Wiccans need to spend more time discussing what hugging and kissing and other ritual expressions of affection mean so that everyone can give their consent in a meaningful way, rather than feeling vaguely pressured to go along with it.

Not everyone is comfortable with being hugged; not everyone is comfortable with being kissed. The only people I kiss are my immediate family, my partner, very close friends, and my coven. When offering a hug to another person, I usually "telegraph" that a hug is on offer (by opening my arms in a hugging gesture), so they can decline if they want to. However, if you do not know the other person very well, it is always best to seek verbal consent to a hug, as they may prefer not to be hugged, and non-verbal cues can be missed.

It is reasonably well-known that the Wiccan third degree initiation may involve sexual intercourse. It does not have to, and whether it does or not is a matter for the initiator and the candidate. However, there is a power difference between the initiator and the candidate, in that the initiator has something to bestow.

There is a general view among Gardnerian and Alexandrian Wiccans that doing the Great Rite "in true" (with sexual intercourse) is somehow better than doing it "in token" (symbolically or with energy exchange). Even the phrases used to describe the two options give greater weight to the sexual version of the Great Rite. But in fact, doing it symbolically or energetically may be more powerful and meaningful than doing it with sexual intercourse. If the circumstances of a sexual Great Rite may involve trying to become sexually aroused with someone the candidate does not know well, or a need to focus on the mechanics of the sex, then a symbolic Great Rite may actually help the candidate focus more completely on the movement of energy. Of course, this problem is greatly reduced if you do the Great Rite with your partner or with a close friend.

Most Wiccans approach the third degree and the Great Rite with delicacy and tact. Even so, care needs to be taken to prevent either the candidate or the initiator from feeling pressured into doing the sexual version of the Great Rite. The initiator and the candidate need to have an open and honest conversation about the possibility of ritual sex, at least a month before the ritual, in a way that does not pressure the candidate to engage in ritual sex: they must be offered a completely free choice between a symbolic ritual and engaging in ritual sex. This conversation does not reveal anything that detracts from the overall impact of the ritual.

Working as a Group

One of the aims of a Wiccan coven is to create an atmosphere of "perfect love and perfect trust". All the members of the coven have been through the same initiation ritual, which is designed to be a transformative experience; they do ritual together naked; and they usually socialise together and share their joys and sorrows with each other. All these practices promote love and trust. A high degree of mutual empathy arises, often referred to as the "group mind" or "egregore". In this atmosphere, it is hoped that people will wish to avoid harming each other. However, with that degree of openness, we also become very vulnerable to each other, and so it is possible to get hurt. Yet the joy of being so open with other human beings generally outweighs the risk. People should be aware of group dynamics, though, and mindful of the possibility of hurting other coven members in such an emotionally charged atmosphere.

When people are in an altered state in ritual, they are less likely to say no to things they do not really want to do. This may be partly because they do not want to disrupt the flow of the ritual, but also because they are in a dreamy and otherworldly state of mind where they are less likely to react negatively. But if something uncomfortable occurs in a ritual where participants feel subtly compelled to cooperate, it leaves a bad feeling behind that can erode the trust of the group. So it is always a good idea to discuss rituals beforehand and make sure everyone is comfortable with them, and discuss any special requirements people have, such as being unable to stand for long periods, or unable to lie down, or kneel down.

In larger gatherings of Wiccans, "perfect love and perfect trust" does not necessarily apply, because different groups may have different values and people will feel more vulnerable in a group of acquaintances. Consequently, they are likely to be less open and trusting. Nevertheless, there are some powerful triggers at large Wiccan gatherings which make people want to let down their guard – the pleasure of meeting with other witches, all the cues being present that tell us that we are in a safe space, and the general atmosphere of bonhomie. It is a good idea for organisers of large gatherings to have a code of conduct which includes a safeguarding procedure and an anti-harassment policy, together with a designated group of people who can be contacted if the policy is violated. The organisers then need to commit to acting decisively if the policy is violated.

Wiccan Mythology

As a polytheist Wiccan, I have the whole of Pagan mythology to draw upon to gain insights about consent, but let us look specifically at Wiccan mythology.

Wiccan mythology largely focuses on the Moon Goddess and the Horned God, sometimes referred to as the Lord of Death and Resurrection. In the various stories associated with them, they are often given a choice of actions. In *The Legend of the Descent of the Goddess*, the Goddess is offered a choice between staying in the realm of Death and allowing him to scourge her. She consents to what happens to her. In the stories of the death of the Corn King, he consents to his death when he offers himself to the Goddess. There is no explicit discussion of consent in these stories – but there are distinct moments when the protagonists give their consent.

Paying Attention to Consent

Wicca has several counter-cultural practices – in the sense that they go against prevailing norms, and that the practices mean something different in Wicca than what they mean in mainstream culture. Accordingly, considerable attention needs to be paid to issues of consent in Wicca. Consent is required for kissing, nudity, hugs, binding, scourging, and the sexual version of the Great Rite.

Fortunately, there are already built-in safeguards in the liturgy to offer choices and opportunities to give meaningful consent (or to opt out). Not enough attention is paid to these issues and people are uncomfortable with discussing them, so people who are uncomfortable with kissing and hugging and other forms of touch need to feel safe to articulate that discomfort, and be enabled to move towards consensual intimacy if they wish to do so.

However, we need to examine our practices and be sure that they are consistent with giving informed and genuine consent. Discussing issues of consent and promoting consent culture with your group and with other experienced witches is a good beginning. Beyond that, we need to develop a positive consent culture that celebrates informed, freely given, and genuine consent, and removes any sense of obligation to comply with social norms around accepting unwanted intimacy, whether they come from Pagan culture or mainstream culture.

Learning from Consent Practices in Kink

We can learn from the way that people in the BDSM community work with consent. Most kinksters establish a detailed understanding of what the parties involved consent to *before* they start any form of kinky activity or scene. This is because, once you are in an altered state of consciousness, your ability to give informed, genuine, and freely given consent may be different.

It is important to note that people cannot give meaningful consent when intoxicated (drunk, under the influence of drugs), and that their ability to consent is impaired when in an altered state of consciousness.

Another important concept in kink is hard limits and soft limits. A hard limit is something you are very clear about not wanting to do. A soft limit is something that you do not think you want to do but may be curious about trying with the right person or can only cope with for a certain amount of time. In these areas of ambiguity, it is important to establish in advance how you are going to communicate during the scene, session, or ritual that you have changed your mind.

One way to deal with communication within the session or scene is the use of the safe word. This was developed because sometimes people would say no in the middle of a scene (a kink session), but not actually mean it. Instead, a clear and unambiguous word that would be out of context in the scene is used. Some kinksters adhere to the traffic-light system, where saying 'green' means 'this is okay now but might not be in a minute'; 'amber' means 'still okay but very near my limit'; and 'red' means 'stop right now'.

The most important thing about kink and consent is that consent must be constantly present and can be withdrawn at any point during a scene, without argument. This should of course be the case for vanilla sex too, but some people assume that once consent is given, it cannot be withdrawn. This is obviously not the case, as the excellent "Consent and Tea" cartoon, article, and video make very clear.

Discussion

What are the ethical boundaries of group practice?

What do you think are the warning signs that a group is unethical?

How do you identify and negotiate consent in your group? Could your communication in this area be improved?

What ritual behaviours can you identify in how people negotiate friendships and relationships?

When is it acceptable to charge money for teaching about magical and spiritual things?

How does money affect personal relationships?

Exercises

Practice giving and receiving consent to hugs with your group.

Practice turning down a hug - how did it feel to say no? How does it feel to be turned down for a hug?

Now try asking if you can touch a specific part of the other person's body. Remember that the whole point of the exercise is that they can say no if they do not want you to touch them there.

See www.paganconsentculture.com for more exercises.

13. Ritual nudity

Much ink has been spilled in trying to figure out why doing ritual naked is so peculiarly satisfying. Gerald Gardner said that his initiators told him that it was because clothing makes it harder for the body to emit magical energy, and other books on Wicca have repeated this claim [72]. Others have pointed out that magical energy must be rather feeble if clothing inhibits it. This explanation does not seem very convincing. Nonetheless, the feeling of working skyclad does have a magical quality of freedom, trust, and a return to wildness, and it is possible that clothes alter the flow of the energies of the etheric body.

According to Ronald Hutton, other Wiccans he spoke to said that it facilitates a feeling of democracy and equality [73]. This is partly true, because class and socio-economic distinctions would be greatly reduced by removing clothing (though there would still be other cues available such as accent and dialect), but it cannot be the whole explanation. As Ronald Hutton points out, many covens are quite hierarchical, which would tend to reduce any feelings of democracy and equality.

For myself, I have always found it to facilitate a change in consciousness - not because there is anything inherently magical in taking your clothes off, but because it is slightly transgressive, and you make yourself vulnerable by removing your clothes. As Ronald Hutton explains, the practice of ritual nudity requires a great deal of trust between members of the

---

[72] Ronald Hutton (2003), *Witches, Druids, and King Arthur*. London, Hambledon and London. (p. 193)
[73] *Ibid.*

coven, and acts as a test of harmony in the group. In a religion like Wicca where we are working on the transformation of the psyche and exposing our innermost thoughts, it would be very difficult to create effective ritual without a high level of trust. [74]

Witchcraft ritual includes candlelight, incense, and chanting. These sensory stimuli suggest to the subconscious that something out of the ordinary is happening; the participants have moved from ordinary everyday consciousness to a space where consciousness can be transformed. Any nervousness felt by the participants can contribute to the sense of otherness and liminality, increase the participants' sensitivity to stimuli, and enable them to create more powerful ritual.

This explanation of why ritual nudity (known as working skyclad) is so effective fits my experience of it. In addition to all this, I think that as a religion of embodiment, we celebrate the body in all its glorious variety - and the human body, of whatever shape and size, looks particularly beautiful by candlelight.

Ronald Hutton goes on to point out that other aspects of Wicca - the celebration of the night, the Moon, and the wildness of Nature - are also countercultural, and that the nudity represents a return to a primal wild state, a resistance to 'civilisation'.[75]

The body (especially the female body) is frequently regarded as 'too much'. The depictions of witches as naked in medieval and early modern art were attempting to show the unbridled

---

[74] *Ibid*, p. 194.
[75] *Ibid*, p. 195.

sexuality of the witches. Hence the body becomes the site of resistance to the hierarchical and kyriarchal powers that attempt to regulate and control the body, sexuality, and pleasure – especially women's bodies, and especially Black women's bodies – because women, especially Black women, are constructed as the Other, the site of resistance to the kyriarchy. Because our existence provokes fear of the Other, fear of wildness, fear of sexuality, fear of letting go – our bodies and our hair (traditionally hair is a source of magical power) must be controlled, groomed, reduced, covered, suppressed. If we cover too much, we are censured for prudery; if we do not cover enough, there is slut-shaming. If our bodies are too hairy, they must be shaved; if they are too generously proportioned, they must be reduced in size.

The secret of witchcraft is that is there is no secret, only the mystery which cannot be spoken: the ability to reside in one's body without shame, without fear. (Actually, "reside in" is too dualistic, implying that the spirit "resides in" the body, like a person in a house – but this is a limitation of the English language. Witchcraft enables us to BE our bodies without shame or fear.)

The body manifests in many different shapes and sizes and colours. There are female bodies, male bodies, intersex bodies, modified bodies, disabled bodies, ebony-coloured bodies, tattooed bodies, scarred bodies, ivory-coloured bodies, pink bodies, caramel-coloured bodies, chocolate-coloured bodies, hairy bodies, smooth bodies, short bodies, tall bodies. There are bony bottoms, and bottoms that spread like the sheltering boughs of a chestnut tree. There are small breasts and large breasts, perky breasts and full breasts, six-packs and beer-barrels. The body reflects our embodied histories as people.

Gravity and age conspire to make breasts head south, but it does not make them any less beautiful.

The body is not a commodity for positioning ourselves in some marketplace of attractiveness. The body is not a "vehicle" or an "overcoat" for the soul. Perhaps, in some mysterious way, it is the soul made manifest. (Your views are likely to vary according to your theology.)

Bodies, whatever size and shape and colour they are, are beautiful. Especially when lit by candlelight or firelight. But most of all, a body is a person – it is not just an appendage attached to a head, it is part of the person, and worthy of respect.

Throw away your preconceived ideas about slimness and muscle tone and learn to appreciate bodies as people. Throw away the pre-packaged concepts of beauty imposed by the kyriarchy; learn to look at bodies the way an artist would: as compositions of line and tone and form, of light and shadow.

Look at the Venus of Willendorf – really look at her. Look how the sculptor loved the generosity of her curves, the abundance of food that her body-fat represented. Look at the sculpture of the Sleeping Lady of Hal Saflieni – another large woman celebrated by an ancient culture. Look at the sculpture of the laughing Buddha. If deities can be fat, then people can be fat, and vice versa.

There are also sculptures of thin deities. If deities can be thin, then people can be thin, and vice versa. Deities come in all shapes and sizes, and so do people.

Celebrate the curves of the land, and the hills and valleys, and see them reflected in the bodies of your cuddly friends. Look at the slender trees, see them reflected in the bodies of your thin friends. Celebrate the beauty and diversity of the human body.

Ritual Nudity in History

In all other ritual and magical contexts where nudity appears, it is used either as a symbol of a return to Nature, a rebirth, or a transformation. Ronald Hutton offers numerous examples from European and other cultures: the Jain Digambra sect, who practice symbolic nudity as a withdrawal from worldliness, from which we get the term skyclad; a Tantric ritual involving naked practitioners sitting in a circle, alternately male and female; the sadhus of India; various folk-beliefs about witches in Africa, where the witches are thought to be naked because they have left their beds at night without bothering to get dressed. The notion of witches working malevolent magic by night and in the nude is widespread across many cultures; but Wicca is almost unique in having made this a positive image.[76]

Most other religions that practice nudity do so mostly for initiations or for specific festivals, with the sole exception of Voudun, which does so regularly. An example of a naked initiation is the famous fresco in the Villa of the Mysteries in Pompeii. Both Wicca and Voudun value the night, the Moon, sexuality, and the wilder side of life, all of which are associated with nakedness.

It seems then, that the early twentieth century witches did not invent the practice of ritual nudity; rather, they were drawing

---

[76] Ronald Hutton (2003), *Witches, Druids, and King Arthur*. London, Hambledon and London. (p. 208)

on a widespread and ancient body of folklore about naked witches. They drew upon the ideas of wildness, untrammelled sexuality, nakedness, the unconscious, dreams, the Moon, and the night to build a powerful set of interconnected ideas which would appeal powerfully to those seeking to escape the repressive atmosphere of the 1930s, 40s, and 50s - and would really take off in the countercultural 1960s and 70s.

Consent and Nudity

Not all covens work skyclad, so if you are uncomfortable with it, you can generally find a coven which does not work skyclad. However, it can be so transformative and liberating that you might want to give it a try before ruling it out altogether. Perhaps go to a nudist beach for the day, or something.

In my previous book, *All Acts of Love and Pleasure: inclusive Wicca*, I wrote that I consider working skyclad to be a core practice of Wicca. How does the promotion of something as a core part of a tradition work with ensuring that everyone can meaningfully consent to it? A very simple answer to this question would be "don't join a coven that works skyclad" but that is not quite good enough. If someone has significant issues with working skyclad, but is willing to try it most of the time, then you could establish the option of a veto - that if even one person doesn't want to work skyclad on any given day, then no-one does; or just decide that the circle is "clothing optional". If we were genuinely comfortable with nudity, then having some people clothed and some not would not be so awkward. Generally, however, it feels like a person who is clothed has more power than someone who is skyclad, because nakedness feels vulnerable. The best thing is to discuss it openly and honestly with your group and see how everyone feels; see if you can arrive at a consensus.

Most covens who do work skyclad wait until after initiation to practice skyclad working. Even then, people who are menstruating or similar often prefer to keep their knickers on and perhaps wear a sarong. That's what I do in circle; not because I think menstruation is icky or anything; just because it is private, and also messy - one has to be careful around cross-contamination of bodily fluids (in case of communicable diseases). Some people feel comfortable with just a tampon; others feel more comfortable with knickers and a sarong. This is really a matter for personal choice. People with incontinence might prefer to wear knickers and a sarong (but of course do not have to if they do not want to). And some people may want extra support for their breasts whilst lactating or menstruating. Basically, if there is potential for leakage, whether incontinence or menstruation or breastfeeding, then of course the person should be able to prevent leakage by whatever means they are comfortable with. Though if you were doing a ritual to celebrate menstruation, some people might not want to prevent free flow. If you are planning such a ritual, it is very advisable to discuss it thoroughly with all participants first, because not everyone will be comfortable with it.

I have a personal pet hate of robes, because they don't go with my earthy and liminal style of magic; so if I am in a non-skyclad situation, I prefer to wear street clothes, or a loose top and trousers that I have set aside especially for ritual.

I feel very strongly that going skyclad should not be restricted only to people with so-called "perfect" bodies. I find working skyclad empowering precisely because I am obese. But if someone is embarrassed by some aspect of their body, they should not be forced to go skyclad. Working skyclad is about creating 'perfect love and perfect trust' and that is not going to happen if someone is forced to do something they do not want to do.

The aura and the etheric body

Occult tradition holds that, as well as the physical body, there is also an etheric body. The etheric body is the vitality that sustains the physical body; it departs upon death. Depending on the way that the person died, the departure of the etheric body can be abrupt and painful, or gradual and easeful.

It is possible to experience the etheric body by sensing the auras of others. You can increase your own sensitivity to auras by gradually moving your hands closer together (but not actually touching), until you can feel a very slight pressure as your aura meets itself. It is a bit like the feeling of resistance when you bring the south or north ends of two magnets close together. A fun way to increase your sensitivity to the pressure of your aura is to have a bath with bubble-bath mixture, and get some bubbles between your hands, and bring them slowly together. The subtle pressure of the bubbles is about the same as the pressure of the aura meeting itself.

A very pleasant exercise to do with your coven is aura-brushing, where one person stands in the middle of the circle and the others gently move their hands over that person's aura, feeling for any gaps, cold spots, or hot spots, and smoothing them out.

The aura extends a long way beyond the body and becomes more subtle and nebulous as it gets further away from the body. It can also vary in intensity depending on your mood. You can test this by thinking of a sad memory and getting your coven-mates to feel where the edge of your aura is. Then think of a neutral memory and repeat the exercise. Then think of a happy memory, and repeat. Usually, the aura expands while thinking a happy thought, and contracts while thinking a sad thought.

The etheric body also contains the chakras and meridians discovered by Eastern religions and spiritualities. Taken out of the context of Eastern philosophy, meditation techniques, and wisdom about the body, the concept of chakras easily becomes distorted. [77]

The meridians are lines of subtle energy found in the body by practitioners of shiatsu and acupuncture. They can become blocked, and practitioners can unblock them by applying pressure to specific points around the body. Again, taken out of the context of Chinese philosophy and concepts of the body, they can be misunderstood. Western philosophy tends to see spirit and matter as two separate phenomena; Eastern philosophy (and physics) tends to see matter as a denser form of energy. The separation of spirit and matter is illusory.

In whatever way we conceptualise the energetic body - as chakras, meridians, the etheric body, or the aura - it is clear that the body does emit energy. Nerves are activated by

---

[77] *Playing with Fire.* Interview with Reginald Ray. *Dharma Life*, issue 26. http://www.dharmalife.com/issue26/playing.html

electrical current, and electrical current creates an electromagnetic field.

In Feri witchcraft, the soul has three aspects. The first of these is Sticky One, the part of us that is sensual and playful, and corresponds to the concept of the etheric body, innocence, wisdom, vitality, and our animal nature. The second is the Shining Body, which is the intellect and the aura, gathering information from the world around us. This is the aspect that senses when there is someone behind you. The third aspect is Sacred Dove, the spark of divinity within, the link to the divine, to ancestors, and to the wisdom of the multiverse. When these three aspects are aligned and working together, the witch comes more fully into their power.[78]

---

[78] T Thorn Coyle (2005), *Evolutionary Witchcraft*. Penguin Books, USA. (Chapter 2)

Discussion

Why do we work skyclad? Is it necessary?

Do we need special clothing (such as robes) for ritual?

Does ritual nudity create a special atmosphere or enhance magical energies?

Why is there a cultural taboo around certain bodily fluids?

Exercises

Try aura-brushing. First move your hands gently over the other person's body, feeling for cold or hot spots, and then repair any gaps by smoothing them over.

Try feeling where the edge of someone's aura is, depending on whether they are thinking a happy, sad, or neutral thought. (It's good to finish with the happy thought, so you don't end up feeling sad.) Walk slowly towards them from at least six feet away with your hands stretched out in front of you.

Try bringing your hands together and feeling the slight pressure where the aura meets itself. If you cannot feel it, increase your sensitivity by doing it with a handful of bubbles in between your hands.

14. The Erotic and Spirituality

The erotic and spirituality have always been overlapping realms. Because authoritarian religions want to control people's direct access to the spiritual, this link has often been denied in exoteric and hierarchical religions. But anyone who reads *The Song of Solomon* with an awareness of the erotic potential of spirituality, and/or the spiritual potential of the erotic, can hardly miss the connection:

> Let him kiss me with the kisses of his mouth: for thy love is better than wine.
>
> Because of the savour of thy good ointments, thy name is as ointment poured forth, therefore do the virgins love thee.
>
> Draw me, we will run after thee: the king hath brought me into his chambers: we will be glad and rejoice in thee, we will remember thy love more than wine: the upright love thee.

Pagan rituals are performed with the whole body as well as the mind and the heart. They have an erotic quality – not overtly but sublimated and transmuted. Ritual is sensual and involves all the senses. This erotic aspect of worship is frequently expressed by medieval Jewish and Christian mystics, Sufis like the poets Rumi and Hafiz, as well as contemporary Pagans. (Worship is a frequently misunderstood concept, but it means the celebration of that which is of ultimate worth.)

The mood-swing of Western culture against the body, women and sensuality is said by historians to have begun around 500 BCE and reached its height in about 500 CE. At its worst, it was profoundly anti-women. It had a lasting influence on the Christianity of later centuries, and because of it, people no longer associate the erotic with spirituality. But if we are to reclaim an embodied spirituality, we need to re-sanctify the pleasures of the body.

Bound up with this fear of women, sexuality, and the body was the fear of the dark, which relates to the feminine, nature, and wilderness and has been reviled for most of Christian history. In patriarchal culture, the assertive and sexually active female is regarded as dark, dangerous, and malevolent, and characterised as a witch. The passive female is elevated as the model for how women should be: silent, virginal, and modest. For patriarchy to function, female sexuality must be suppressed and controlled, and men must be taught to fear it and abuse it; and the wilderness must be conquered and tamed. In mysticism, alchemy, and the occult tradition, however, darkness and the feminine principle (wild, untamed, sensual) were and are recognised as the gateway to a direct experience of the Divine. Their writings were deeply sensual and erotic, and extolled the dazzling darkness of God, the ultimately unknowable and mysterious aspect of the Godhead.

Judaism never entirely abandoned its respect for the body and for women, and making love remained an act of worship. It was and is strongly encouraged in Judaism to make love on the Sabbath Eve, because making love reunites the exiled Shekhinah (the immanent feminine aspect of the Divine) with the Godhead. According to many Jewish theologians, the Shekhinah is exiled in the material world, and seeks to be reunited with the transcendent male Godhead. We can help her by making love and performing acts of kindness, which are known as Tikkun Olam, repairing the world. Progressive Jewish theologians affirm that same-sex lovers also reunite the Shekhinah and the Godhead.

Spirituality and sexuality are intertwined. The most profound sexual experiences involve an abandonment of the centrality of the ego and opening to the beloved other; this can become surrender to the Divine Beloved. This experience is reflected in the erotic and spiritual poetry of the Sufis. The Sufis loved the night, which was viewed as the time when the soul was most open to the Divine Beloved.

Similarly, the deeply spiritual is also erotic, and opening and self-abandonment to the Divine can resemble a relationship with a human partner. The ancient Greek story of Eros and Psyche represents the Divine visiting the soul. In India, the story of Krishna pleasuring a thousand cow-girls simultaneously also symbolises the erotic relationship with the Divine. Medieval mystical poetry is full of erotic yearning for the Divine. In the medieval period, among both Jewish and Christian thinkers, the Song of Songs was regarded as an allegory of the soul's relationship with God.

Erotic ritual for lovers

With your lover, you can use anointing, massage, kissing, and caressing to heighten the sense of sacredness and sensuality before and during lovemaking, or in a sacred space. Kissing specific parts of the body, accompanied by sacred words, is a beautiful way to honour the sacredness of the body. Brushing them with a feather, soft brush, or your hair can make them feel adored and blessed. Taking a bath together, with candles, wine, and incense, can be a beautiful and intimate thing to do.

Making love in the circle (known as the Great Rite) can be an amazing and powerful experience. This practice should always be entirely consensual (which is why I personally would advise against doing it as part of any initiation ritual, especially if it is seen as expected or required). In the Great Rite, we become embodiments of divine lovers, and partake in the nature of the deities. I prefer to do the Great Rite with someone whom I know well (and I am in a monogamous relationship with my partner, who is also my high priest).

Myths of divine lovers, and divine and human lovers, can be acted out in a circle to honour the erotic connection between lovers. Eros and Psyche, Hadrian and Antinous, Hermes and Crocus, Sappho, Athena and Gaia, Agido and Hagesichora, Pomona and Vertumnus (a potentially genderqueer deity), Hades and Persephone, and many more, can all be celebrated in ritual.

In her novel, *The Fifth Sacred Thing*, Starhawk includes a Beltane blessing for past lovers: all the lovers who have shaped you and blessed you over the years. It is a lovely blessing and could be included in Beltane rituals for polyamorous and monogamous people alike. Jumping over the Beltane fire with your best beloved is also a joyful rite of Spring.

Deepening levels of intimacy and commitment with your lover could be negotiated through meaningful ritual. The first time you make love could be in a setting that is neutral but sacred, neither your personal space nor theirs, but a sacred place in the landscape. Many people regard the first time they farted in front of their lover as a significant moment. Many lovers celebrate the anniversary of the first time they met, the first time they made love, when they moved in together, the moment of commitment, as well as the anniversaries of engagement and handfasting. These moments are like crossing a threshold or entering into a new realm; they deserve to be marked.

The ultimate commitment ceremony is of course a handfasting or Pagan wedding. The handfasting has several essential features: the tying of the couple's hands with a cord; the exchange of rings and vows; and jumping over a broomstick to symbolise crossing the threshold into their new life together. Each of these is accompanied with special words and done with both mirth and reverence.

Sensuality and sensory pleasures

The concept of the erotic also includes the sensual and the sensory. If you are asexual, aromantic, celibate, or monogamous, you can still access the sensual and the sensory without being overtly sexual.

The erotic can be expressed through sensuality, involving all five senses. Ritual includes visual elements: the magical tools, the altar, flowers, candlelight, jewellery, and pictures. These create an intimate space, soft, inviting, cave-like. The candlelight glints off the polished wood of a wand, or the bronze patina of a censer. The firelight illuminates the naked bodies in the night, and the branches of the trees.

Ritual can include scent – the smell of flowers, incense, good moist earth, baking bread, wine, fruit. Smell is the most subtle and evocative of all the senses, and smells can transport you instantly to a memory of the past or an intimation of future bliss. Different incenses, oils, and resins can evoke different moods, different deities. There are many magical correspondences of incense and oils. Oils can also be used for anointing and consecration.

Ritual can include taste – the taste of food, mindfully and appreciatively savoured, shared amongst friends. Jewish worship in the home includes food, as in the well-known ritual of the Seder (Passover meal) with its various symbolic foods.

Many Pagan rituals include the use of food. Different tastes (salt, sweet, sour, and bitter) can be associated with the four directions and the four elements. In *The Sea Priestess*, a novel by Dion Fortune, Miss Le Fay Morgan, the sea priestess of the title, prepares a feast at full Moon consisting entirely of white food. You could also have a feast of yellow or red food for the Sun (strawberries, oranges, raspberries, lemon meringue pie); red and hot and spicy for Mars (ginger, cumin, chilli, a tikka masala perhaps); cool and green and nutritious for Venus (broccoli, courgettes / zucchini, watercress, lettuce); purple for Jupiter (eggplant / aubergine, purple broccoli, beetroot); orange for Mercury (mangos, peaches, guava); dark food for Saturn (black pudding, wild black rice, puy lentils); and earthy food for Pluto in his role as lord of the underworld (potatoes, artichokes, and other root vegetables, with a pomegranate in honour of Persephone).

Ritual can include touch and movement – hugging, dancing, joining hands, gestures, warming oneself at a fire, anointing with oil and water, body-painting, ceremonial kissing, the feel of rich earth, planting bulbs, experiencing the textures of silk, or stones, or earth.

Aura brushing is a beautiful way to care for fellow coveners. The one who is to be aura-brushed stands in the middle of the circle, and the others all stand round them, brushing and smoothing their aura with their hands - not actually touching their skin, just the edges of their aura, about six to eight inches away (15 to 20 cm) from their body. Those doing the brushing look for cold spots and hot spots, try to smooth out the energy in the aura, and repair any gaps. When one person has been thoroughly pampered in this way, the next person steps into the middle, and they are brushed too, until everyone in the group has been aura-brushed.

Ritual includes sound, but there is not as much singing in Paganism as there could be (presumably a reaction to the singing of hymns in Christianity). The lyrics of Pagan chants are sometimes a bit trite. In Hinduism however, the classical raga form goes through stages, firstly of yearning for the Divine Beloved, then making contact, and finally achieving union. The erotic aspect of this encounter is clearly celebrated in the music.

The erotic aspects of spirituality are present in Paganism (especially Wicca) but not much talked about, because they are so easily misunderstood. The erotic can be sensual, passionate, tender, mysterious, alluring, mystical; it does not have to be explicit or acted upon.

Our rituals are performed with the whole body, not just with mind and heart. This is how we integrate our spirituality with everyday life. As Mary Oliver so memorably put it, "Let the soft animal of your body love what it loves."

Let us welcome Eros into the bridal chamber of the psyche, for only then can we make the shift from the domination of the ego (the rule of law) to the balance of all aspects of the psyche (the religion of love). Let us descend into our own depths to encounter the darkness and silence, be dazzled by the unknowable mystery of the Divine, and surrender to the oceanic bliss of union with the ground of all being.

Cakes and Wine

In Wicca, cakes and wine are consecrated and shared among the coveners. The wine is consecrated by touching it with an athame. Various words may be used to accompany this consecration, for example: "As the lightning struck the primordial waters, bringing forth life, so when the athame touches the wine, the union of lover and beloved is accomplished." These were the words I wrote for my handfasting.

The words used in many inclusive Wiccan rituals are "As the athame is to the lover, so the cup is to the beloved". This includes both same-sex and different-sex lovers. You might also want to think about the meeting of self and other, spirit and matter, divine and human, too.

The Two Chalices Ritual

One of the rituals of inclusive Wicca is the two chalices ritual. This has evolved over a couple of decades to become something more than I originally envisaged, as is often the way with traditions, which are evolving and fluid. It started life as a ritual for women-loving-women, and evolved into a ritual for everyone, but retaining its original symbolism.

Back in 1995, I was asked to call a quarter and consecrate some cakes and wine with another person. The person I chose to do it with was another woman, so we scratched our heads over the whole business with the athame and the chalice.

Some traditions give the athame to a woman in the rite of Cakes and Wine; others give it to a man. The athame is generally considered to be a "masculine" tool, and the chalice is generally considered to be "feminine". If a woman holds the athame, it symbolizes the idea that everything contains its opposite, like the little dot of yang in the middle of the yin, and the little dot of yin in the middle of the yang. If a man holds the athame, it represents his masculine energy.

So, whichever one of us ended up with the athame or the chalice, someone was going to jump to conclusions about which one of us was being the 'man', and which one of us was being the woman in the usual ceremony. But, as the saying goes, asking a same-sex couple which one is the man and which one is the woman in the relationship is like asking a pair of chopsticks which one is the knife and which one is the fork.

I cannot now remember which of us held the athame and which of us held the chalice. But the whole experience got me thinking. What if there was a way of consecrating wine for two women? As the chalice symbolizes the vulva, it was a fairly obvious move to have two chalices. This reminded me of the Temperance card in the Tarot, which is usually depicted as a person pouring liquid from one receptacle into another.

The esoteric meanings of the Temperance card are about flow, balance, harmony, blending, and connection.

It was some time before I was able to try out consecrating wine with two cups in a Wiccan circle; I think the first time was around 2002. After that I did it a few times whenever I was working magic with another woman.

The breakthrough came in 2015, when I shared the ritual with a group of LGBTQIA+ Wiccans at a workshop. We started by pouring a full cup of wine into an empty cup; and then someone had the idea of passing the now empty cup to the next person in the circle and filling it again. And then someone came up with the beautiful words, "I fill your cup with love". It did not matter who the next person was, you just filled their cup with a blessing. The ritual developed a life of its own and changed because it was shared with a group of people.

If you use this ritual in your own circles and covens, please tell the story of how it came about, and emphasize that it was developed by a community of LGBTQIA+ Wiccans.

How to do the Two Chalices ritual in a group

Say you have person A, B, C, D, and E standing in a circle.

Person A passes the empty cup (2) to person B. A pours the full cup (1) into the empty cup (2), and says, "I fill your cup with love".

Then A passes empty cup (1) to person C. Person B then pours the full cup (2) into empty cup (1), being held by person C. Each time the wine is poured, the person pouring it says "I fill your cup with love." And so on.

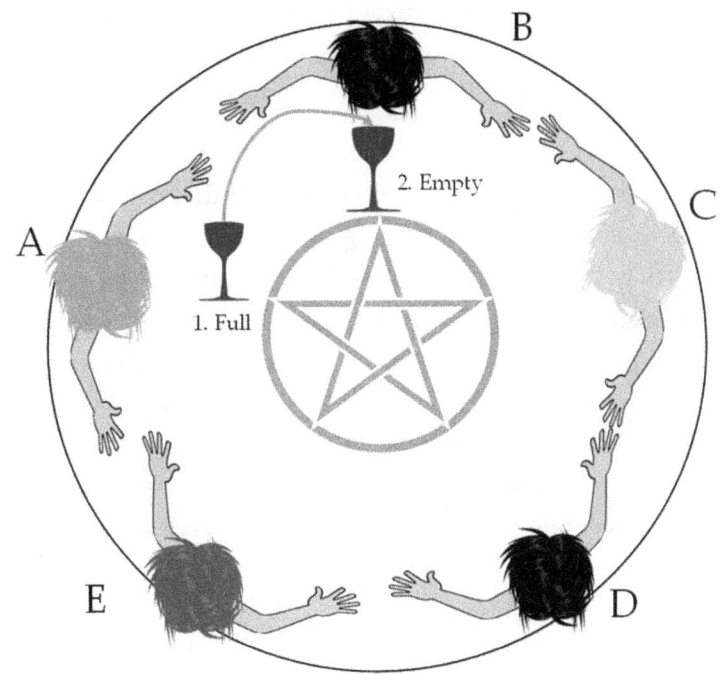

Kink and Spirituality

Practitioners of erotic spirituality have often discovered a hidden path to ecstasy: the release of endorphins by means of inflicting pain. Others find their ecstasy on paths of servitude or ordeal: the complete surrender of the ego, and the submission to pain as a means of transcending the ego.

Contemporary society, with its ideals of individuality, freedom, and equality, has difficulty accepting these ways of relating. This is because we usually associate dominance with the twisted notions of hierarchy found in the authoritarian worldview, which arrogates power and authority to itself as if it had a right to it. If such relationships are freely chosen, without coercion, and see dominance and submission as a beautiful gift and a sacred responsibility, then they can be healthy and fulfilling for the participants; and this should be the criterion on which they are measured.

In many ways, a BDSM 'scene' or session is very similar to a ritual. Both are planned and structured, with a beginning, a middle, and an end. Both have opportunities for spontaneity. The participants should be mentally and physically prepared, and ready to get into an altered state of consciousness. This means that consent should be given for what happens in the ritual, or in the scene. Not a blanket consent to everything, but a carefully discussed and negotiated consent. And consent should be enthusiastic, informed, and freely given (otherwise it is not consent at all). As Raven Kaldera writes, "one has to be able to say No in order for one's Yes to be worth something".[79]

Both rituals and scenes should have the option of a 'safe-word' – a word that is out of context and means "I need to stop now".

There are several paths to ecstatic altered states within spiritual kink. There is the ordeal path; the creation of spiritual ecstasy through pain and the release of endorphins; the use of control, followed by release; the use of shame and guilt (be careful with these, they are extremely powerful and potentially difficult); the gift of surrender and submission; and the path of dominance as a sacred trust.

---

[79] Raven Kaldera (2006), *Path of Service and Mastery: Spiritual Dominance and Submission*.
http://www.paganbdsm.org/articles/power-exchange/spiritualds.html

The ordeal path has been used for centuries and is a test of physical endurance. Legend has it that a druidic initiation involved placing the candidate in a stone bath and placing rocks on their chest, which they had to hold up to prevent themselves slipping into the water. A squire who was to be knighted in the morning would keep vigil with his weapons in a chapel overnight. Young warriors would be tested with ordeals such as tattooing and scarification or killing their first wild aurochs and then being smeared with its blood. Kinksters can achieve these altered states with bondage and flagellation. [80]

The use of pain to induce altered states has also been known for centuries. A flagellation ritual is depicted in a wall-painting from Pompeii. Various cultures have used piercing and scarification to induce altered states. Endorphins are released and can cause visions and feelings of release, ecstasy, and deep embodiment. The transcendence that people experience because of this is a journey deeper into the body, a sense of being larger than life, and fully inhabiting the body; it is not usually an out-of-body experience.

Bondage and restraint can give a sense of control, feeling where the boundaries of the body are. Careful use of knots can be used to control blood flow. The inability to move focuses the senses inwards, into the depths of the body. Giving control of one's body to another person is an example of perfect trust;

---

[80] Raven Kaldera (2005), *The Ordeal Path: Introduction to Neo-Pagan BDSM*

http://www.paganbdsm.org/articles/intro.html

you would not allow them to bind you unless you trusted them completely.

Shame and guilt can be powerful and corrosive, and can cause considerable discomfort, because they reveal to us the characteristics of our shadow side, the aspects of ourselves that we prefer to forget and ignore. Some feelings of shame and guilt are useful. If you have violated your current set of ethics, then there is nothing wrong with feeling ashamed or guilty; these are healthy emotions that will discourage you from violating your code of ethics again. Some feelings of shame and guilt have been instilled in us by mainstream culture, and these are often unnecessary and unwanted.

Sometimes people can, if the space is safe enough, achieve catharsis of unhealthy feelings through kink. It may be an acceptance of feelings that we do not want to examine, or it may be the process of overcoming feelings that have been instilled in us by mainstream culture. Either way, the main goal of catharsis is dismantling that which prevents us from facing our true selves. It is very important that this catharsis is given in a loving and supportive way, with plenty of aftercare. What aftercare involves is different for different people, so this should also be negotiated.

The gift of surrender and submission, and its corollary, the path of dominance as a sacred trust, is the most misunderstood aspect of BDSM. Here, spirituality can help by creating a sacred framework for the gift of surrender and submission, and the acceptance of that gift by the dominant. Raven Kaldera writes [81] that "the spiritual expression of …

---

[81] http://www.paganbdsm.org/articles/power-exchange/spiritualds.html

mastery should be more like 'mastering' the violin, which is a process that takes years of work and patience, and learning to work with the instrument rather than merely attempting to violently coerce it." He and Joshua Tenpenny have stated that one "cannot honorably serve a dishonorable master", and this is written into their contract [82]. The gift of submission cannot be expected or demanded; it can only be freely given, by one who has fully and freely chosen to offer it. This path is not for everyone; but those who walk it say that it is like monastic or military commitments. The submissive feels protected and enclosed by the dominant; but they should also be careful to retain their individuality and wildness. No dominant worth their salt should want to master a submissive who is not a powerful being in their own right. A person who knows what it is like to submit and to serve makes an excellent leader, because they will not demand too much of those they are leading, but will use the model of servant leadership to empower those they lead and prepare them to lead in their turn. If you have power over someone (that they have freely given to you), you have a responsibility to use it for their growth and spiritual enlargement, and not for the aggrandisement of your ego.

The practice of sacred kink can be a powerful and transformative set of tools; it is also full of pitfalls for the unwary, so tread carefully. Do not try everything at once; take it slowly and carefully, gradually working your way up to more powerful experiences. Read articles and books by BDSM practitioners such as Clarissa Thorn, Raven Kaldera, Joshua

---

[82] Raven Kaldera and Joshua Tenpenny, *Joshua's Contract*. http://www.paganbdsm.org/rituals/joshcontract.html

Tenpenny, Patrick (Pat) Califia, Janet Hardy and Dossie Easton, Mark Thompson, Thista Minai, and Lee Harrington. Get involved in your local BDSM community and learn from more experienced practitioners. Learn to use the tools of kink (rope, floggers, cuffs, etc) safely.

Done properly, this can be a path to bliss and transcendence; done badly, it can be a source of shame and distress. The practice of BDSM is not for everyone, but for those who enter it freely and joyfully, it can be a hidden door to the mysteries.

Discussion

What are the connections between embodied spirituality and sacred sexuality?

What can vanilla people learn about consent and communication from the BDSM community?

What is your own history regarding sexuality and the sacred?

Exercises

Meditate on the different areas of your body, especially cherishing the bits you do not like very much. Focus on telling your body you love it, and thanking it for all the bodily functions it performs (breathing, digestion, orgasms, walking, etc.)

Pamper yourself with a bath using scented oils, incense, candles, and other sensual props.

Work with your partner or lover to create a ritual to pamper each other and bless each other's bodies.

15. The inner aspects of the festivals

There are eight festivals in the cycle of the year. They consist of two interlocking cycles, the Celtic quarter days (Samhain, Imbolc, Beltane, and Lughnasadh or Lammas), and the solar festivals (Yule, Spring Equinox, Midsummer, and Autumn Equinox).

The festivals can also correspond to the vegetation cycle, the reproductive cycle of animals, and the phases of human life.

The vegetation cycle unfolds throughout the seasons of the year. In autumn, the fruit ripens and falls from the parent plant; then it rots down, revealing the seed, and providing nutrients for the seed. Sometimes the seed is eaten by birds, and the bird's faecal matter provides nutrients for the germinating seed. The seed germinates in the cold earth of winter and begins to strive towards the light. Meanwhile the parent plant has lost its leaves and stands naked in the wind. In the spring, the first shoot of the seedling can be seen on the forest floor, and the full-grown plant puts forth leaves and blossom. Bees and other insects fertilise the flowers. Later the petals fall, and the fertilised flower matures into fruit.

Autumn Equinox: Ripening of fruit; harvest of fruit.

Samhain: Leaves turn gold and fall from tree; seed falls from parent plant.

Yule: Turning point; cold conditions enable seed to germinate. Mature trees dormant; forestry work may be undertaken.

Imbolc: First red twigs indicate the start of new growth. Cherry and blackthorn begin to bloom.

Spring Equinox: Seed sprouts; sap rises in mature trees.

Beltane: Leaves fully out; in a good year, hawthorn in blossom.

Midsummer: Flowers are fertilised; beginnings of fruit production.

Lammas: Completion; seeds begin to form.

(based on an idea by Nigel Pennick)

The eight seasonal festivals can also be associated with specific trees, appropriate to the qualities of the festivals. Others may prefer a different schema, but my personal attributions for each festival are as follows:

Samhain	Elder (for the Crone); Apple (fruit of the Underworld)
Yule	Holly (sacred to Saturn etc.); Mistletoe
Imbolc	Blackthorn (flowers around Imbolc)
Spring Equinox	Great Sallow or Goat Willow (*Salix caprea*), sacred to Freyja.
Beltane	Hawthorn (flowers around May 1st)
Midsummer	Oak (sacred to Jupiter etc.)
Lammas	Gorse (sacred to Lugh); Ivy (often twined round the last sheaf of the harvest).
Autumn Equinox	Apple (for the cider harvest)

The seasonal cycles have many mythological patterns within them. The patterns outlined above are derived from English folklore and mythology. Each culture has a different cycle of festivals, depending on the climate changes, agricultural or pastoral customs, landscape, flora, and fauna of the place where they live.

Tides of the year

Each part of the year corresponds to a different tide.

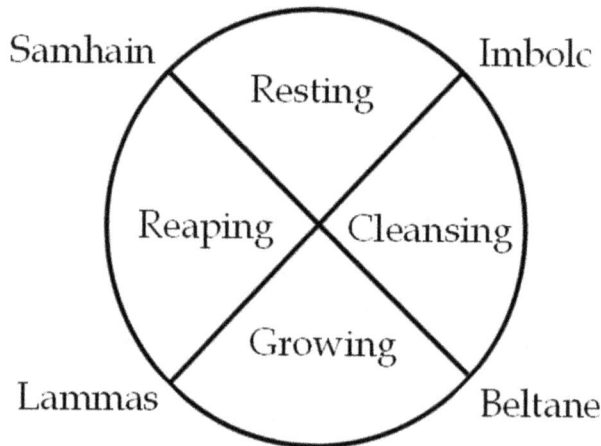

Resting: during the late autumn/early winter when everything lies still in the earth. Psychologically, this is when we sit by the fireside and tell tales, go within ourselves.

Cleansing: during the late winter/early spring when the frost breaks down the earth and decayed matter. February was the month of cleansing in ancient Rome. Psychologically, a time for clearing old habits, spring-cleaning the house.

Growing: late spring/early summer, everything is growing. Psychologically, the time of new projects, branching out into new ideas, being creative and extrovert.

Reaping: The time of harvest when the fruit and corn ripen and can be gathered in. Psychologically, the time of bringing things to completion and fruition.

The festivals and tides of the year also correspond to tides in the inner self, and phases of human life. Hence the festivals can also be correlated to the story of the goddess of agriculture, and her consort who represents the crops, cut down for the good of the people. This story is reflected in several myths, such as Inanna and Dumuzi, Ishtar and Tammuz, John Barleycorn, Isis and Osiris (Aset and Ousir), Cybele and Attis. It is a good idea when constructing rituals about these myths to engage deeply with the original myth, and not mix them together to try to create an über-myth or ur-myth. These stories were created in the context of a specific culture, history, and landscape, and deserve to be experienced in their original rich context.

Over the years, as I have celebrated the Wheel of the Year, the festivals have become an increasingly important part of my inner life. I measure time by them, I feel the energies changing as the wheel turns, and I feel bereft if I miss the celebration of one of them. I have written and performed various rituals over the years, exploring different aspects of the meaning of the festivals, and have also repeated certain key elements from the rituals I was passed as part of the Wiccan heritage. These beloved items of liturgy can often reveal new meanings when you revisit them, as you experience them differently depending on the phase of your life or the circumstances in which you find yourself. That is the joy of poetry and symbols, that they can mean different things to different people, and that the reader and the writer create a nexus of shared meanings and understandings. That shared process of creation is what makes poetry and liturgy live.

Different people will experience different inner meanings for the festivals, but here are some thoughts on what they mean from an inner point of view.

Yule (21 December)

At Autumn Equinox, we begin the descent into winter. At Samhain, we remember and honour the ancestors and the beloved dead. At Yule, the furthest point in the descent of the Sun, we begin to emerge from the creative and introspective phase of winter and start thinking about the first stirrings of Spring. The sun represents the core aspect of the personality in many esoteric symbol-systems, and so its descent into the underworld represents a journey into our own subconscious, our own depths, to bring up fertile material to feed a time of creativity. Of course, we know that the Sun doesn't really descend into the underworld, but in many mythologies, that is where the sun god goes.

Yule is also a time for enjoyment; the harvest is over and done, there is little work to do in the dark time of the year, so it is time to feast, sing, dance, make merry, and kindle plenty of lights (to make up for the lack of sunshine, and to remind the sun that we would like it to start rising further north again!)

Yule is a great time to be creative with crafts, song, music, cookery, art, poetry, or whatever works for you.

Imbolc (2 February)

Imbolc is a festival celebrating the lactation of ewes, the coming of lambs, and the first stirrings of spring. The name may be derived from either "ewes' milk" (Oimelc) or "in the belly" (im bolg) - but these meanings are disputed.

In Ireland, Imbolc is the feast of Brigit, originally a Goddess, and now a saint. The Goddess Brigit is associated with healing, poetry, and smithcraft. The saint is associated with them too, and with the perpetual flame tended by the nuns of Kildare - which possibly goes back to pre-Christian times. There are numerous folk-customs and stories associated with Brigit.

Imbolc is traditionally focused on the increasing light and life as the days lengthen; it is the time when the trees start to blossom and bud.

Imbolc is a great time to begin a new project, group, or enterprise. This can be symbolised by the lighting of a new fire or the weaving of a new Brighid's cross. It is a time of beginnings and gestation, forging and annealing. The processes of smithcraft are analogous to the processes of psychological change. First, air and fire and earth come together to make the hot fire of the forge. Then the metal is heated in the forge; then it is hammered into shape. Finally, it is plunged into water to fix the new form. In *The Way of Wyrd* by Brian Bates, the protagonist has a vision in which he is broken and remade by the dwarf smiths of underworld. In a process of psychological change, first there are external changes of circumstance, and then these begin to impact on the inner self, melting our resistance to change. Then we feel the hammer-blows of the change acting upon the psyche; and finally, things settle down, and begin to flow again.

When the process of change is initiated from the inner self (as opposed to by external situations), it is perhaps triggered by an upwelling of new material from the unconscious, but a similar process happens.

Spring Equinox (21 March)

Spring Equinox is a festival of balance, as day and night are equal (but after this the days get longer). It is also the time when the coming of spring is really becoming apparent. According to Bede, the ancient Germanic pagans honoured a goddess called Eostre who was associated with hares and the Moon and eggs; however there is no reference to this goddess in any other text, so much of the modern mythology associated with her is extrapolated from Bede, and does not have any basis in older mythology. That does not mean that it is not valid as mythology, just that people should not claim ancient origins for it.

The inner aspects of this festival are particularly rich with meaning. The concept of balance can be explored in many different contexts. I once wrote a ritual relating this festival to the concept of courtly love, and the court of women in which violators of the codes of courtly love were tried. The balance of light and darkness is also a favourite theme, but the balance, polarity, complementarity, and dynamic interaction of any pair of opposites can be explored: active and passive, yin and yang, morning and evening, air and earth, fire and water, civilisation and wildness, and so on. When constructing a ritual around these themes, it is often helpful if the apparent conflict between the two is symbolically resolved in some way.

Beltane (1 May)

Beltane is a festival celebrating sacred sexuality. It is typically celebrated by jumping over fires and dancing round maypoles. Pagan rituals often include symbolic expressions of sexuality. It could also include celebrations of the senses, and something to honour the coming of spring and the renewal of life.

An inclusive celebration of Beltane could include celebration of sexuality in all its forms, and hence a social justice element. It could also include celebrations of the senses, and something to honour the coming of spring and the renewal of life. It would preferably be held outdoors.

Many people enjoy leaping the Beltane fire as a sign of commitment in their relationships. Fire symbolises a threshold or a transformation and has traditionally been used in rituals of purification. Fire represents sexuality, warmth, passion, intimacy, but also destruction, greed, anger, and war.

Anger can be a useful emotion. It is designed to warn us when we are threatened by predators and oppressors. Repressing it can lead to depression, as the anger turns inwards. Anger is a legitimate response to oppression and provides the energy to propel us out of the risky situation and change things.

A Beltane ritual could also celebrate the transformative effects of fire, creating space for new growth and new life.

Midsummer (21 June)

Midsummer is a festival celebrating the Sun. At this time of the year, the days are at their longest, so the Sun is said to be at the height of its power. However, after Midsummer, the days will get shorter, so the Sun is said (symbolically) to descend into the underworld. The Sun is a metaphor for our consciousness; as we descend into the depths of winter, the self goes inward and becomes more introspective.

A celebration of midsummer could focus on the aspects related to consciousness and emphasise the shift from outward to inward preoccupations. This could be symbolised by the crossing of a threshold, or the turning of a lined cloak from the outer colour to the colour of the lining.

Lammas (1 August)

Lammas commemorates the death of John Barleycorn, the dying-and-resurrecting vegetation god. The corn was believed to be inhabited by the corn-spirit, which was killed at every harvest and resurrected in the planting of the new corn. In Ireland, Lammas was celebrated with games in honour of the goddess Tailtiu, the mother of Lugh the sun god, and was called Lughnasadh. The harvest is an important symbol of cyclicity, growth, and change. The wheel turns, and what has grown must die, so that the seeds can be planted for the new cycle of growth. From an inner perspective, this is a time to shed old habits and preoccupations that have been outgrown and plant the seeds for new activities and habits and thoughts to replace them.

Autumn Equinox (21 September)

At the Autumn Equinox, day and night are equal (but after this the nights get longer), so most Pagan rituals focus on this, and on the importance of balance. The festival also honours the Celtic god Mabon, who was imprisoned in a tower for many years. It is also the fruit harvest; for this reason, I associate it with the Roman deities Pomona and Vertumnus. A celebration of Autumn Equinox could focus on the sensual delights of food and the harvest of work and creativity, as well as the balance of light and dark.

In Taoism, the way of harmony is the balance of opposites – yin and yang, night and day, life and death, eternally cycling around each other in the great dance of existence, the dynamic equilibrium of nature. Equilibrium means "equal freedom" – freedom to move, to grow and to change; freedom of choice.

This dynamic balance of opposites can also be seen in the dance of the seasons. The wheel of the year turns; falling in the autumn, rising in the spring. As it falls in the autumn, and the nights draw in, we turn inward, towards home, and hearth, and spiritual things; baking, and making jam and wine; creative projects.

In Pagan tradition, there are three harvests; the corn harvest at Lammas; the fruit harvest at Autumn Equinox; and the harvest of meat at Samhain, when some of the cattle were slaughtered and preserved for the winter.

The Autumn Equinox can be viewed as a mirror image of the Spring Equinox. Day and night are equal at Spring Equinox, but daylight is in the ascendancy; at Autumn Equinox, night is in the ascendancy, and it is time to descend into the underworld, exploring the depths of the psyche, and meeting the hidden aspects of ourselves.

Samhain (31 October)

Samhain is a festival honouring ancestors. It is also the "harvest of meat" when cattle would be slaughtered before the winter. To the ancient Celts, however, Samhain was a festival of liberation from oppression. Many Wiccans use Samhain rituals to honour, remember, and commune with their loved ones who have passed on.

Samhain is the Irish word for the month of November. The ancient Irish festival held at this time was about the renewal of freedom – legends associated with it tell of heroes who freed their people from bondage. The association with the dead was probably imported to this country by Christianity, as this was the feast of All Saints and All Souls.

Pagans tend to focus on the preciousness of this life, not some future one beyond death. Hence many traditions want to celebrate and remember the lives of our ancestors. Ancestors can be relatives and friends who have died, or people from the past whom we admire (we often honour both). These people have shaped who we are now – given us life, given us inspiration, guided us, comforted us, and nurtured us – and it comforts us to remember them and commune with them. Our ancestors may have come from many parts of the world, and ultimately of course, all our ancestors came from Africa.

Many covens include a section in the Samhain ritual where people can remember loved ones who have died. That would include LGBTQIA+ members of the coven remembering LGBTQIA+ loved ones who died if they want to. And if we are remembering ancestors of spirit, then queer ancestors might be remembered.

There is a very important remembrance event for LGBTQIA+ people in November: the Transgender Day of Remembrance. Some Pagans and polytheists have devised the Transgender

Rite of Elevation, which culminates on the day of remembrance.[83]

Many people believe in reincarnation, and that the consciousness resides in an in-between place between lives. In Paganism, the dead are seen as not being very far away – only a heartbeat away – and many Pagans say that "the veil between the worlds is thin" at Samhain, because the tides of life are on the ebb as winter approaches, and because the encroaching darkness of winter is seen as a time for contemplation, remembrance, and introspection. For some people, of course, the veil is always thin. For them, the importance of Samhain is the opportunity to come together as a culture to remember and honour our beloved dead.

Pagans do not see darkness and death as evil, but as part of the cycle of life, death, and rebirth. If there was no death, there would be no growth, no change, and no birth. If there was no darkness, the seeds could not gestate in the warm darkness of the earth; if there was no night, there would be no sleep, and no stars and moonlight. If there was no winter cold, there would be none of the beauty of autumn, the seeds would not germinate, and germs would not be killed by the frost. Darkness is the Yin spoken of by the Taoists – part of the divine dance of the cosmos.

In the West, death is swept under the carpet, ignored, and feared. If we acknowledge it (at least once in the year), it becomes an invitation to live more fully and mindfully. If we ignore it, it becomes part of the shadow, the part of our psyche

---

[83] Transgender Rite of Ancestor Elevation, https://trans-rite.tumblr.com/

that we reject and that contains our fears and follies, and which we project onto other people: the Other, the outsider, the transgressor.

If we recognise death as being part of the natural cycle, like the seasons of the year, then we can live more integrated lives.

Samhain is also the time when, as the nights get longer and the winter grips the land, we descend into our own depths. Summer is a time for being extrovert, creative and expansive; winter is a time for curling up by the fireside and going within oneself to find the poetic, the spiritual and the quiet side of ourselves – the forgotten aspects, perhaps even the side of ourselves that we have repressed and need to examine.

The presiding deity of winter is the Crone Goddess. She has been feared and denigrated in recent centuries – people speak of old wives' tales, haggard old witches muttering in corners, and so on. But traditionally, old women were the ones who were the keepers of stories and other traditional wisdom such as herb lore and midwifery. She is the midwife and the one who washed, anointed, and laid out the dead, the one who cuts the cord of both life and death. She represents merciful release; but she also possesses the wisdom of old age. Wisdom is traditionally represented as a feminine being or quality. Wisdom is the joining of instinct and experience and knowledge. It is the wisdom of the body, the knowledge of when to act and when to refrain from acting, when to speak and when to keep silent. Wisdom comes from reflection upon experience and knowledge.

The Crone is also the Goddess of the Waning Moon, which represents a time of letting go and ebbing away, so it is traditional at Samhain to let go of aspects of your life that you do not need or want any more.

Discussion

How do the inner aspects of the festivals manifest for you? How are they reflected in your life?

Do your rituals reflect and stimulate the inner processes associated with the festivals?

How can we deepen our relationship with the cycles of the seasons?

Exercises

Meditate on the Wheel of the Year and its interlocking cycles.

Meditate on the vegetation cycle and how it relates to your life.

Meditate on the four seasons and how they relate to the phases of human life.

Draw a mandala of the interlocking cycles of the festivals, the seasons, and the tides of the year.

16. Grounding and Centering

Many rituals begin with this simple practice, especially Pagan circles. It comes from the Taoist tradition originally. There are several different versions of it.

Its purpose is to allow you to feel connected to the Earth (grounded), not floating away into fantasy-world, not obsessing about the past or the future, but being present in the now. The centering part of the practice allows you to feel connected to the cosmos and the four sacred directions, which are associated with the elements.

Begin by focusing on your breathing. There is no need to breathe in any special way, just notice how your breath comes in and out of your nostrils, and how your belly rises and falls.

As you breathe in and out, feel your feet planted firmly on the ground. Relax your hips and your knees and imagine a thread extending from the top of your head to the centre of the sky (this helps to align your spine with the axis of the Earth).

Imagine that your feet are tree roots. Extend your roots deep into the earth. Your roots push down into the earth, through the rich soil, finding their way among rocks, and down deep into the molten core of the Earth. As you breathe out, extend your roots; as you breathe in, draw up energy from deep within the Earth.

As the energy makes its way into your body, draw it up through your legs and feel it gathering and pooling in your solar plexus. Note the colour of the energy.

Now extend a tendril of energy up your spine. Imagine that your spine is the trunk of a tree. Extend your aura at the top of your head, growing branches. Extend your branches up into the sky, beyond the atmosphere, and reach for the energy of the starlight. As you breathe out, extend your branches; as you breathe in, draw the energy down from above. Feel it gathering and pooling in your solar plexus, mingling with the energy from below.

Now draw energy from both above and below at the same time, and let the energies mingle in your solar plexus. As you breathe in, draw in the energy from above and below; as you breathe out, feel it spiralling and swirling.

Now allow the energy to fill your whole body, extending out to your feet, your fingertips, the top of your head. Feel how you are aligned with the cosmic axis.

Now acknowledge the four directions: North for Earth, representing the body, sensation, physicality, and structure; East for Air, representing intellect, thought, inspiration and breath; South for Fire, representing passion, intuition, and spirit; and West for Water, representing emotion, the Moon, dreams, and the blood that flows in your veins.

17. Making an Altar

There are as many ways to set up an altar as there are spiritual practitioners, but I can give some useful hints and tips for a working altar.

Working altars

Our coven came up with three rules for how to lay out a working altar.

1. It is your altar. Your choice.
2. Put the things you will need first in the ritual nearer the front so you can get to them easily.
3. Put the candles at the back so you do not burn yourself reaching over them to get the things you need.

A Wiccan altar

A Wiccan altar is a focus for working magic. The focus of devotion in a circle happens when a deity is invoked into a person. Some covens prefer to have the altar in the North, or in a suitable niche in the temple room. Some covens who are lucky enough to have permanent temples have an altar in each quarter devoted to the element of that direction. These are decorated with symbols, statues, and objects appropriate to that element.

If you do not have a permanent temple space, you might set up your altar afresh each time, or you might keep it permanently set up in a corner of your living room. It depends how much space you have available, and whether you mind getting questions from non-witches. I had my altar in the corner of my living room for years, and most non-Pagans seemed completely unaware that it was an altar. Someone even put their cup of tea on the corner of it once.

A Wiccan altar generally contains some or all of the following: candles, the eight working tools of Wicca (athame, burin, pentacle, sword, wand, cords, scourge, and censer), deity statues, cakes, wine, and perhaps flowers. Most Wiccans have statue or pictures of the Moon Goddess and the Horned God. If the coven has specific patron deities, then they may have statues of them. Queer Wiccans may have genderqueer or transgender deities, or deities associated with same-sex love. Polytheist Wiccans may have several statues or pictures on their altar, or images of specific deities associated with the festival being celebrated.

Some people apparently assign the left side of the altar to the Goddess and the right side to the God. As a polytheist who does not subscribe to the gender binary, my reaction to that is: Nope.

Others will try to tell you that there are specific things you should have on the altar and they should be in specific places. That is not very helpful to people who are just starting out, as you do not necessarily want to buy all your magical tools at the same time; it is better to allow for serendipity and wait until you find the things that are just right for you.

I like to have my magical tools on the altar, but I do not lay them out according to any scheme, except putting the things on the altar in approximately the order in which I will use them.

If you or your coven has a patron deity or deities, it is nice to have something on the altar to represent them. If you are working with a specific deity or pantheon, it is good to have symbols associated with them, or images of them.

Some people like to put fresh flowers on the altar. Most people like to have some candles. I usually have three.

It is a good idea to decide on a specific aesthetic for your tools, and stick to it. Do you like the rustic, home-made, handcrafted look? Go for it. Or the high magic, very ornamental look? Or something in between? Have at it. I have ended up with some rustic looking altar items, and some silver ones. So now I have them on two separate altars.

It is worth looking at the sources of what you have on your altar and making sure that it is sustainable. If you have crystals, make sure that they were not strip-mined. If you have candles, try to get beeswax or soya candles. If you have incense, make sure it is ethically produced. My magical tools tend to have a home-made and slightly rustic feel to them and are made from found objects and natural materials.

Devotional altars

Another type of altar is the devotional altar, where you create a sacred focus on a deity, a pantheon, your household deities, or your ancestors (they can be people who you find inspiring, genetic ancestors, or people who lived where you live now). Devotional altars typically have pictures of the beings to whom the altar is dedicated, plus candles and flowers and sacred objects.

There is considerable overlap between the two types of altar and both types may contain elements of the other.

Creating an altar should be an enjoyable experience that makes you feel happy and connected to your Craft, not a chore or an exercise. You can put things on it that are sacred to you.

A devotional altar is a focus for devotion, prayer, or meditation. It can be simple or complex, small or large. It can have no images, a single image, or multiple images. It can be themed around an idea, deity, inspiring person, or festival. You can have more than one altar or shrine around your home.

If your altar is for meditation or prayer, choose a spot in your home that is quiet and peaceful. Consider how you will use your altar. If you are going to place flowers on it, or use it in ritual, make sure there is space for everything you need, and that the altar is easy to keep clean. Some people like to light a candle or ring a bell before they start their ritual, meditation, or prayer.

The typical devotional altar might have a bell or singing bowl, some sacred pictures or statues, some natural objects such as pebbles, shells, feathers or wood to make a connection with Nature, a candle, prayer beads, and perhaps a sacred book. It may be a shrine to a deity, saint, Buddha or bodhisattva, or to multiple sacred foci.

In Orthodox Christianity, the shrine at which the family prays is known as the Beautiful Corner and is decorated with icons of favourite saints. Icons are regarded as windows into Heaven. They depict the transfigured face of the saint. Before praying, people will light a candle and cross themselves.

In some traditions, people build altars or shrines at specific times of year. In Mexico, people build shrines for El Dia de los Muertos (the Day of the Dead) to commemorate their loved ones who have died. There might be photos of the loved one, together with their favourite foods, and flowers. Many Pagans around the world have borrowed this idea.

Clarissa Pinkola Estes, in her classic book *Women who run with the wolves*, describes how women built altars to commemorate losses in their lives, and how this helped them to grieve properly and to recover from the trauma. You could also build altars for rites of passage, such as the transition from childhood to adulthood, or for marriage or divorce. The altar might include symbols of the phase that is coming to an end, and symbols of the new phase to be embarked on. You could even build one altar for each phase, and then have a ritual progression from one phase to the next. Another way of making an altar is to find a special tree or rock and decorate around it with found (but biodegradable) objects arranged in a pattern, such as twigs, leaves, berries, and feathers.

There is no right or wrong way to make an altar. Each altar is personal and special. If you are following a specific spiritual tradition, it may have specific ways of making altars, but even within that, there is plenty of scope for creativity.

Discussion

Should the altar be in the centre of the circle, the East, or the North?

How does the position of the altar affect the group dynamic, the shape of the space, the flow of the ritual, and the movement of energies?

What do you regard as essential tools or things that must be on an altar?

Exercises

Create an altar for a specific occasion, or an ancestor altar, or an altar for a specific deity or pantheon.

Create a deity shrine and practice daily devotion to a deity or deities.

Meditate in a specific place every day and see if the energy changes - does it become a shrine or an altar, just because it has been the focus of ritual?

18. The Fire and the Hearth

I remember watching driftwood burning in my grandparents' fireplace as a child — there would be all sorts of colours in the flames from the salt: green and blue and turquoise flames.

There is a great tradition of magical fire making. In *The Sea Priestess*, Dion Fortune describes the making of a Fire of Azrael:

> The fire is laid of Juniper, Cedar, and Sandal. After the flames die down, it produces a clear, glowing ash which is used in clairvoyance, much as a gazing crystal is, to induce as vision, or to provide a bridge between conscious and sub-conscious.

In the book, Morgan Le Fay makes the fire on the rocky shore of Brean Down in Somerset. The book never names the place, but the description in the book is so good that it describes every feature of Brean Down.

Another type of sacred fire is the needfire, which is made with nine sacred woods, as described by Nigel Pennick in *Pagan Magic of the Northern Tradition*.

The purpose of a needfire is to banish sickness from cattle. All other fires must be extinguished and then the fire must be lit using a fire-bow or the friction of two pieces of wood. According to Nigel Pennick, it was traditionally made with nine sacred types of wood. However, it is not entirely clear how ancient this requirement is, and presumably the availability of the trees would vary from place to place, and so would the list of preferred types of wood.

The making of a Beltane fire is also a special magical activity. It is very similar to the making of a needfire.

Ronald Hutton has identified a line across Britain, south of which people erected Maypoles for May Day, and north of which they made Beltane fires.

The name Beltane means bright or shining fire[84], from a Common Celtic root, *belo-te(p)niâ.

Sacred fires were also lit at Samhain, when the cattle were brought down from the high pastures and those that couldn't be overwintered were slaughtered and the meat preserved.

Why is fire so magical? Imagine the time before electricity and easy ways of making fire, like matches and lighters. It is dark, and someone makes fire with a fire bow or a fire drill, or the friction of two sticks. Suddenly there is a circle of light and warmth, where before it was dark and cold. That is probably one of the reasons why the circle is sacred too. The flames seemed to come from nowhere, springing out of the wood like the first buds of springtime.

You can also use fires for scrying. Look at the shapes made by the flames, let your mind drift, and see what comes to you.

The Hearth

The hearth is the heart of the home. A home without a hearth lacks focus (or perhaps the focal point of the living room becomes the television). This is interesting because the word focus is Latin for hearth, and can also mean fire, point of convergence, and the bringing together of energies.[85]

---

[84] https://en.m.wikipedia.org/wiki/Beltane
[85] Online Etymology Dictionary
http://www.etymonline.com/index.php?term=focus

The concepts of hearth and home were linked in Roman thought too. In ancient times, the hearth, as the sole source of heat in the home, would have been massively important. Now that we have radiators and central heating, we tend to forget about the importance of the hearth. But in ancient cultures, the hearth was the place where you made offerings to the family gods and spirits, the lares and penates (household spirits in Roman religion). The notion of 'familiar spirits' originally meant the deities and spirits honoured by your family. In Vedic culture, the making of the sacred fire was a very important ritual.

The hearth - photo by Yvonne Aburrow.

Several cultures have domestic spirits, often associated with ancestors, such as the Cofgodas (cove-gods) of Anglo-Saxon paganism. The English and Scots believed in house Brownies, also known as urisk in Lowland Scots. Slavic cultures believed in Domovoi, which were originally ancestral spirits in Slavic paganism. There are also Aitvaras (Lithuania), Dimstipatis (Lithuania), Ev iyesi (Turkey - known as Sahab or Kimsene in Anatolia), Hob (North and Midlands of England), Kikimora, or Shishimora (Russia), Kobold (Germany - possibly related to the Anglo-Saxon cofgod), Olys' (a hearth spirit of the Komi people of northern Russia), Lares (Ancient Rome), Pūkis (Latvia), Pukys (Lithuania), Tomte (Scandinavia), and Zashiki-warashi (Japan).

In cultures that use stoves, they have also acquired resident spirits and folklore as well. Domovoi live in stoves. In Tove Jansson's Moomintroll novels, there is an ancestor who lives in the stove. In Swedish, he is called Förfadern, like the English word forefather.

So, from this brief survey of the folklore, we can see that the hearth is traditionally the place where you honour your ancestors and household gods and spirits, usually by making offerings to them. The fire would have been kept burning all the time, so it would be a good place to make offerings.

The English word hearth is derived from the Old English word heorð (hearth, fireplace, an area of a floor where a fire is made). It represents house, home, and fireside. It comes from from West Germanic *hertho (burning place) and is connected to Old Saxon and Old Frisian herth, Middle Dutch hert, Dutch haard, German Herd, from proto-Indo-European *kerta-, from the root-word *ker- (heat, fire; related to carbon).[86]

---

[86] *Online Etymology Dictionary*
http://www.etymonline.com/index.php?term=hearth

The hearth was the heart of the home, and the spirits that were honoured at the hearth were at the heart of the family's ritual observance. For example, the Lares and Penates were very important in ancient Roman culture. They were guardian deities in ancient Roman religion. It is unclear what the earliest form of lares were. They may have been hero-ancestors, hearth guardians, field spirits protecting boundaries or fruitfulness, or a combination of all of these. They were believed to protect, watch over, and influence everything that happened in their domain. Statues of domestic lares were placed on the table during meals, and their blessing was sought for all important family events. These spirits were not only domestic, however; they also watched over roads, seaways, agriculture, cattle, towns and cities, and even the state and the army. The lar of a specific neighbourhood (vicus) had a shrine at the crossroads. These shrines (compitales) served as the focus of community devotions. [87]

The offerings made to these spirits were usually a part of whatever food was being prepared. In Ancient Rome, both Lares and Penates were associated with the hearth, and were offered food. These customs continued long into the Christian era, and in some places, were never eradicated. In 1703, John Brand wrote about the people of Shetland making offerings to the house brownie. Milk churning and brewing both involved making an offering to the house brownie. Part of the milk was scattered all over the house; and a portion of beer was poured onto a special stone with a hole for offerings, which was called the Brownie's stane. [88]

---

[87] https://en.wikipedia.org/wiki/Lares
[88] https://en.wikipedia.org/wiki/Brownie_(folklore)

If you want to recreate these customs but you do not have a hearth, you could have a chimenea or a fire-pit in your garden, or a shrine with candles in your house. If you do have a fireplace with a real fire, or perhaps a wood-burning stove, then you could have a bowl for offerings on the hearth and set aside food from your meals for the ancestors. You can also make offerings in the fire itself.

The poem *To Lar*, by Robert Herrick,[89] gives a glimpse of the variety of offerings that may be made to hearth spirits:

> No more shall I, since I am driven hence,
> Devote to thee my grains of frankincense;
> No more shall I from mantle-trees hang down,
> To honour thee, my little parsley crown;
> No more shall I (I fear me) to thee bring
> My chives of garlic for an offering;
> No more shall I from henceforth hear a choir
> Of merry crickets by my country fire.
> Go where I will, thou lucky Lar stay here,
> Warm by a glitt'ring chimney all the year.

---

[89] *To Lar*, Robert Herrick (1591-1674). Online, available from: https://www.wwnorton.com/college/english/nael/noa/pdf/27636_17th_U04_Herrick-1-7.pdf

Discussion

How do the functions of the hearth differ from those of the altar?

In what ways does the kitchen function as the modern hearth?

How can we cultivate a sacred relationship with our own hearths?

Exercises

Meditate on your hearth and try to contact your hearth spirit.

Decorate your hearth as a shrine to the domestic spirits (the brownies, lares and penates, the domovoi, or whatever spirits live in your house).

If you have an open fire, sit and watch the flames and allow pictures to form in your mind as you watch the flames dancing.

19. Food in ritual

The sharing of food and drink is one of the most ancient and basic rituals of hospitality and reciprocity. It is surrounded by symbolism and ceremony.

A nice cup of tea and a sit down

The Japanese tea ceremony is the ultimate form of this hospitable practice; in it each movement is choreographed, and the tea is prepared and served mindfully and gracefully. The ritual has deep meaning and resonance for the participants. However, the preparation and drinking of tea has a restorative effect on many people. The fragrance of the tea, the effect of drinking it, and the relaxation of sitting and being focused on the pleasure of tea, is all good for you. It is even better if it is accompanied by conversation with a friend. The title of this section is taken from the excellent website entitled "A nice cup of tea and a sit down" [90] which extols the pleasures of this activity, or should I say inactivity?

The health benefits of tea are also significant. It is a mild stimulant, enabling people to continue working when they are tired, and it is also astringent and antibacterial, preventing infections of the gut such as cholera.

Shared meals

Many religious traditions have shared meals as part of their practice. Jewish tradition has the Seder or Passover meal, in which specific symbolic foods are eaten, representing different aspects of the Passover story. The youngest person present

---

[90] http://www.nicecupofteaandasitdown.com/

must ask, "Why is this night more special than all other nights?" and various other symbolic actions are performed, such as leaving the door open for Elijah, and raising a toast to the idea that one's next Seder will take place in Jerusalem. Christianity has the Eucharist, which commemorates both the Last Supper that Jesus had with his disciples, and the meal he is said to have shared with them at Emmaus after his resurrection. The meal consists of bread and wine consumed in a sacred manner. There has been much conflict throughout Christian history about what the Eucharist means, who can partake of it, and what its effects are. Nevertheless, it is a powerful ritual. Stephen Lingwood, a Unitarian minister, suggests that communion represents Jesus' radical hospitality – his willingness to eat with people marginalised by society, such as prostitutes, tax collectors and publicans.

In Wicca, the shared meal is known as cakes and wine, and is usually consecrated by a woman and a man (but it can be a same-sex couple), and then shared among the participants in the ritual. A portion is kept for offering to the deities as a libation.

In some Hindu traditions, a portion of the food is offered to the deities while it is being cooked, and blessed food is known as prasadam.

The ancient Greeks had a custom of sharing wine and intellectual conversation, which is where we get our word symposium, which literally means 'together drinking' (and is related to *sympotes,* 'drinking companion'). In ancient Rome, there were dining clubs devoted to the god Bacchus (god of wine), which presumably had a ritual or spiritual aspect.

Many religious traditions (including Paganism) give thanks for their food before eating. Typically, the meal blessing might include thanks to all the beings and processes that went into creating the food, and a wish that everyone in the world might have enough to eat.

Cooking can also be a spiritual practice. It is in many ways akin to alchemy (the transformation of one thing into another); indeed, a cooking vessel invented by a medieval female alchemist – the bain-marie – founds its way from the laboratory to the kitchen. In Jewish tradition, the preparation of food has special rituals associated with it. The magic of a lovingly prepared meal is powerful stuff, restoring both body and mind.

Kitchen witchcraft restores the spiritual aspect of cookery. Someone who cooks in a mindful way can create beautiful dishes which restore one's faith in humanity. These dishes are created with love and imbued with meaning. The witch can also use the process of cooking for sympathetic and imitative magic; or they can imbue the food with healing energy and feed it to the beneficiary of the spell. They can also use specific ingredients to imbue the food with specific qualities (see the section on Symbolic Foods below).

Four Elements, Four Flavours

The herbalist Susun Weed has associated the four cardinal directions with the four main tastes that are detected with the tongue. She has also associated the more subtle flavours with the directions.[91]

She assigns four of the tastes to the four directions, using the Native American correspondences for the directions. Her system applies mainly to herbs and is used to determine which herbs should be used to treat which ailments. I can see some parallels here with the symbolic foods of the Passover Seder, where the bitter herbs represent the travails of the people of Israel in the desert.

I have done a ritual where I gave different foods to the participants at the four quarters to represent the different tastes. In my ritual based on Susun Weed's ideas, I think I assigned bitterness to the North and sourness to the West, so we had cress and radishes in the North, capers and pickles in the West, wheat in the East, and salt in the South.

You could also assign different foods to the four directions depending on where they were grown or ripened - so fruit might be assigned to Air, root vegetables to Earth, sun-ripened vegetables to Fire, and things that grow in the sea, ponds, or rivers, to Water.

Using the qualities of the four elements from the Western magical tradition, you might get a different arrangement of ideas:

---

[91] Susun Weed (2003), "Herbal Medicine Chest... The Medicine Wheel of Plant Uses." *Weed Wanderings*, July 2003, Volume 3, Number 7.
http://www.susunweed.com/herbal_ezine/july03/herbalmedicine.htm

East	South	West	North
Air	Fire	Water	Earth
Hot & Moist	Hot & Dry	Cold & Moist	Cold & Dry
Spring	Summer	Autumn	Winter
Fruit	Sun-ripened vegetables	Seaweed, watercress, rice	Root vegetables
Sweet	Sour	Salty	Bitter
Sticky	Spicy	Moist	Astringent

Symbolic Foods

Foods are also traditionally associated with specific festivals - sometimes with great symbolic meaning, sometimes just because they are available at that particular time of year, or because it is comforting to eat warming and stodgy food in winter, and cooling and soothing to eat salad and lighter fare in summer.

One of the Pagan festivals that I particularly love is wassailing, which happens on Plough Monday (17 January). Plough Monday was traditionally the day when the farmer would go out to his field and test how cold and hard the earth was by putting his bare buttocks on the earth. If it was not too cold and hard to sit on, then it was ready to be ploughed.

Wassailing is the practice of waking up the apple trees by banging pots and pans, firing shots into the branches, and singing them wassail songs. The traditional wassail drink is mulled cider[92] with "lambswool" (stewed Bramley apples) in it.

Some of the eight festivals of the Wiccan and Druid Wheel of the Year already have foods associated with them through long tradition; others need a tradition to develop based on their symbolism. Here is a list of traditional and suggested foods for the festivals.

In our consecrated circles, we generally only eat vegetarian food, but I have included meat in the list of correspondences, as it is also symbolically associated with the festivals.

Samhain	Yule	Imbolc	Spring Equinox
Parkin Pumpkin Turnip Root vegetables Stewed meat	Pudding Oranges Baked apples Roast meat Mince pies	Milk Cheese Yoghurt Tofu Coconut Almond	Eggs Meringue Cress Spring greens Lamb's lettuce

---

[92] Note for North American readers: in Britain, cider refers to the alcoholic drink that you call "hard cider". What you refer to as cider is what we call apple juice.

Beltane	Midsummer	Lammas	Autumn Equinox
Aphrodisiacs Oysters Edible flowers Asparagus Fiddlehead ferns [93]	Strawberries Raspberries Oranges Lemons	Wheat Barley Beer Bread Blackberries	Nuts Pomegranate Persimmon Apples Cider

In her novel *The Sea Priestess*, Dion Fortune describes a ritual involving food associated with the Moon. Lunar food is white in her symbolic system. You could associate different foods with the classical planets and do a ritual to attune people to the planetary energies using symbolic foods. [94]

The magical and mystical correspondences of food are endless and vary from one culture to another.

Different regions have different seasonal produce, so the corresponding foods for each festival are clearly going to vary depending on what is available at that time of year in that region.

---

[93] Fiddlehead ferns are a delicacy on the East Coast of Canada and the United States

[94] A huge list of magical food correspondences and recipes can be found at http://witcheslore.com/bookofshadows/herbology/food-magic-for-witches/2908/

Sun	Moon	Mercury	Mars
Oranges Lemons Limes Strawberries Bay leaves Cinnamon	White cheese Tofu White bread White fish Mooli Eggs Bamboo shoots Ice cream	Astringent Basil Marjoram Parsley Almonds Caraway seeds	Spicy foods Red foods Mango Chocolate Banana Chives, leek, garlic, onions
Venus	**Jupiter**	**Saturn**	**Pluto**
Aphrodisiac Oysters Edible flowers Asparagus Wine Pears Quince Beets	Puddings Heavy foods Broccoli Sage Oats Aubergine (eggplant) Anise Maple syrup	Tamarind Thyme Quince Pickles	Root vegetables Mushrooms

Food comes from the Earth, and enables you to relate directly to your environment, especially if you have grown your own vegetables or raised your own livestock. If you have your own allotment or garden, then it is good to have rituals to honour the spirits of the garden and the plants and the animals and birds that live there. The first time you turn over the soil in your garden, the first time you plant seeds, the first time you gather fruit or vegetables, all can be marked with ritual and suitable offerings such as a libation. At Imbolc, we have started to bless the garden tools (spade, fork, rake, and trowel).

The point of all this ritual and symbolism is to bring us closer to Nature, and to bring us into right relationship with our Mother, the Earth.

Discussion

How does food connect the body to Nature and the seasons?

How do different religious traditions relate to food and the body?

How can we cultivate a healthy relationship to food?

Exercises

Try cooking and eating in a sacred and mindful manner. Make the cooking of a meal a ritual activity, and then eat the food in a sacred manner.

Make a list of the foods you associate with the different festivals. Draw a mandala of the festivals and their associated foods.

Make an edible mandala, and then eat it.

20. Walking

Meditative Walking

There are several different types of meditative walking, from various spiritual traditions.

The theologian St Augustine famously wrote "*Solvitur ambulando*" (It is solved by walking), by which he presumably meant that as you walk, the problems that were at the forefront of your mind are put on the back burner and there solved. I have experienced this process myself.

Walking is also more environmentally friendly than other means of locomotion.

Eastern Orthodox Christians practice the prayer walk, which is a form of processional walking, with stops for prayers at various intervals.

The practice of walking labyrinths is a very ancient practice dating from pre-Christian times, but also used by Christians in labyrinths such as the famous one at Chartres. In a Chartres-style labyrinth, you never know quite how near or far you are from the centre, so as you twist and turn through the labyrinth, walking slowly and meditatively, you are reminded of the twists and turns of life, and sometimes solutions to problems come to mind as you walk.

Some Buddhists practice the walking meditation, which is where you walk slowly and mindfully, place one foot in front of the other in a slow and deliberate way, silently reciting a mantra as you walk.

Another way of walking mindfully is to walk in a garden and walk towards the first thing – perhaps a plant, perhaps a stone, or a leaf on the ground – that attracts your attention, and then really look at it. What colour is it? What is its texture? How is it structured? Is it growing or decaying? Smell it, touch it. Does it make a sound? Follow the patterns on its surface. When you have really observed it with all your senses, thank it and move on to the next thing that attracts your attention. At the end of your walk, you might like to draw what you have seen, or write a poem (perhaps haiku) about the experience.

Labyrinths

Walking the labyrinth is a very ancient form of meditation, very relaxing, and it is well worth giving it a try. It is very personal and inwardly focussed, and yet shared with your fellow-travellers in a wordless communion.

Each person's journey into the labyrinth is unique, although the labyrinth has a single pathway to the centre. We all travel on the same pathway, but each person goes at a different speed, travelling in a different way. Rather like life, the path twists and turns, in and out, and you never know how close to the centre you are. When the path appears to take you furthest away from the centre, you are nearer, and when you appear to be closest, you are further away.

The centre – the goal of the journey – can mean different things to different people. For me, it is a metaphor for the Divine: always present, always hidden. In Pagan labyrinths, the centre symbolises the underworld, the inner realm; in Christian labyrinths, it represents the goal of the pilgrim, Jerusalem, with Christ at the centre.

The centre is a place to meditate and reflect on the journey, connect with the Divine, or just look within yourself. The space at the centre is shaped like a flower, or like the rose window of a cathedral. Each of its petals represents one of six kingdoms: mineral, vegetable, animal, human, angelic and the unknown.

The journey back from the centre depicts bringing back the blessing and insight from the other realm to share with your community. As you cross the threshold once more into the outer world, it is a good idea to meditate on the experience, and only gradually ease back into normal conversation.

Pagan labyrinths generally have the path winding through one quadrant at a time, possibly so the walker can meditate on each of the four elements in turn. Christian labyrinths have the path winding back and forth between the quadrants, so that you never know where you are. This is in many ways a more powerful experience because you never know how close you are to the goal of the journey, so it is a revelation when you reach it. One such labyrinth is the one in Chartres Cathedral, which was constructed around 1200.

The oldest labyrinth design is the Cretan labyrinth, which is a very simple design and can be drawn quite quickly; it is easy to make out of pebbles in your garden or at a camp.

A Brief History of Mazes and Labyrinths

Mazes are recorded in Egypt, Rome, Scandinavia, England, India, and the American Southwest. They are generally believed to symbolise the soul's journey through life, or the journey of the dead to the underworld.

There are two types of maze: the unicursal (single path) maze and the puzzle maze. Both are referred to as a labyrinth and a maze. However, in the myth of the Minotaur, the labyrinth in which the Minotaur dwells is clearly a puzzle maze (i.e. having dead ends), as Theseus needs a thread to find his way through to the centre. Apparently, the legend of Theseus and the Minotaur refers to the maze-like palace at Knossos, which burned to the ground in the 15th century BCE.

The Classical Maze comes in four types, the Serpentine, Spiral, Simple Meander, and Complex Meander. The Roman ones were usually square, but these designs work as circular mazes too.

The principle of the maze was probably discovered in the Neolithic. The earliest recorded mazes were in Crete, 4000 years ago. In Egypt, there was a huge palace complex on the shores of a lake seven days journey up the Nile from the pyramids in form of a labyrinth. This was built by pharaoh Amenemhet III in the 19th century BCE. It consisted of thousands of rooms and twelve large maze-like courtyards, which were probably intended to keep out unwelcome visitors. Amenemhet also created a maze inside his nearby pyramid to thwart tomb robbers. Most Roman labyrinths, on the other hand, were too small to have been walked, and are typically found on the floor near the entrances to houses and villas; many have small city walls (perhaps indicating the walls of Troy) drawn around them. This suggests they served a protective function and were perhaps believed to have warded off evil influences or intruders — a common function of the labyrinth in many other cultures as well. The tomb of Lars Porsenna (an Etruscan king) at Chiusi in Italy was said to be surrounded by a labyrinth.

The turf mazes of Britain and Scandinavia may have served a similar purpose, but in the Middle Ages they acquired an additional association with May games; hence the name "Robin Hood's Race" or "Julian's Bower". The Celtic name for a maze was Caer Droia, the place of turning, and this was transliterated into English as Troy Town. It was widely believed that England was founded by Brutus fleeing Troy, and the mazes were believed to represent Troy. Mazes in Finland were often called Jericho, referring to the legend that it was destroyed by the Israelite army marching around it seven times. A maze called 'the walls of Jericho' also appears in a Hebrew manuscript.

Pilgrimage

Pilgrimage is a spiritual practice in many different traditions. One of the most powerful experiences I have had was visiting the witch's cottage, the building where Gerald Gardner and the Brickett's Wood coven met. I was profoundly moved to think that here was where the Wiccan tradition really got going, and to think of all the rituals that took place there. I also enjoyed visiting Charles Darwin's house and walking along the path where he used to take his morning walk and think about the theory of evolution. Of course, I and my companion talked about evolution and natural selection. Another profound pilgrimage experience was visiting Canterbury Abbey, where thousands of pilgrims went to visit the shrine of St Thomas à Becket.

Each of these pilgrimage experiences was different. The witch's cottage was because of a personal connection with the tradition and the people who met there. The visit to Darwin's house was more because of the very important idea that emerged there. And the Canterbury Cathedral visit was more because it was a place where many other people had had a profound spiritual experience and made a connection with the numinous. The literary connection with Chaucer also contributed; and I have always liked Thomas à Becket because he was kind to the poor.

The excellent book, *Art of Pilgrimage* by Phil Cousineau,[95] links the pilgrimage to the idea of the hero journey outlined by Joseph Campbell. First there is the call to adventure - the urge to go on pilgrimage. Then there is the meeting with magical helpers - these can be companions on the journey, or the helpful tools you take with you. Then the crisis - feelings of conflict, futility, or an encounter with difficulty. Finally, the goal is reached - the destination of the pilgrimage. Then you need to bring back the blessing of the pilgrimage to the everyday world. Phil Cousineau suggests making a collage of images and found objects from the journey, or drawing, or writing a journal (or all of these). He also advocates plenty of time spent meditating and contemplating both the journey and the destination. Ritual performed at the place (like Muslims perambulating around the Ka'aba) is also a good way to engage with the destination.

One of the important things about a pilgrimage is the effort expended to get there. If it does not involve effort, it is probably just a visit. There's no need to actually suffer to reach your destination, but the opportunity to take time out of from the mundane world to have an adventure, be alone or with people other than your usual companions, and be reliant

---

[95] Phil Cousineau (1998 / 2012), *Art of Pilgrimage: The Seeker's Guide to Making Travel Sacred*. Conari Press.

on your own resources, is part of the process. That is why people walk as part of a pilgrimage. Just as entering the labyrinth involves a journey to the centre of everything, so does a pilgrimage.

Many of the places that ancient Pagans might have visited on pilgrimages have gone, but there are still many Pagan temples in Greece and Italy and Turkey, megalithic sites in Britain and Ireland and France, and beautiful landscapes everywhere. The pathways that people might have travelled to get to them may have been turned into roads, however.

You can get inventive with pilgrimages and visit places associated with your personal heroes and heroines. I have visited most of the sites associated with the Tolpuddle Martyrs (early trade unionists). It is exciting to be in the place where something of personal significance to you happened.

Long-distance walks along the Ridgeway and other ancient trackways are also excellent, both for the changing scenery and the number of sacred sites they pass through. Hadrian's Wall has a Mithraeum and some excellent museums devoted to Roman statuary and funerary monuments, and amazing views over the surrounding countryside.

The beauty of walking, whether it is over a long distance or a short one, is the changing scenery, the ancient monuments, the flowers, birds, trees, and animals you see along the way, the companionship of fellow-travellers, and the many excellent pubs that can be found tucked away in country villages. There is something particularly healing about the act of walking, the focusing on something else, the placing of troubles on the backburner, and the change of scene.

Discussion

Why is a walking meditation or a walk across the landscape so effective for shifting one's perspective and solving problems?

How do walking, pilgrimages, and labyrinths relate to each other?

How does the design of a labyrinth relate to Pagan cosmology?

Exercises

Do the mindful walk described in the first section of this chapter: walk in a garden, and walk towards the first thing – perhaps a plant, perhaps a stone, or a leaf on the ground – that attracts your attention, and then really look at it. When you have really observed it with all your senses, thank it and move on to the next thing that attracts your attention.

Walk across your favourite landscape several times over the course of the seasons, and observe how it is different in spring, summer, autumn, and winter. Keep a note of the birds, flowers, and animals that you see.

Look back over the times you have visited a special place that has major significance for you. Was it a pilgrimage?

Carry out a pilgrimage to a place associated with someone you admire, or the temple of a deity. Note the stages of the journey and how they feel. What blessing can you bring home with you?

21. Gardening

Gardening is well known to be therapeutic, but it also serves to connect us with all of life, and with Nature. It is a process of fostering life, of working with the land and Nature to create beauty – part of the inner work.

Embodied spirituality is about responding to the world with wonder, creativity, and joy; it is not some abstract process – it is about connecting the inner with the outer.

The planting of the seeds in the ground teaches us hope and care for small growing things. Watching the seeds come up is an experience of hope rewarded. Then we must care for the tender seedlings, watering them, planting them out, protecting them from being eaten. We create patterns in the garden – arrangements of plants that flower and fruit in their season. The plants might be herbs that heal, or flowers with scent and colour, or leafy trees, or fruit and vegetables. Plants have symbolism and mythology and folklore associated with them.

The word paradise means an enclosed garden; the earliest gardens were oases of fertility in the desert, such as the famous Hanging Gardens of Babylon, which must have required considerable watering. The fabled Garden of Eden was the mythological model for such gardens. Clarissa Pinkola Estes' uncle Zovár said that the Garden of Eden was really the whole Earth, because everywhere on Earth is capable of flowering like a garden, and is full of the divine presence if you know how to be aware of it.

Composting (an essential aspect of gardening) is a wonderful metaphor for the process of change and transformation. We compost our dead matter (past experience) and it helps to fertilise new growth (the wisdom that comes from experience).

Gardens are often associated with witches, because the properties of herbs (poisonous and healing, psychotropic and psychedelic) are part of the traditional lore of witchcraft. Rue, wormwood, and many other plants were associated with the witch. Fern seed was said to make you invisible. The mysterious ingredients of flying ointment (if the fabled brew ever actually existed outside the fevered imaginings of the Inquisition) were said to cause hallucinations of flying to the witches' sabbat.

If you are going to use herbs for healing, it is best to get yourself a really good herbal like Mrs Grieve's *A Modern Herbal*.[96]

You can also grow your own vegetables and flowers. Even on a balcony in the middle of a city, it is possible to grow herbs, flowers, and vegetables like courgettes (zucchini) in pots. Climbers like beans, nasturtiums, and peas are great for small gardens; and the scent of honeysuckle and jasmine and roses are wonderful on a summer evening. Planting flowers for bees is also important, because of the decline of bees due to pesticides, specifically neonicotinoids. Make sure any plants you buy for your garden have not been pre-treated with these chemicals. Single flowers (such as dahlias) and purple or blue flowers (such as lavender, rosemary, thyme, alliums, buddleia, catmint, cornflower, aquilegia, astilbe, campanula, sea holly, globe thistle) are favourites with bees. They also like

---

[96] M Grieve (1931), *A Modern Herbal*. [Available online.] http://www.botanical.com/botanical/mgmh/mgmh.html

tubular-shaped flowers such as foxgloves, honeysuckle, penstemons and snapdragons. Spring flowers (daffodils, bluebells, cherry blossom, and apple blossom) are also great for bees. They need both nectar-bearing and pollen-bearing flowers throughout the growing season.[97]

Trees and flowers have symbolic associations with deities, elements, and planets, so if you want to create a magical garden, you may also want to consider these associations. My earlier books on trees, *The Enchanted Forest: the magical lore of trees*, and *The Sacred Grove: Mysteries of the forest* provide comprehensive lists of symbolism, folklore, and mythology. If you live in Britain, it is worth buying Richard Mabey's *Flora Britannica*,[98] which provides a massive compendium of the contemporary folklore of flowers. *A Witch's Natural History* by Giles Watson[99] is essential to any witch's bookshelf, and highly recommended. Another favourite of mine is Barry Patterson's *The Art of Conversation with the Genius Loci*.[100]

Gardens are places where we can reconnect with Nature, and create a sanctuary for bees and other insects, birds, and small mammals. And maybe faeries as well, if any live in your vicinity. But remember that the Fair Folk are not the pretty winged beings of popular imagination, but something much

---

[97] *Plants for Bees*. Gardeners' World. www.gardenersworld.com/plants/plant-inspiration/plants-for-bees/
[98] Richard Mabey (1996), *Flora Britannica*. Penguin Books.
[99] Giles Watson (2012), *A Witch's Natural History*. London: Troy Books.
[100] Barry Patterson (2003), *The Art of Conversation with the Genius Loci*. Capall Bann Publishing.

more powerful and primal, and to be treated with caution and respect.

If your garden is big enough, you may be able to keep chickens or bees. If you do keep bees, it is customary to tell them all your news, whether happy or sad - especially if there is a birth or death in the family. More details of the folklore of bees can be found in my earlier book, *The Magical Lore of Animals*.

I have a small garden and two cats, so I do not put out bird food, as when the seed falls on the ground, the birds fly down to eat it, and are then vulnerable to cats. But if you do not have cats, it is lovely to have a bird feeder - especially in the winter when food is scarce in the hedgerows. In North America, hummingbird feeders are very popular, and it is amazing to see a hummingbird up close. You can grow specific nectar-bearing flowers that hummingbirds will enjoy, too[101]: abutilon, agastache, aloe, anisacanthus, aquilegia, caesalpinia, callistemon, chilopsis, fuchsia (also popular with bees), hamelia, justicia, kniphofia, lobelia, lonicera, monarda, penstemon, salvia, tecoma.

A garden is a microcosm of Nature, a little piece of paradise, a sanctuary from the noise and hubbub of the world, offering restoration and healing to the spirit. The fascinating thing about gardening is that we are co-creators of the garden - we place the plants in a specific place, and introduce a new species, and tend the rambly plants to make space and light

---

[101] *Hummingbird Flowers - The Best 18 Plant Families for Natural Nectar.* http://www.hummingbirdsociety.org/hummingbird-flowers/

for the smaller ones - but we are in partnership with the plants, and the sun, and the rain, in the making of a garden.

Discussion

How is the experience of being in a garden different from being in a wild place?

What is the symbolism of gardens?

What deities are associated with gardens? Why?

Exercises

Design your own herb garden.

Meditate in your garden and try to contact the spirits of place.

Create a small shrine in your garden.

If you do not have a garden, create a shrine involving house plants, or on your balcony if you have one.

22. Spirits of the Land

I have always liked the description of Paganism as nature religion (however inaccurate and unhelpful that may be). The idea of being connected to Nature was one of the things that drew me towards Paganism. I also really liked the old gods, but woods, mountains, the sea, chalk hills, ancient trackways, burial mounds, stone circles, and liminal places have always attracted me. I think I first tried talking to trees when I was about 12 years old. I get withdrawal symptoms if I do not get out into the countryside regularly. I also feel the urge to converse with the spirits of the land.

Land Spirits and Deities

The Otherworld does not consist only of deities. There are also land wights, landvaettir, genii loci, land spirits, and spirits of the hearth and home.

If you want to be in relationship with deities, it is a good idea to talk to your local land spirits, ancestors, and household spirits. Deities exist in the context of other spirits.

Start by identifying the sacred places in your local area, such as hilltops, hollows, wells and springs, crossroads, and other liminal places. Then go and spend time in those places and feel the energies and presences there. If you leave offerings, it is best to leave inconspicuous ones that do not harm the environment or the animals and birds that live there. Rather than tying ribbons to trees, tie a strand of your hair to a branch instead. Rather than leaving flowers or crystals, make a temporary mandala of leaves, pebbles, pinecones, twigs, and/or berries that you find on the site. Even better, clear up any litter on the site.

Land Spirits in North America

Many people in North America are worried that if they approach the land spirits, it will be cultural appropriation. But you need to devise your own rituals for approaching them, not appropriate the rituals of First Nations people, which will probably not fit in a Pagan context anyway.

When I contacted the land spirits of Ontario in a ritual, they seemed keen to talk to me, so I feel that trying to enter into relationship with them is a good thing. You do need to be respectful and not try to use Native American / First Nations terminology or offerings unless you are specifically invited to do so by Native Americans / First Nations people[102] themselves. This is because they are specific to that culture and tradition (not for genetic reasons, but for cultural ones), and are likely to be poorly understood outside of that culture. The land of the indigenous people was taken away from them, and land treaties were repeatedly broken by the colonial powers. There was also genocide of the indigenous people in both Canada and the USA. This means that in many cases, their religious traditions are the last thing they have left that is their own. A similarly cautious and respectful approach

---

[102] The collective term for the indigenous peoples of North America can vary. In Canada, the preferred term was for a while 'First Nations'. In the USA, the term Native American is disputed by some indigenous people (because anyone born in North America is a 'native'). Some people call themselves Indians (possibly from Spanish *'in dios'* - in God), some use the term Natives. It is also worth bearing in mind that there are many different languages and cultures involved. Either way, I am using the terms that feel most respectful to me.

should be adopted in Australia and New Zealand, for similar reasons.

Land Spirits in Europe

Contacting land spirits in Britain and Europe is even easier (because these are not colonised lands – unless you live in the northern regions of Scandinavia). Go into the landscape and listen. Finding a sit-spot and going there regularly is a very good way of connecting with a place. When you go to a sacred place in the landscape, always approach it with respect and ask the local spirits for permission to be there, especially if you are planning a ritual. What I do is pause at the entrance to the site, ask if it is okay, and wait for a sense that it is alright to proceed.

One of the finest books on Paganism I have ever read is *The Art of Conversation with the Genius Loci* by Barry Patterson. It explains in some depth how to see things from a non-human perspective, how to relate to your local landscape, and how to make connections with the land and the spirits that dwell there. It is so good that I have said to people, "If you only read one book about Paganism, make it this one".

Each landscape (especially in Britain with its very varied geology) is unique and takes some getting to know. There is the geology, the flora, the fauna, the history, the folklore, and the archaeology (a palimpsest of human occupation and land-use). Take your time to get to know all of these, and to connect with all of it. Get to know your local trees, especially the ones that seem neglected.

Building and repairing relationships with land spirits entails doing something to repair our relationship with nature. This will mean different things for different people. Personally, I have felt much more attuned to Nature since I stopped owning a car. Your approach may be different, and I do not presume to dictate what it should be (because not everyone can manage without a car).

Discussion

Are connecting with Nature, the Earth, and the land the same experience or process?

What aspects of Pagan and witchcraft practice assist with connecting to Nature, the Earth, and the land?

Do any aspects of Pagan and witchcraft practice hinder the process of connecting with Nature, the Earth, and the land?

Exercises

Draw a sacred map of your local landscape, with the prominent landforms (hills, rivers, mountains, lakes, woods, meadows, marshes, sacred trees, stone circles, burial mounds) and their mythological associations.

Walk through your local landscape in a sacred manner and make offerings (the sort that will not harm the flora and fauna) to the local spirits. The best offerings are clearing litter from the land, poetry readings, and non-permanent offerings.

23. Meditation, Visualisation, Contemplation, Prayer

Often people use the terms visualisation, meditation and pathworking interchangeably, but they are different techniques, with different purposes and histories of development.

A **meditation** invites you to focus on your breathing, your body, or your feelings; it does not usually involve visualising. It is designed to increase awareness of your body. Typically, meditation techniques are drawn from Taoism or Buddhism. It can also focus on an external pattern or design such as a mandala. Many meditation techniques in witchcraft and related traditions involve moving energy through and around your body, such as the Iron Pentacle and Pearl Pentacle exercises in the Feri tradition.

It is important to note that several studies have found that meditation and mindfulness meditation can increase the symptoms of anxiety and depression, or even cause their onset, for about 8% of the population [103]. If you are one of those people, this is not a failure on your part, it is just the way you are wired. I have found that I get especially disoriented by any meditation that asks me to focus on a specific part of my body for a long period of time, or that asks me to travel outside my body. If you experience any adverse symptoms, such as increased anxiety, depression, disorientation, or nausea, stop doing the practice straight

---

[103] https://bit.ly/3iFwTi9 Mindfulness and meditation can worsen depression and anxiety. *New Scientist*, 14 August 2020.

away. I find that I need to earth myself by eating something and hugging a tree if this happens.

Another related technique is **contemplation**, where the practitioner focuses on a deity, virtue, or quality (such as love). The technique is used in both Christianity and Islam. It was also advocated by Plato. Examples of contemplation include contemplative prayer, centering prayer, and lectio divina. Some people contemplate Nature as a spiritual practice.

A **visualisation** invites you to focus on specific images; sometimes it tells a story or involves travelling through a landscape (real or imaginary); sometimes it is intended to bring about a specific result – this is known as creative visualisation. Visualisation is popular with both Pagans and New Agers.

Visualisation is a journey of the imagination (though not necessarily an imaginary journey).

It can be as simple and low-key as visualising an apple, or it could involve astral travel, and everything in between. It is different from meditation in that the symbolic or archetypal qualities of what is visualised are important. It often involves encounters with mythical beings or archetypes. It is also part of the technique of pathworking. Visualisation can be used as a spell-working technique, both to change consciousness and to bring about more material changes.

A **pathworking** takes you on a journey through an inner landscape. Pathworking as a technique is derived from magical uses of the Kabbalistic Tree of Life. In that system, a pathworking is a journey along one of the 22 paths of the Tree of Life, each of which has a specific set of landscape and symbolism associated with it (and corresponds to one of the twenty-two cards of the Major Arcana of the Tarot).

I would say that guided meditations were suitable for large groups; guided visualisations and path-workings should probably be used in smaller groups where the person leading can be more aware of participants' emotional responses. When I lead a visualisation, I do the visualisation, and at the same time, try to remain aware of participants' emotional responses and internal energy states.

Some visualisations are not safe (e.g. ones that invite you to visualise going out of your body) and should not be attempted by the inexperienced. People often think that it is all happening in your head and therefore you can visualise whatever you like with no consequences, but that is not necessarily the case. Magic (often defined as "the art of changing consciousness in accordance with will") does have real effects, even if they are only psychological effects.

I never pre-record either visualisations or meditations – I prefer to do them live and feel the mood of the participants, going slower or faster depending on whether I feel the participants are following, and adding bits for the specific audience. I always try out a visualisation myself before leading others in it.

I tend to leave as much as possible to the imagination of the participants; for example, if there are trees, animals or birds, let them decide what type of trees, animals, or birds; if there are people, let them decide what they are wearing, and what gender they are, unless it is relevant to the symbolism you are trying to convey. This makes the visualisation more satisfying for them, because then it is filled with their ideas and imagery, instead of something imposed from outside.

It also helps if the visualisation has between three and seven key symbols, which are linked together by a logical association or train of thought. This is because the human brain can retain somewhere between three and seven ideas (the optimum number of five).

I have come across a lot of people who cannot visualise at all. For small group work, I always ask if there are people who cannot visualise and try to adapt by talking about feelings and spatial cues as well as visual imagery.

You can test whether someone can visualise by getting them to think of an orange – most people can manage to see an orange sphere in their mind's eye, and if they can't, the chances are that they are one of those people who cannot see with their mind's eye. I, and several other people that I know, can taste on my mind's tongue (and smell on my mind's nose) but many people cannot do this. Not being able to visualise has a name, aphantasia, and psychologists are researching it.

You can check whether people can experience all five senses with the orange visualisation – imagine touching the pitted surface, prising the fruit open with your fingers, hearing the noise of the tearing peel, smelling the orange oil from the skin and the juice inside, then tasting the fruit, and feeling the juice on your tongue. For people who cannot visualise in any sense modality, get them to remember the emotional feeling they get when they eat an orange; you can then use the same approach for other visualisations.

Prayer

There are several different types of prayer:

- contemplative prayer (communing with a deity, usually in silence)
- intercessory prayer (praying for help for someone else)
- petitionary prayer (praying for help for yourself)
- thanksgiving
- adoration, devotion
- prayer of approach (preparing to enter a deity's presence)
- invocation (asking a deity to be present)
- bidding prayer (a suggestion to participants to pray for a specific thing)
- confession and penitence (though not that many Pagans do this, as we do not tend to regard wrong acts as injuring a deity, only as injuring the physical person(s) who were harmed by them)
- words of reassurance (for the benefit of the participants of the ritual)
- healing prayer
- expressing aspiration (e.g. "may we be blessed")
- reflection (reflecting on events).[104]

Prayer is not just asking a deity to do things for you. It can be used as a means of creating a sacred context for your activities, by opening proceedings with a prayer. An invocation of a deity is a form of prayer. An evocation of an elemental spirit is a form of prayer. Many Pagans dismiss

---

[104] Thanks to Vernon Marshall, whose excellent workshop on prayer inspired some of this section.

prayer as "passive magic" (as opposed to doing spells, which they class as "active magic"). This reduces prayer only to petitionary and intercessory prayer – but there are many other kinds of prayer, as you can see from the list above (which may not be a complete list).

There are also different modes and techniques of prayer: for example, centering prayer, contemplative prayer, and body prayer (using dance or other special movements in prayer).

Centering prayer was developed by an interfaith dialogue group of Christians and Buddhists. These Christians admired the technique of Buddhist meditation but didn't want to cultivate the awareness of the Void recommended by Buddhist tradition; so instead they decided to choose a single concept and focus on it during the meditation, which they called "centering prayer". For instance, you might choose one of the Nine Noble Virtues[105] of Heathenry, or the Eight Wiccan Virtues[106], or one of the Roman virtues[107], to focus on during the prayer. The technique is similar to that of meditation, in that you relax your breathing and focus on the body, but you hold the concept you wish to focus on in your heart for the duration of the prayer, perhaps repeating the chosen word.

Contemplative prayer is an age-old tradition of mystics. It is quite similar to centering prayer but doesn't involve focusing on a specific concept; it's more of a wordless communion with a deity. It is usually preceded by more verbal forms of prayer, which lead into contemplation or meditation.

---

[105] http://en.wikipedia.org/wiki/Nine_Noble_Virtues
[106] http://www.cauldronliving.com/showthread.php?t=7313
[107] http://www.novaroma.org/nr/Roman_virtues

Body prayer is where you involve your whole body in the act of prayer. This might be gardening and praying, or dancing and praying, or walking and praying. Walking a labyrinth can be a prayerful act, as you deliberately focus on the spiritual journey. Another example of body prayer is the Dances of Universal Peace, a dance tradition in their own right, designed to engender peace and love in the participants; another example is the Salute to the Sun found in Yoga (which is a sacred Hindu practice designed to stimulate spiritual growth).

What is the purpose of prayer? I do not think it is only for the benefit of the deity being prayed to. I think it is for the benefit of the one doing the praying. The practice of cultivating awareness of the greater life of the universe, and of examining our own conscience, and being aware of the suffering and joy of others – these are beneficial for the soul.

Ceisiwr Serith produced *A Book of Pagan Prayer* [108], which is an excellent starting point if you are new to this practice. The book suggests a lot of different types of prayer, and to many different deities.

Prayer can be personal and private, or collective. When sharing a prayer with others, it can be difficult to express your theological viewpoint without excluding others. One proposed solution [109] is to say, "this is a prayer from my tradition" and perhaps invite people to "translate in their heads" if it does not quite work for them.

---

[108] http://books.google.co.uk/books/about/A_Book_of_Pagan_Prayer.html?id=tquqpfeL7BsC

[109] http://www.thorncoyle.com/blog/2014/02/18/on-prayer-and-privilege-pantheacon-2014-1/

There are prayers in many different Pagan traditions, including devotional polytheism, Feri, Reclaiming, Wicca, Druidry, and many others. The theological stance of these prayers may vary from monism to 'hard' polytheism. A prayer does not have to be to a deity; you can also pray to spirits of place, or commune with Nature. I do not think there is anything wrong with adapting prayers to fit your own theology (if you state your sources, to avoid plagiarism, if you are praying the prayer in public).

You do not have to close your eyes or kneel down to pray. Many people (e.g. Eastern Orthodox Christians) pray with their eyes open and their hands extended to indicate that they recognise the divine in the world. You could experiment with different positions. Some traditions use prayer beads; there are some lovely Pagan prayer beads [110] available.

A prayer can be nothing more than time taken to set an intention for the day, or to contemplate the day's events before going to sleep. It can be time spent communing with a deity or holding others that you care about in your awareness and wishing them well. It can take place at your personal altar, or just in your head. It can be spoken or unspoken, formal or informal, and involve stillness or movement. It can involve descending into your own depths to find a connection with all-that-is; or it can be reaching out to a deity or spirit of place; or some other process. Different people experience it differently.

---

[110]

http://paganwiccan.about.com/od/godsandgoddesses/ss/How-To-Make-Pagan-Prayer-Beads.htm

The sit spot

An important part of embodiment is experiencing yourself as part of the world. As climate activists have said, "we are not defending nature - we are nature defending itself". [111]

A really great way of experiencing yourself as part of nature is to incorporate the sit spot into your practice. The sit spot is a place in nature where you can sit comfortably for around fifteen minutes. While there, you slow your breathing, quiet your mind, and listen to the sounds around you: the rustling of the wind in the leaves, water flowing or falling, bird song. You return to the same spot on a regular basis, to become attuned to that particular place and its sounds, energies, spirits, seasons, and moods.[112]

Útiseta

The sit-spot meditation is like the ancient Heathen magical practice of 'sitting out', known as útiseta. This is a practice for communicating with land-wights and should only be used if you specifically need help or answers.

It was used by practitioners of seiðr, the völvur, and spækona - women who arguably fulfilled the same social niche as witches. Some sources describe it as sitting out in the sense of sitting between the worlds; others interpret it as sitting out-of-doors. A thirteenth-century Icelandic law outlawed útiseta at

---

[111] http://www.theecologist.org/News/news_analysis/2986467/cop21_actions_go_ahead_we_are_not_defending_nature_we_are_nature_defending_itself.html

[112] http://www.adrianharris.org/blog/2011/03/the-sit-spot/

vekja trǫll upp ok fremja heiðni (sitting out to wake up trolls and practicing heathenry). [113]

Focussing on the Body

Depending on the aim of your inner life, it is advisable to choose techniques that are compatible with the goals of your inner work. If your goal is to connect with Nature, then select practices which are compatible with that goal, such as techniques to help you live more fully in your body and perceive its continuity with the environment in which you live.

Much of Western culture seems designed to cause us to live in our heads and ignore the body. Traditional spirituality includes a lot of techniques for focussing on the body.

Ignatian spirituality has a technique for becoming aware of different parts of the body and offering them accompaniment through pain. Ignatius Loyola was the founder of the Jesuits, and his spiritual techniques were intended to help the practitioner "to conquer oneself and to regulate one's life in such a way that no decision is made under the influence of any inordinate attachment." Some of his ideas are compatible with a Pagan inner life; others may not be.

For people who find it difficult to relax (which includes me), a very effective prelude to meditation or visualisation is to tense each muscle in the body for a count of three, and then relax it. You can start from your head and work your way down to your feet. Alternatively, you can start from your feet and work

---

[113] http://www.northernshamanism.org/utiseta-breath-and-mound-sitting.html

your way up to your head. Try both and see which you prefer. Make sure to include the inside of your mouth, facial muscles, the back of each limb, the back of your head, and your back muscles.

We spend far too much time treating the body as a workhorse and ignoring aches and pains which are often warning signs of stress and illness. This is especially true if you work in an office and do not get up and move around every so often.

Contemplative Prayer

I have been trying sporadically to get into praying to Pagan deities for some time. I started with Ceisiwr Serith's *A Book of Pagan Prayer*, which is excellent. I have also occasionally practised *lectio divina*. Pagan prayer does not assume that we are the passive recipients of favours from the deities; nor that Pagan deities are all-powerful or rulers of the universe. Pagan prayer is about an encounter with deities.

Being a relatively lazy person, and not that great at keeping in touch with people, I am not that great at maintaining a spiritual practice. Therefore, any practice that I engage in must be simple, with no barriers to engaging in it, no effort to set it up, and of variable length.

Contemplative prayer is a practice that is simple to understand, but which may take a lifetime to master. The person doing the prayer sits quietly, usually upright on a chair, and often uses a prayer word to focus the mind. When thoughts arise, do not follow the train of thought, just let it go, and refocus on the prayer word (or your breath, if you are not using a prayer word).

In contemplative prayer, we descend into the depths of the psyche, and encounter the collective unconscious, and thereby the formless depths of the divine realms. Contemplative prayer is not solely an internal experience; it is an encounter with the divine that transcends the individual (note that I am referring to epistemological transcendence, the experience of something greater than oneself, and not ontological transcendence, which is the idea of something existing outside the universe).

I learnt a lot about contemplative prayer from reading two excellent books from the Christian tradition: *Into the Silent Land* and *A Sunlit Absence*,[114] both by Martin Laird. The first book (*Into the Silent Land*) deals with the stages of contemplative prayer and how one can deepen one's practice. The second book (*A Sunlit Absence*) deals with the pitfalls and difficulties of contemplative prayer (boredom, distraction, feelings of dryness, lack of a sense of divine presence). Both are written entirely in the context of the Christian tradition, so as a Pagan and a polytheist, I needed to "translate in my head" as I went along. Nevertheless, these are outstanding books which explore the techniques and mental states of contemplative prayer in considerable detail.

---

[114] Martin Laird (2006), *Into the Silent Land: A Guide to the Christian Practice of Contemplation*, Oxford University Press.
https://books.google.co.uk/books?isbn=0199779430
   Martin Laird (2011), *A Sunlit Absence: Silence, Awareness, and Contemplation*, Oxford University Press.
https://books.google.co.uk/books?isbn=0195378725

In Pagan contemplative prayer, the focus of the practice might be the name of a virtue that you wish to cultivate; the spirit of a place you wish to connect with; the name of a deity whom you worship; an image or statue of a deity; a rune or a Tarot card; or a mandala. Focusing on an external image may make you reliant on the external image for maintaining your focus, but it can be useful, especially if the image is seen as a gateway or window onto the Otherworld, rather than merely an image. The point of contemplative prayer is not necessarily to ask for anything, but just to enjoy the presence of the deity you are communing with. You can, however, combine it with other forms of prayer if you wish.

My personal practice is to sit quietly, saying the name of the deity I wish to commune with, and maybe adding a few words in praise of their deeds, attributes, or qualities. I then recite their name, saying it once on the in-breath and once on the out-breath. I find I need to spend at least five minutes, preferably ten or fifteen, to really experience the presence of the deity. I usually try to commune with at least two deities (the patron deities of Wicca, and some of the deities with whom I have a personal connection).

Discussion

What is the difference between visualisation, meditation, contemplation, and prayer?

Is prayer an exoteric or esoteric practice? Does it matter?

Why do you think so few Pagans engage in prayer?

What are the benefits of visualisation, meditation, contemplation, and prayer?

Exercises

Choose a deity to focus on and spend at least five minutes each day contemplating that deity (or choose seven deities and contemplate one for each day of the week).

Choose a favourite poem and meditate on it.

Visualise an orange and the feel of its skin, the sound of the peel tearing, the taste of its juice, and the smell of its essential oils.

Tense and relax each muscle of your body in turn for a count of three (see the section Focussing on the body).

Find a sit-spot in a garden, park, or forest, and meditate there as often as possible.

24. Creativity and Embodiment

Storytelling and poetry (which were once far more intertwined as art-forms) are the ways in which traditional cultures are transmitted. The stories of Robin Hood and King Arthur were transmitted through ballads. Folktales, such as those collected by the Brothers Grimm, were transmitted through both story and song. Traditional values appear to have been an odd mixture of conformity and freedom: sometimes patriarchal and sometimes revolutionary. Women seem to have had our own traditions to a certain extent; and in the Jewish tradition, women were often the shapers of the Yiddish language, and the stories and oral culture that went with it. [115]

The history of uprisings and revolts against oppression (the Peasants' Revolt, the Peterloo Massacre, the Tolpuddle Martyrs, and many others) and the complaints of the oppressed over enclosure and other injustices is recorded in ballads and songs, some passed down over generations. These songs and stories which resist the narrative of the victors and the Whig interpretation of history (that we will get our rights if we just wait quietly in line) are our common heritage.

Poetry

Poetry is related to theology and magic; they use the same twilight mode of consciousness. Spells and ritual words often take the form of poetry – Doreen Valiente was very good at that. There are many different meters and poetic devices such as assonance, alliteration, and the caesura, which can be used

---

[115] Leo Rosten (1971), *The Joys of Yiddish*. McGraw Hill.

to great effect in the writing of ritual poetry. Poets, like comedians, see connections that others have missed. Both comedy and poetry are sacred arts, showing the world hidden connections and undercurrents.

For me, writing poetry is a sacred vocation, and one that no-one can take away from me. One is a witch in community, one has a job title conferred by an employer: but one can be a poet without approval or sanction from anyone else. Even a child writing their first poems may call themselves a poet. I love that.

A poem can transform your perspective and perceptions, it can be an incantation (listen to WB Yeats reading *The Lake Isle of Innisfree*; [116] it is as if he is reading a spell), or it can be an invocation to change the world.

The process of writing poetry often involves impulses and sensations within the body. For me, a poem starts to build up like a pressure inside me, and then it bursts like a bubble and I get the first few lines and start writing, and then it all comes out in a big rush. Later, I start to refine it, rearranging the lines here and there – but most of my editing is pretty light after the first rush.

I write small pieces of prose in response to the beauty I see all around me, which could get turned into poems, and I think that is my "poetic eye" responding to the world. I once wrote a poem about my creative process where I likened it to the bends – bubbles rising from the depths. I also write poetry for

---

[116] https://www.youtube.com/watch?v=hGoaQ433wnw

ritual, and that tends to be more "written to order" (and sometimes I create spoken poetry extempore in ritual).

If you are not accustomed to writing poetry, or you tend to only write poetry that rhymes, take some time to study poets like Sylvia Plath, W B Yeats, Algernon Swinburne, Hilary Llewellyn Williams, Dave Bonta, Sarah Sadie Busse. Have a look at Anglo-Saxon poetry. This will show you a range of styles and techniques. Get a good modern poetry anthology and dip into it. Work your way through Stephen Fry's guide to writing poetry, *An Ode Less Travelled*. Practice writing sonnets, and haiku, and limericks, and sestinas. Try out different metres (the iamb, the anapaest, the spondee, the trochee, and so on) and get a feel for how they affect the mood of the poem. Comic poems are also good for tricks of metre, rhyme, assonance, and alliteration; Paul Jennings' poem about galoshes springs to mind, which contains the wonderful line "Galoshlessness is foolishness when sharply slants the sleet".[117] When writing rituals, repetition, alliteration, and rhythm can all help to create mood and atmosphere. Try not to include too many tongue-twisters or unfamiliar words that people might stumble over.

Poetry can help to excavate and articulate feelings that are buried deep in the body or the subconscious; it is very cathartic and transformative, and as such, an essential item in the witch's toolbox. Speaking poetry aloud is a form of incantation or enchantment, and one of the ancient bardic arts.

---

[117] Paul Jennings (1961), *I Said Oddly Diddle I?* Max Reinhardt Publishing.

Haiku

The haiku is a Japanese form of poetry which evolved out of the philosophy of Zen Buddhism. Traditional Japanese haiku have 17 syllables, but it has been suggested that English haiku should have more syllables, because English is a more long-winded language than Japanese, and you can pack a lot more concepts into 17 Japanese syllables than you can into 17 English syllables. However, I tend to stick to the 17-syllable structure, divided into 3 lines of 5, 7 and 5 syllables. Haiku also traditionally include a *kireji*, a 'cutting word'. The cutting word divides the poem into two contrasting sections with imagery that adds a surprising twist or contrast to each other. It's difficult to find 'cutting words' in English, so haiku writers in English use a dash to separate the two sections of the poem.

Haiku are essentially poems about Nature, so Japanese haiku also have a season word, to indicate in what season the action of the poem takes place. The season word does not have to be the name of the season; it can be obviously associated with that season – for example, plum blossom would indicate that the poem was describing spring. The imagery of a haiku is simple and unpretentious, and generally does not use similes to achieve its effects. The natural phenomena described may very well be metaphors for something else, but the haiku may also be enjoyed for the images of natural beauty, and the human response to it, that it conjures up.

Haiku poets would often gather to compose haiku on the spot. One poet would begin, and then another poet would respond with a haiku of their own, and in this way a series of linked haiku (known as *haikai-renga*) would be composed by the group.

Sometimes haiku would be combined with travel writing or other prose. The most famous example of this form is *The Narrow Road to the Deep North* by Matsuo Basho,[118] which describes Basho's travels to the far north of Japan. The combined haiku and prose form is known as haibun.

Writing haiku teaches one to strip things back to the essentials, to distil experience into its pure form, and to observe Nature closely. It is a very satisfying process, because haiku are so short, and so complete in themselves.

Theatre and ritual

Theatre and ritual are intimately connected. Indeed, theatre has its origins in ritual, and both have some of the same functions. They are both cathartic and transformational, but there are also some significant differences.

My ex-husband, Nick Hanks, [119] who studied both theatre and the archaeology of ritual spaces, first pointed out to me some of the differences between theatre and ritual.

The fourth wall

In theatre, there is a "fourth wall". The proscenium arch of the theatre is seen as a sort of transparent wall through which the audience observes the action of the play. It is kind of weird, and sometimes even uncomfortable, when that fourth wall is breached. Examples of breaching the fourth wall include theatre-in-the-round, and asides to the audience.

---

[118] Matsuo Basho (1689 / 2005), *The Narrow Road to the Deep North and Other Travel Sketches*, translated by Nobuyuki Yuasa. Penguin Classics.

[119] http://nick-hanks.co.uk/sitemap/

In Wiccan ritual, the audience is the gods, the numinous, the divine. Since the ritual is done in a circle, the "doorway to the divine" is either visualized as the altar, or as being everywhere, since the divine realm is inter-permeable with ours. We generally do our rituals in secluded places where we are not likely to be disturbed; there is no audience. Most religions have a requirement for their most sacred ritual to be members-only; having people who are observers and not participants is uncomfortable, for both the participants and the observers; this is especially true if participants are making themselves vulnerable in some way, either because they are skyclad or because they are being open about their feelings.

Sacred drama

Theatres were first formalized in Ancient Greece, but doubtless sacred drama is as old as ritual. It is from the ancient polytheistic Greeks that we have written dramas, comedy, tragedy, and theatrical concepts like the chorus, catharsis and the *deus ex machina*.

Many anthropologists and archaeologists have speculated on the origins of ritual. It could lie in the practice of imitative magic; or it could lie in the human need for a story to make sense of our lives; or the need for rituals to negotiate changes in our lives, such as the transition from childhood to adulthood. Many cultures have rituals for these transitions (see chapter 25, Rites of passage).

Sacred dramas are often performed as part of a ritual, but they are not the entirety of the ritual. The purpose of the sacred drama is often to achieve catharsis. Theatre often provides a secular form of catharsis.

Catharsis, Verfremdungseffekt, and transformation

A key feature of both theatre and ritual is catharsis. It is a major part of the purpose of ritual, but perhaps more of a side-effect in theatre.

Catharsis (from Greek κάθαρσις, *katharsis*, meaning "purification" or "cleansing" or "clarification") describes the purification and purging of emotions, especially pity and fear. Catharsis is brought about by art or any extreme shift in emotions, resulting in restoration and renewal. Catharsis was originally described by Aristotle in *Poetics*, where he compared the effects of tragedy on the mind of a spectator to the effect of catharsis on the body.

The purpose of catharsis can be transformational, or its purpose can be to reconcile the individual to the status quo, the consensus view of reality.

That is why Brecht wanted his audiences to experience the Verfremdungseffekt (distancing effect) instead of catharsis. He wanted them to look askance at the consensus view of reality, the status quo, and ask why it was like that.

Some rituals are intended to be transformational. Their purpose may be to accustom the participant to their new status in life (which is the case with rites of passage), or it may be to awaken them to new ways of looking at the world, in which case it is more like the Verfremdungseffekt (distancing effect), which provides a new perspective on life.

Deadly, Holy, Rough, Immediate

Peter Brook identifies four types of theatre. Deadly theatre is conventional, boring, lifeless, and obviously theatrical and artificial. Remember the Actors from *Blackadder the Third*? They were the epitome of deadly theatre.

Ritual can also be deadly when performed in a highly stylized and over-dramatic way.

Then there's holy theatre, which is any theatre that dramatizes true emotions, rather than the empty shell of the outward expression of those emotions. Good ritual should also be holy theatre. The emotions invoked by holy theatre can be destructive as well as helpful; what makes it holy theatre is the genuineness of the emotions evoked.

Rough theatre is theatre that is not artificial, grand, lofty, or attempting to make a point. It is street theatre, puppets, mummers' plays, and other seasonal entertainments. Ritual can also be rough theatre; but beware of over-use of rhyme and rhythm, which all too often turns ritual into deadly theatre. Quite often the purpose of rough theatre (and rough ritual such as the Boy Bishop and the Bean King) was to let off steam and restore the status quo.

And finally, there's immediate theatre, which is improvisational, extempore, emergent. The meaning and the story emerge during the performance; they are a collaboration between the actors and the audience. This can often happen in ritual if people are comfortable with extemporizing. It can also happen with storytelling; a friend of mine who is a storyteller mentioned that on one occasion he told a story and the audience found it really sad; on another occasion, the audience laughed when he made a sound-effect, and this changed it to a comic performance of the story.

The purpose of theatre and ritual

Both ritual and theatre are intended to create meaning, to dramatize meaning, the body it forth in stories. Both can be cathartic, transformational, and either reinforce the status quo, or seek to challenge it.

Whilst the theatre was originally a sacred art, eventually a secular version of the theatre emerged. The origins of theatre lie in polytheist antiquity, where both comedies and tragedies were sacred, but Christianity initially had no use for sacred theatre (until the Mystery Plays emerged in the Middle Ages). After the Reformation, Christianity divorced itself even further from the theatre, and so the secular theatre was born.

The main difference between theatre and ritual lies in the intended audience and the structure of the performance.

The structure of a ritual

For a Wiccan ritual, we usually take some time to create a sacred space and create the sense of the numinous. We sweep the space, cast a circle, and call the quarters; the purpose of this is to create the circle as a microcosmic representation of the cosmos.

In a theatre, the establishing action is to draw aside the curtains concealing the stage, revealing the world of the play. The fourth wall has been made transparent and we can now view the action.

At the end of a ritual, we have cakes and wine, a communal meal with the gods, and then we close the sacred space.

In a theatre, the actors bow to the audience and receive their applause. Some of Shakespeare's plays (and probably those of his contemporaries) end with a reminder that the play is now ended and normality is restored (and anything else you may be experiencing is therefore your own problem).

> Our revels now are ended. These our actors,
> As I foretold you, were all spirits and
> Are melted into air, into thin air:
> And, like the baseless fabric of this vision,
> The cloud-capp'd towers, the gorgeous palaces,
> The solemn temples, the great globe itself,
> Yea, all which it inherit, shall dissolve
> And, like this insubstantial pageant faded,
> Leave not a rack behind. We are such stuff
> As dreams are made on, and our little life
> Is rounded with a sleep.

> William Shakespeare, *The Tempest*, Act 4 Scene 1

The playwright confesses that everything you have just witnessed was an illusion created by the actors. It is possible that this was a new thing, caused by the secularization of theatre.

That is not the intention of most rituals. Most rituals are intended to put their participants in touch with a deeper unseen reality (even if that is just your subconscious or your inner self, rather than the divine realms). That is why ritual begins with a process designed to put its participants in touch with their inner selves and with the cosmos, and ends with a process of gently closing down the perceptions that have been opened up, so that the participants can function effectively in the mundane spaces that they regularly inhabit. It is all very well to cleanse the doors of perception and touch the infinite, but sometimes we really do need to focus on the finite.

Participants in a ritual wear clothing that represents their inner self, their spiritual self, hopefully their most authentic self. Sometimes (such as for a rite of passage) they wear new clothing, to symbolize either a ritual state of purity, or an entrance into a new phase of life, or both. Actors in a play wear clothing designed to perpetuate the illusion that they are someone else.

Another purpose of ritual is to create community, and to share sacred meals, and sacred experiences, with other members of the religion. That is one of the reasons why not being able to practice religion in groups during the lockdown is so painful: religion is a communal and embodied experience.

Theatre is also best experienced in person, in the theatre, with its magical atmosphere, but it is not designed to bring about group cohesion or group experiences. Unless the play is very cathartic, it is rare to come away experiencing an identification, or a sense of belonging to a group, with other members of the audience. Each member of the audience has their own personal experience of the play.

Both theatre and ritual are extremely important ways of connecting with other humans, experiencing empathy, catharsis, storytelling, distancing effects, connection with community, and the magical art of acting. They are both similar and different; the main difference being the location of the fourth wall.

Storytelling

Most spiritual and religious traditions have a corpus of stories which transmit their values and beliefs, and the stories of their saints and heroes. It is also good to create stories. In his essay, *On Fairy Stories*, JRR Tolkien expressed the view that when we create stories, we are exercising a gift from the Divine, the gift of 'subcreation'. [120]

One way of creating new stories is to practice storytelling in the round. One person starts off a story, and then when they have run out of ideas, the next person in the circle takes over. You can augment this practice by using cards with images or words to suggest ideas to the participants.

Storytelling is an art which it is very satisfying to learn. To memorise a story, you first strip it down to its essential details, which can be a series of bullet points on an index card. The plot points of a traditional story are always retained, but the way you tell it is unique to you, a specific performance, and the relationship you forge with an audience.

Having stripped the story down to its bare bones, you must now rebuild it again. When retelling it, to make your story come to life, include details of colour, taste, smell, sound, and texture; imagine how the characters in the story feel about their situation.

Traditional storytelling does not go into much detail, but it gets across the experience with directness and immediacy.

You can also add your own personal twist to well-known stories, such as telling the story from the point of view of

---

[120] http://www.tolkien-online.com/on-fairy-stories.html

another character – how about the story of *Little Red Riding Hood* from the point of view of the wolf, for instance?

Try to find and listen to traditional storytellers and learn from their technique.

Reading

In the eighteenth century, reading novels was regarded as a frivolous pastime, and there was even a sort of moral panic about women crying over the fate of imaginary characters while their children were crying for bread, as one anti-novel rant described it.[121] One of the sources of this panic was that anyone who was literate could read novels, and get ideas from them (even as late as 1960, the chief prosecutor in the obscenity trial of *Lady Chatterley's Lover* asked if it were the kind of book that 'you would wish your wife or servants to read'). Some of the accusations levelled against novels were rather like modern complaints about pornography. According to Ana Vogrinčič, people thought that novels would create expectations which everyday life would crush, and by constantly exposing readers to emotional scenes, would exhaust their sympathy and compassion.

I would argue that the ability to identify and empathise with characters in novels is an excellent thing, as it extends our ability to try to understand the motivations and impulses of other people (if the novel is sufficiently well-written). The experience of reading a novel can be cathartic, transformative, and deeply moving. This is especially true if you read it

---

[121] Ana Vogrinčič (2008), *The Novel-Reading Panic in 18th Century in England: An Outline of an Early Moral Media Panic* - available from: http://hrcak.srce.hr/file/49661

creatively, performing the different parts in your head as well as you can, visualising the events that take place, and identifying with one or more characters.

The ability to imaginatively enter into the world of a novel is in many ways similar to the abilities required for magical workings: empathy, imagination, visualisation, and creativity.

Novels (especially speculative fiction, also known as science fiction and fantasy) enable us to imagine and enter fully realised alternative worlds and explore what would happen if the starting conditions were different. When women started to write novels with female protagonists, many of them found that they had to discover new ways of writing, because their perspectives were very different. Many novels explore different value systems, some of which are akin to the Pagan worldview. Therefore, my lists of recommended reading for seekers of the Pagan path usually include a lot of novels.

Many people feel that they have had their lives changed by novels, poetry, and nonfiction books. My friend Sue Woolley[122] calls these life-changing books "Ah! books". Some of these books have influenced a lot of people: *Jonathan Livingston Seagull* by Richard Bach [123], *The Prophet* by Kahlil Gibran [124] are two books that everyone seems to have on their shelves. It can be helpful (and fun) to make a list of the books that have influenced you along the way, and what insight you gained from them. It can reveal a lot about who you are as a

---

[122] Sue Woolley (2016), *Gems for the Journey*.
[123] Richard Bach (1970 / 2015), *Jonathan Livingston Seagull: A story*. Harper Thorsons.
[124] Kahlil Gibran (1923 / 2009), *The Prophet*. BN Publishing.

person, and about your journey through life. It is also worth discussing this with friends, as it may turn out that you got a completely different insight from the same book.

The life of the imagination is incredibly important, as it is how we create alternatives to the world as it is at present. Whenever a right-wing government gets into power, the first thing it wants to do is to crush the life of the imagination. Novels, storytelling, and poetry are dangerous to the would-be totalitarian because they encourage empathy and compassion and creativity; they encourage us to walk a mile in someone else's shoes; and they enable us to imagine ways of overcoming tyranny and oppression.

Imagining Other Possible Worlds

Science fiction, particularly the writings of Ursula le Guin, explores hypothetical alternative societies, cultures, futures, and histories. Both fantasy and SF present alternative visions of the world. Some of these visions are helpful, and others are not. Some are dystopian, some are utopian. Some are hierarchical, some are egalitarian. Some have individual heroes; others have resistance movements. Some inspired whole Pagan movements, such as the Church of All Worlds, inspired by Heinlein's *Stranger in a Strange Land*. There are a surprising number of parallels between Paganism and SF, and a lot of Pagans read SF, too.

What is the difference between fantasy and SF?

Science fiction usually offers an explanation (however tenuous or inferred) of how the world, and the technology in it, came to be the way it is. Science fiction can include alternative histories, what-if scenarios, extrapolations into the future, utopias, and dystopias. It has many sub-genres. There's hard science fiction, which mainly deals with the effects of technology on society; soft science fiction, which looks at things from a social science perspective (anthropology or sociology, sometimes linguistics or psychology). There's steampunk, where the technology is mostly steam-driven, with lots of cogs and brass (this emerged out of the alternative history sub-genre). SF is sometimes called speculative fiction.

In fantasy, the underlying technology is generally magic. Fantasy also has several sub-genres. There is the sword and sorcery tale. There's space opera (which is basically fantasy masquerading as SF). A lot of fantasy seems to be set in a very hierarchical medieval or feudal world, and often in a magic kingdom which is reached by a magic door (or wardrobe, or mirror). There are many interesting and classic fantasy novels, but in many ways the genre was put out of joint by the sheer weight of *The Lord of the Rings*, which has had many imitators, most of them bad (I really like *The Lord of the Rings*, but for goodness' sake, get your own plot, fantasy authors). And quite frankly, the Harry Potter books are basically a school story with magic in it (though I heartily approve of the egalitarian behaviour of "Dumbledore's Army", and of the brilliant caricature of OFSTED in the person of Dolores Umbridge). A marvellous exception to all of this is Philip Pullman's brilliant *His Dark Materials* trilogy, which is deeply anti-authoritarian, and has quite a lot of crossover with science fiction, with parallel worlds, and even a slight steampunk feel to some of the worlds in it. And of course, there's Terry Pratchett's brilliantly insightful Discworld novels, which are arguably Pagan theology at its finest.

Urban fantasy, on the other hand, is set in our reality, into which fantastic elements emerge, and it uses these to comment on things in our world. Examples include most of Neil Gaiman's oeuvre, Seanan McGuire's hilarious *InCryptid* series, which is about the adventures of a family of cryptozoologists, the Storm trilogy by R A Smith, and *The Last Changeling* by F R Maher.

In fantasy novels, when someone resists the encroachment of evil, the evil is usually rather obvious, and frequently relies on a supernatural source of power. It is a Dark Lord (Voldemort, Sauron, etc). Better quality fantasy novels have more subtle tyrants, like Saruman, who started out trying to resist Sauron, but because he tried to use Sauron's power to do so, ended up becoming like Sauron himself. Another example of a subtly drawn tyrant is Mrs Coulter in *His Dark Materials*, who works for the Magisterium, and indeed Lyra's father, Lord Asriel, who is something of an ambivalent character. The protagonist of these novels is usually especially gifted with magical powers to resist the evil (the Old Ones in The Dark is Rising; Harry Potter; even Lyra), or has been fated to be the one to resist since the beginning of time, or since their birth. One of the clever things about The Lord of the Rings is that there is nothing all that special about Frodo Baggins, except perhaps the ordinariness of hobbits. As Tolkien himself pointed out, it is Frodo's vulnerability and smallness that fitted him for the task.

In science fiction novels and dramas, the evil or oppression to be resisted is often systemic, and identifiable as a human construct, the outcome of a complex web of causality (though sometimes, as in Isaac Asimov's story *The Caves of Steel*, it's the consequence of the environment). Because the evil or oppression is usually systemic, the means of resisting it is usually co-operative and collaborative; not led by one single hero but requiring the input of many people working together. In *Babylon 5*, for example, although Sheridan is important as a leader of the resistance, he couldn't have done it without Delenn, Ivanova, Garibaldi, Franklin, the resistance on Mars, the co-operation of the security people who didn't collaborate with the regime, and so on. In Starhawk's *The Fifth Sacred Thing* and *City of Refuge*, the resistance consists of many different individuals coming together to bring about change.

Bertolt Brecht, Darko Suvin, and cognitive estrangement

In his ground-breaking essay, *Estrangement and Cognition* (1968, 1979, 2014), where he analyses the difference between SF and fantasy, Darko Suvin, a Croatian-Canadian literary critic, wrote that science fiction engages in 'cognitive estrangement'. Suvin says that fantasy and myth is estranged from everyday reality, but it does not ask us to think about why; we accept the magic door, and other magical effects, as *a priori* necessities in the fantastical universe. Literary fiction, set in our universe, is not estranged, though it may be cognitive and require us to think about cause and effect. Science fiction, on the other hand, is set in an alternative world, but it is one we are required to think about, and to actively construct in our imaginations by looking for clues in the text about how the world, and its technology, works; how the society of the SF novel came to be the way it is.

Suvin based his interpretation on the Russian theatre technique of ostranenie, a term coined by the playwright Shklovsky, and meaning 'making the familiar strange'. This is like Bertolt Brecht's use of Verfremdungseffekte (often translated as 'alienation effects', but Suvin's translation, 'estrangement effects', gets the idea across much better). It is possible that Brecht was told about the ostranenie technique on a visit to Moscow in 1935. Brecht created his plays and poetry to get people thinking, and to do that, he did not want them to identify with the characters and achieve a cathartic effect or a discharge of emotion. Instead, he wanted people to think about what they would do in a similar situation, or about the causes of the situation. Why does Mother Courage go round and round in circles, getting poorer and more miserable? Why do the characters of *The Threepenny Opera* have such terrible lives? Brecht wants us to analyse the underlying causes, as well as having a general solidarity or empathy with the characters.

The beauty of the science fictional setting, of course, is that it is already strange, and so it makes the reader think about what is happening, so that they can piece together how this fictional world works. In his essay on science fiction in Speculations on Speculation, Samuel R Delaney quotes a sentence, "I rubbed depilatory soap over my face and rinsed it with the trickle from the fresh water tap" (from Pohl and Kornbluth's The Space Merchants). As Delaney points out, this single sentence lets you know that there is a water shortage in this world, because there is only a trickle from the fresh water tap, and the fact that it is labelled fresh tells you that there's another tap with non-fresh water. This leads the reader to ask, why is there a water shortage? Has there been an environmental catastrophe, or is it a desert world?

Fantasy, on the other hand, does expect the reader to identify with the characters, and to achieve an emotional catharsis through the dramatic journey that they experience. Readers of fantasy, however, know that the hero will restore the proper order in the end, and defeat the evil tyrant, because that's how fantasy works. They also know that it is the job of the predestined hero with the special powers to defeat the evil tyrant. And of course, they know that in the real world, the odds may be stacked against the hero. Fantasy does not provide much of a roadmap for defeating a whole system of tyranny. It is very good on overthrowing the Dark Lord with a magic sword, but what if the Dark Lord has loads of minions waiting in the wings who are just as obnoxious as he is?

Science fiction, on the other hand, is set in ostensibly the same universe as the one we live in, with the same physical properties, and the same sort of people (barring the occasional telepath). Because it deals with whole systems of oppression or flourishing, it is much better placed to provide us with roadmaps for change. Of course, there are exceptions to the picture I am painting here, but it is mostly true.

Resistance is collective. Yes, there are those who dare to dream bigger and better, and do something, and they are extremely important as catalysts – but a catalyst is no good unless it is followed by a reaction. In order to bring about change, we need to create a mass movement of people who are tired of racism, tired of homophobia, tired of misogyny, tired of austerity, tired of exploitation, globalisation, putting profits before people, and the widening wealth gap. We need to inspire them to dream something different. And we need to show them the blueprints for change, not just tell them that it is possible.

Most fantasy merely provides an excursion from the normal order of things, in the same way that carnival and Saturnalia were an inversion of the normal order, a letting-off of steam in order to facilitate a return to business-as-usual. It would be good to see more fantasy that challenges the usual tropes of fantasy – which is why urban fantasy is such a refreshing change.

Science fiction, on the other hand, provides a blueprint for other ways of being, other ways of thinking, other ways of feeling. It puts the characters in a hypothetical situation and asks what the human reaction to that situation would be; not the superhero reaction, but the human one. It can posit whole different ways of organising society, or gender, or sexuality, or the economy, and explore in depth how they would work, and how people would flourish or struggle in that environment.

Photography, embodiment, and memory

Another form of creativity which can create a sense of connection is photography. Looking at a photograph can create a sense of wonder, almost as much as seeing the view depicted. But for the person taking the photograph, the camera can create a sense of detachment from their surroundings.

It's a curious thing, but when you're behind a camera, especially one where you have to put your eye close to the viewfinder to see the field of view, you sometimes forget to really look at things and take them in properly. It starts to feel like the camera will do the remembering for you.

There is a photograph of me when I was little, poking a twig between the wooden slats of a bridge. I think my body remembers standing on that bridge, bending over and carefully inserting the twig in the gap. But maybe my memory is overlaid by the photograph.

When I got handfasted, one of the best bits of advice was to 'photograph it with your brain'. As the pivotal moments went by, I tried to record them visually in memory. This is us leaping the broomstick, putting rings on each other's fingers, the first dance, cutting the cake with a sword. But there are also photographs of each of these moments which can easily overlay the more ephemeral memory that is stored in your brain.

One of the great things about taking pictures on a cellphone is that you don't need to put the viewfinder right up to your eye, and the process of framing the scene is a lot quicker than with a large SLR (big camera with a lens, for the non-technical). The advent of digital cameras made photo editing and cropping much easier too; and you can try out umpteen different filters at the click of a button. This makes the photographer less like a cyborg and restores them to the social context.

You can also have a phone in your pocket and forget (more or less) that it's there, whereas if you have a large chunky SLR, you don't forget that it's there, and walk around looking at the scene around you as a series of photographic compositions, instead of as a place or landscape in its own right.

I once went to the temple of Asklepios on the island of Kos, and the first time I went, I had my SLR camera with me, so I was looking at it as a series of photos. I went back a second time without the camera, and it was a completely different experience.

When I have visited sacred sites with a cellphone or digital camera in my pocket, I can put it out of my mind and focus on the atmosphere of the place, and stop framing it as a series of compositions.

The advent of Instagram has created a tendency to create art photographs depicting the 'perfect Instagrammed life'. I caught myself doing this when I stopped to take a picture of a beautiful sunset, and carefully positioned myself so that the telephone cables and large bins that I was standing near to take the photograph were not in the picture. Maybe we should start taking one perfect arty shot, and then follow it up with another picture showing the full scene, including what we edited out of the first photograph.

Discussion

Why are creativity, folktales, storytelling, and poetry important?

How can we pass on stories to the next generation?

How do storytelling and poetry relate to embodied spirituality and the inner work? How do they empower us to change the world?

Are novels more powerful than non-fiction?

What is the purpose of reading?

Do you prefer science fiction or fantasy? Why?

What is the difference between theatre and ritual?

Which of Peter Brook's four types of theatre do you prefer?

How can you make your photographs more 'real'?

Do you dissociate yourself from the scene around you when you are taking photographs?

Do you find that photographs tend to 'overwrite' memories?

Exercises

Storytelling in the round. Sit in a circle with a few good friends. One of you starts the story, and when they run out of ideas, or have created a bit of a cliff-hanger moment, they pass the story on to the next person.

Write a haiku about your day.

Write a poem about your hands, or the face of someone you love.

Make a list of your Ah! books and how they influenced you.

25. Cultivating the virtues

The inner work of ritual is informed by Pagan values and seeks to manifest Pagan virtues in the participants and in the world. Pagan ritual often seeks to cultivate Pagan virtues in the participants (though indirectly and subtly rather than didactically).

Ancient pagan philosophers advocated the cultivation of the virtues. The philosophy informing this practice was called Virtue Ethics, and some philosophers believed that the way to a good life (harmony, balance, and increased happiness) was through the cultivation of virtue. [125]

The embedding of virtue as a character trait is important because then it becomes instinctive, rather than merely utilitarian and expedient. If doing the right thing is merely convenient, what is to stop people doing the wrong thing when they can get away with it, and it benefits them more? But if they have decided to cultivate the virtues, they will do the right thing for the sake of their own virtue and happiness, not merely for utilitarian reasons.

The virtuous person knows when to apply a specific virtue to a situation because they possess *phronesis*, practical wisdom. It is possible to have too much of a virtue (to be generous to a fault, or to have silly compassion, for example), so they need to be balanced and applied with wisdom. We also need to consider whether the practice of a virtue will contribute towards eudaimonia (true happiness).

---

[125] Virtue Ethics, *Stanford Encyclopedia of Philosophy*, http://plato.stanford.edu/entries/ethics-virtue/

Pagan values and virtues

Pagan values are grounded in an appreciation of life and the enjoyment of being physically embodied, and the desire for others to enjoy the same experience. A value is shared norm or expectation of a group; something that is considered desirable. A virtue is a quality of a person or a group that is considered desirable. Traditionally, most Pagan ethical codes were lists of virtues which were considered desirable, instead of a set of rules to be kept. The cultivation of virtues by the individual was said to lead to eudaimonia, a happy state of being.

Hospitality

This was and is a hugely important virtue in just about every traditional culture and governed the behaviour of both guest and host. Imagine you are travelling in a strange land, like Gawain in the story of *Gawain and the Green Knight*. The offer of a nice warm bed, and a feast every night, would be an absolute godsend if you were riding through a howling wilderness at midwinter. Imagine you were shipwrecked on a strange coast, like Odysseus in the story of *The Odyssey*. Rescuing and looking after shipwrecked travellers would be a sacred obligation in an age when there were no coastguards and few lighthouses. But the guest must also behave honourably towards the host. Many cultures still have the beautiful custom of the guest-gift - something that the guest brings the first time they visit your house. Being inclusive and welcoming to all could be said to be a logical extension of hospitality.

Reciprocity and balance

This is linked with the idea of hospitality. "A gift for a gift" says the *Hávamál*. Connections between people are maintained by the exchange of gifts (not necessarily physical objects, but the gifts of time and attention). Everything in Nature is balanced, and the same is true of society and culture - as in the saying "what goes around, comes around". This is related to the Pagan concept of cyclicity, which maintains that everything goes in cycles: night and day; the seasons; birth, life, death, and rebirth.

A common treasury for all

The land is sacred in all Pagan traditions, and looking back at non-hierarchical cultures, we can see that it was held in common by the people, or not owned at all. The persistence of the idea of communal land, despite the Enclosures, the Highland Clearances, and the theft of land from indigenous peoples around the world, shows what an important idea this is.

Honour

The upholding of personal integrity appears in lists of virtues compiled by various cultures and traditions, including the eight Wiccan Virtues, and the Nine Noble Virtues of Heathenry. What honour means to me is being honest in my personal dealings, including all aspects of life, and doing the decent thing: fighting against injustice, speaking up for the vulnerable.

Embodiment: celebrating being alive

Pagans value physical pleasure: eating, drinking, making love, seeing beautiful things. We find that the enjoyment of these things increases our 'spiritual' connection, because we find value in the physical world. We love trees, rocks, mountains, flowers, beautiful art, the ocean, animals, birds, other people, the moon, the night, the sun, rolling hills, water, making love, eating, making merry. Oh yes!

The Charge of the Goddess, written by Wiccan priestess and poet Doreen Valiente, says that "All acts of love and pleasure are [Her] rituals."

The idea that the divine is, or deities are immanent in the world (intimately entwined with physical matter) also contributes to the sense that being alive in this world is to be celebrated and enjoyed.

Sovereignty

"Women desiren sovereigntie", wrote Chaucer, at the conclusion of *The Wife of Bath's Tale*. Sovereignty is the ability to determine your own destiny. Pagans love being free, and not being coerced. We do not like to be told what to think, what to do, or how to live. This extends to bodily autonomy, and not being coerced or cajoled into having unwanted sex or other physical contact. The value of sovereignty is particularly important in Druidry.

Pagan religions are life-affirming, and most Pagans view the physical world as sacred. Pagan values flow from that and embrace it. Pagans do not usually regard spirit as more important or more valuable than matter. Most Pagans view matter as entwined with spirit, or perhaps as a denser form of spirit.

So the inner work of Pagan witchcraft may vary from one witch to another, but it is very likely to involve the realisation of individual, communal, or social goals through the creation of harmony between the inner and outer worlds, and will involve action in both the spiritual and physical levels of existence.

The eight Wiccan virtues

In *The Charge of the Goddess* by Doreen Valiente, eight virtues are mentioned: honour and humility, mirth and reverence, strength and beauty, power and compassion. Each of these pairs is carefully balanced.

Too much honour can mean excessive touchiness on every potential ethical dilemma, perhaps even pomposity. Too much humility could make you a doormat, or a Uriah Heep figure. Taken together and balanced, honour and humility make for dignity and integrity. The word humility derives from humus, earth, and so implies closeness to the earth. This is not false humility or self-deprecation, but rather an accurate assessment of one's powers. This is especially important in magic, where it can be disastrous to overreach one's capabilities. Ideally, leaders in Wicca are not primarily motivated by the aggrandisement of their ego, and are aware of the needs of their coveners, seeking to develop them as independent priests and priestesses. We do not lord it over the initiate, but receive them with humility, aware of the talents and insights they bring to circle. Behaving honourably is also important – keeping one's word and behaving with a high standard of integrity.

Too much mirth can lead to cynicism, and too much reverence can lead to boredom – but balanced, these two virtues can lead to good companionship. Mirth is a wonderful thing, especially for pricking the pomposity of the powerful, but we have all met people who can never take anything seriously, and after a while, one wishes that they would take off the mask of comedy and show their real face. But those who always insist on reverence are rather puritanical, and one wishes that they would lighten up. Hence a balance between mirth and reverence is vital, especially the ability to laugh at ourselves.

Beauty and strength also need to be balanced – a graceful person is often also a strong person, because they are in control of their body and their mind. Beauty alone can be fragile and vulnerable, and strength along can be brutal; but together, they create balance.

Too much power can lead to cruelty, and so can too much compassion. Some Buddhists call compassion without wisdom "silly compassion" – the compassion that gives money or time or effort whilst having no insight into the situation of the recipient can do more harm than good. Too much power can be corrupting, especially if it is not tempered with compassion. When we wield the power of magic, we had better be sure we do so wisely and compassionately.

The balance of these opposites recalls the twin pillars of the Kabbalistic Tree of Life, which are reconciled in the central pillar. Together, Wisdom and Understanding create Gnosis or Knowledge; Strength combined with Mercy creates Beauty; and Power and Glory create the Kingdom. All the Sephiroth (Spheres) of the Tree of Life proceed from the Divine Source.

How does one cultivate a virtue? I would say, mainly by performing actions that express that virtue. Practice being kind and you will become kind. Practice not offering sharp and bitter criticism, and it will become natural to you. Holding others in your thoughts and prayers can help with developing your compassionate side. Finding out why people are homeless, or refugees, or oppressed, can also increase your compassion.

Discussion

Why don't Pagan religions have a set of commandments?

What is a virtue? How is it different from a value?

How can we cultivate the Pagan virtues?

What does it mean to "keep pure your highest ideal, and strive ever towards it"?

Exercises

Honour and humility, mirth and reverence, strength and beauty, power and compassion: what do these virtues mean to you?

Is there another virtue that expresses the combination of the pairs (e.g. honour + humility = integrity)?

Make a list of the eight Wiccan virtues, the eight working tools of Wicca, and the eight festivals of the Wheel of the Year. Can you match a tool to a virtue and a festival? How and why do they match up?

Look at other virtue lists, such as the one for Heathenry, Druidry, and Religio Romana. What are the similarities and differences?

Write a ritual illustrating the Pagan virtues that you hold most dear.

26. Rites of passage

A rite of passage is a ritual to assist transition from one role or identity into another, such as from childhood into adulthood, from single into married, from living as one gender to living as another, from non-parent into parent, and so on.

The term was originally coined by anthropologist Arnold van Gennep in his book, *Les rites de passage*. He came up with the term because he visualised society as a house with many rooms, and the change from one identity or stage to another as being like a passage between one room and the next. He also subdivided the ritual process for easing the transition into three phases. In the first phase, the person withdraws from their old status (van Gennep calls this the preliminal stage); then they exist in some sort of intermediate or threshold state (the liminal stage, often regarded as a bit dangerous and ambivalent); and then they enter into the new status and are reincorporated into society in their new role.

Many new identities involve doing something with the person's hair; for example, nuns, monks, and soldiers have their hair cut on adopting their new role. Many people do this instinctively, as having a haircut implies a fresh start and a new identity.

Mysteries of gender

There has been much controversy over 'women's mysteries' and whether these should be inclusive of trans women. Personally, I would not object even slightly to transgender women attending a ritual about menstruation or childbirth, or any other aspect of being biologically female. Transgender women are women, whether or not they were socialised as girls, and whether or not they have penises. Nonbinary people and transgender men also menstruate and give birth. Gender is mainly about what goes on in your head.

There has been less kerfuffle over men's mysteries, but some trans men have reported feeling excluded from male-bonding type activities such as rugged outdoor things. It is also worth mentioning that not all cisgender men want to do the activities that comes under the category of 'male mysteries'.

I think we need to separate out the notion of biological mysteries from archetypal ones, and separate gender from biological sex. Archetypes are not limited to people with corresponding biology (e.g. warriors, weavers, healers, explorers, carers, can be any gender, and have been throughout history).

Biological mysteries are specific to body morphology, but not to any gender. Cisgender women, some genderqueer people, and transgender men have wombs and may or may not experience childbirth, menses, menopause etc. Cisgender men, some transgender women, and some genderqueer people have penises. Your biology may or may not correspond to your lived gender.

So gender mysteries could be about roles associated with a gender (but I would question why those roles are associated with that gender) and biological sex mysteries would be more about the phases of development, such as the menopause or the onset of menstruation. Gender does not need to have the central role it plays in our culture; and it does not need to be so closely tied to biological characteristics.

Triple Goddesses

Most people, when "the Triple Goddess" is mentioned, probably think of the Maiden, Mother, Crone archetype. However, this archetype can be very limiting, and there are many other triple goddesses who are worth exploring: goddesses of the land and sovereignty, goddesses with many skills and roles, goddesses who are women in their own right, not merely roles in relation to a man.

I find the archetype of the Maiden, Mother, Crone unhelpful for several reasons. One is that it is biologically essentialist. In its most basic sense, it refers to a virgin, a woman who has given birth, and a post-menopausal woman. Yes, biology is important, as it is how we are embodied; but culture and personality and creativity and spirit are also important.

This biologically essentialist model excludes trans women, women who have never given birth, and women who do not identify as motherly types. It can be profoundly upsetting for women who cannot give birth, or who have had an abortion. I once attended an event where two fairly prominent Pagan women were going on about the profoundly mistaken notion that "you are not a real woman until you have given birth", and this really upset two other women, and annoyed me. Yes, many women do become mothers, and that is a beautiful thing; but it is not the only archetype of an adult woman available.

People often get confused by the archetype of the Maiden. According to some interpretations, a maiden or a virgin is a sexually independent woman (not a woman whose hymen remains intact). For feminists, the idea of a sexually independent woman is much more empowering than the idea of a woman whose hymen remains intact. The idea of a woman who "belongs to" her father and will be "given away" to her husband is utterly patriarchal and oppressive and has no place in Paganism. The notion that a virgin is a woman who has not been penetrated by a penis is hopelessly patriarchal and overly privileges penetrative sex.

The notion that a sexually active woman must also be a mother also seems patriarchal to me. It is implying that the ultimate role of an adult woman is to be a mother, and that all sexual activity leads to motherhood. Some people have claimed that Maiden, Mother, Crone is matriarchal, but I do not really want to live in a matriarchy any more than I want to live in a patriarchy. The idea of a matriarchy is gender essentialist, and potentially oppressive for those of us who do not fit in the gender binary model.

The Crone is perhaps a bit more empowering, as it involves facing up to death and embracing the wisdom of old age. But why must the dividing line between mother and crone be the menopause? This once again excludes trans women, genderqueer women, and so on, and is also biologically essentialist. To be sure, the menopause can be a profound and powerful experience for many women, and that is awesome for them; but we are more than just our biology.

The idea of Maiden, Mother, Crone also leaves out lots of other archetypes, such as the priestess, the hag (Dark Moon), the warrior, the poet, the architect, the writer, and many more.

The attributes associated with the three aspects of the Maiden, Mother, Crone imagery are somewhat limiting too [126]. Why is only the Crone seen as the embodiment of wisdom? Why is only the Maiden seen as the Muse? Why can't she create poetry and art in her own right, rather than hanging about waiting for a man to be inspired by her beauty? Can't a woman in her prime also be wise and inspirational and creative?

Even Robert Graves, who more or less invented the Maiden/Mother/Crone archetype, described the Triple Goddess in other ways, such as Mother/Bride/Layer-out and Maiden/Nymph/Hag. Graves seems to have still seen these as Her roles in relation to a man, but at least they are different archetypes.

Sigmund Freud wrote about a Triple Goddess of birth, love, and death, and related her to the Fates, the Seasons, the threefold Artemis-Hecate, and Mother Earth who receives the dead.[127]

Alternative triple goddesses

One very powerful triple goddess is Brighid, who has three roles: smith, healer, poet. At first glance these roles seem unrelated, but the smith re-forges and transforms metal; the healer transforms flesh and spirit; and the poet transforms words. All three are aspects of the creative impulse.

---

[126] Mary Jones, The Triple Goddesses of the Celts, *Jones' Celtic Encyclopedia*, www.maryjones.us/jce/triplegoddess.html

[127] John Halstead (2014), *13 things you don't need to know about the Triple Goddess*

Another important Celtic triplicity was the Matronae, who are frequently depicted in Romano-British statuary. There is an example of these in the Corinium Museum at Cirencester (UK). They are three women, sometimes depicted as married, sometimes as unmarried, with bouquets of flowers, fruit, or wheat. They are the same age. They are sometimes given the name of local goddesses; the depiction at Cirencester was dedicated to the Suleviae, which was probably their local name.

Gwenhwyfar (Guinevere) wife of King Arthur, may have originally been a triple goddess, as she is described as three queens in the Welsh Triads: "Gwenhwyfar daughter of Cywryd Gwent, and Gwenhwyfar daughter of Gwythyr son of Greidiawl, and Gwenhwyfar daughter of Gogfran the Giant."

Another form of triple goddess is found in goddesses of the land, such as the three sisters Eriu, Banba, and Fotla, who are married to the three kings of Ireland, the brothers Mac Cuill, Mac Cecht, and Mac Grienne. Another example is their sisters, the war goddesses Morrigan (sometimes called Anand or Anu), Badb, and Macha.

Most examples of triple goddesses from ancient mythology are either sisters or a single woman with three different roles. There were also male triplicities (Lugh Lamhfhada, the Samildánach; Brian, Iuchar, and Iucharba, the sons of Turenn; Cian, Cu, and Cethe, the sons of Cainte; and Bleiddwn, Hydwn, and Hychdwn the Tall, the sons of Gilfaethwy and Gwydion, in *The Mabinogion*).

Other mythologies also had triple goddesses who were not Maiden, Mother, Crone archetypes. Hecate, a very complex ancient Greek goddess, was sometimes depicted as threefold, but she had several epithets and roles. The earliest depictions of her were not three-formed. The threefold imagery (Trimorphe, three-formed; Triodia/Trioditis, the one who frequents crossroads; and Trivia, a Roman form) came later. Pausanias wrote that Hecate was first depicted as threefold by the sculptor Alkamenes in the Greek Classical period of the late 5th century BCE.

More triplicities are found in the figures of the Three Fates and the Three Graces, who appear in Greek, Roman, and Slavic mythology; and the Three Norns, from Norse mythology. None of these are Maiden, Mother, Crone, either.

In Greek mythology, the Three Fates are called the Moirai (the appointers). They are like the Sudice from Slavic mythology. The Moirai are called Clotho (spinner), Lachesis (allotter) and Atropos (unturnable). Even the gods could not change what had been ordained by the Fates.

In Roman mythology, the Three Fates are called the Parcae. They spun the thread of life, allotted destiny to humans and gods, and cut the thread at the end of life. Their names were Nona, who spun the thread of life from her distaff onto her spindle; Decima, who measured the thread of life with her rod; and Morta, who cut the thread of life and chose the manner of a person's death.

The Norns of Norse mythology were not a direct equivalent to the Fates, but they performed a similar role, controlling the destiny of humans.

Another triplicity from Greek and Roman mythology is that of the Three Graces, or *Charites*. These are deities who create happiness, beauty, and harmony, and are therefore worth celebrating.

Fourfold and fivefold goddess imagery

The Triple Goddess imagery of Maiden, Mother, Crone is often related to three of the phases of the Moon (New, Waxing, and Waning). This misses out the goddess of the Dark Moon, sometimes called the Hag, who is associated with menstruation, wild sexuality, resistance to patriarchy, Lilith, witchcraft, and childlessness. This archetype is very important for liberating people from the restrictions imposed by patriarchal imagery. Erich Neumann identified a fourfold Goddess figure. It is also worth mentioning the Fivefold Goddess image; her five aspects are Birth, Initiation, Consummation, Repose, and Death. These are also mentioned in Robert Graves' book, *The White Goddess*.

Many goddesses

There are many different goddesses. Most are singular in form, and some are triple. The threefold goddesses of antiquity were generally three sisters, three mothers, three queens, and were goddesses of the land, associated with grain, flowers, and fruits. Some were a single goddess with three different roles, like Hecate and Brighid. Some were responsible for weaving fate, like the Norns, the Sulevice, the Parcae, and the Moirai; others were responsible for creating joy, like the Three Graces.

Life stages

Birth

Most cultures have naming ceremonies for babies, and Pagans do too. Pagans generally believe that children should be able to choose whether and which religion to follow when they are old enough, so Pagan naming ceremonies do not include a pledge to bring the child up Pagan - though they may include a desire to instil Pagan values into the child.

Pagans do not perceive a need to purify either the mother or the child after birth, considering that people are born innocent. The child will typically be welcomed into the community and given a name but will not be committed to any particular religious tradition, as most Pagans believe that children should be able to choose their religion when they are old enough. Although the naming ceremony in Wicca is sometimes called a Wiccaning, it does not mean that the child becomes a Wiccan as a result of the ceremony, because it is up to them to choose their religion when they are old enough to choose.

Most Pagans presume that everything is already sacred because deities are immanent in the world. Therefore, rituals of consecration are about creating extra sacredness, or reconnecting us with the deities, the community, or the natural world.

Coming of age

Western culture generally lacks a single unified coming of age ritual. Judaism has one in the form of the Bat Mitzvah and Bar Mitzvah. Many Pagans celebrate the first menstruation of their daughters (if the daughters want to celebrate it). Many indigenous cultures have rites of passage into adulthood, in the form of a vision quest in the wilderness.

Many cultures still have these rites of passage at puberty; others have lost them. It is well worth reinstating them; but be aware that transgender teenagers may not welcome the onset of puberty, and their rite of passage into adulthood is more likely to be gender confirmation surgery.

The lack of a distinctive and unified coming-of-age ritual in Western culture seems to me to be a major source of dysfunction in our culture. People seem to be constantly in doubt as to whether they are really an adult. On the one hand, people tell us that adulting is a serious business, and that when we grow up we will "realise" that you can't have a fair, equitable, and just society, and become right-wing capitalist drones like the people who peddle these lies; if that is 'being an adult', then I would rather not be one. One the other hand, our culture constantly encourages us to avoid adult responsibility; in part, perhaps, because that suits the commercialisation and commodification of everything - we are encouraged to buy more toys to satisfy our hunger for real intimacy and connection. No wonder millennials exhibit anxiety about adulting; I have every sympathy with them.

Part of the solution to this problem might be to have a rite of passage into the sort of adulthood that does take responsibility for the oppressed and for other species and for the planet - one that encourages the young person to develop the sort of values that promote sustainability and equality and diversity.

The key features of a coming-of-age ritual seem to be a period of preparation, followed by an excursion into the wilderness, which confers a sense of one's own skills and abilities, but also the interdependence of all humans. Everyone has a unique combination of skills and abilities, but when these are brought together with others, a sense of community and cooperation is created. By working together in a challenging situation, the young person feels part of a group, and has a greater sense of their own aptitudes.

Some feminists have suggested that male rites of passage are an attempt to mimic the definite sense of transition from childhood to adulthood experienced by young women at their first menstruation. That may be true, but both young women and young men can benefit from rites of passage to help them develop resilience and teamwork.

A ritual to mark the first menstruation is an excellent idea, though it must be with the full consent of the menstruating person, and not if they do not feel comfortable with the idea. A trans man is unlikely to want such a ritual. A nonbinary person might want it, or they might not.

It could involve symbolically crossing a threshold, meditating on the symbolism of blood, the womb, and the Moon, being welcomed to the community of women (preferably by both transgender and cisgender women), and generally affirming that menstruation is part of the cycle of renewal in the womb, and is natural and beautiful. It would also be a good idea to emphasise that menstruation is not what makes you a woman; feeling that you are a woman is what makes you a woman.

Coming out

In 1983, when I was in my teens, my best friend came out to me as gay. The world was very different back then: no same-sex marriage, no civil partnerships, no Internet, no mobile phones, no sat-nav, and obviously no social media either; not even digital cameras.

Remember how, in the film *Pride*, when the everyman character was grounded by his parents, he had no way of getting in touch with any of his friends? That was the reality for everyone.

The age of consent for gay men in the UK was 21. You could still be arrested for cottaging. Most people were homophobic. Most Christians were opposed to active homosexuality. This was just before the awareness of AIDS became widespread in the UK.

So, my friend had very little way of knowing whether coming out to me was a safe thing to do. I had said to others that I was totally fine with him being gay, but I do not know if I had actually said it to him.

There we were, one night, at the theatre, in the corridor, during the interval.

I cannot remember the exact wording of my friend's coming out, or my response, which was something along the lines of it being totally fine by me, and good for him, and other positive noises.

Because one of the foundational texts of Wicca is *The Charge of the Goddess*, which contains the assertion that "All acts of love and pleasure are [Her] rituals", and because I believe that same sex love is part of Nature, I initially assumed that all other Pagans and Wiccans felt the same way. Doreen Valiente certainly did [128]. After all, as the saying goes, homosexuality is found in most species of birds and animals; homophobia is found in only one.

It came as a bit of a rude shock to discover that some early Wiccans excluded LGBT+ people altogether (though that pretty much ceased to be the case sometime in the 1980s, I think) and that much of Wicca is heterocentric. This is especially odd considering the history of queerness and gender variance in magic, witchcraft, and shamanism.

Coming out as LGBTQIA+ is a rite of passage, and usually a very liberating and empowering experience as the person who comes out feels more authentic as a result. Some people have argued that coming out as lesbian, gay, bisexual, or transgender would not be necessary in a society that did not automatically assume that you were cisgender and heterosexual until you indicated otherwise. However, what would probably happen in a society that did not automatically assume people's orientation and identity would be that everyone would have to come out, including heterosexual and cisgender people. Various Pagan parents of my acquaintance did not assume their children would be heterosexual, so their kids came out to them as heterosexual.

---

[128] Doreen Valiente, address to the National Conference of the Pagan Federation, held at Fairfield Hall in Croydon, London on 22nd November 1997, in which she said, "In every period of history, in every country in the world there have been gay people, both men and women. So why shouldn't Mother Nature have known what she was doing when she made people this way? I don't agree with this prejudice against gay people, either inside the craft of the wise or outside it."

Of course, it is worth remembering that coming out is not a single act that you do once – people come out multiple times to multiple people. Some of the best occasions of coming out as bisexual for me were the ones where the other person kind of took it for granted rather than making a big deal out of it. It is also not safe for everyone to come out, so no-one should feel pressured into doing so. Sometimes the sheltering darkness of the closet is the safest place to be.

But an exciting thing for me about the act of truth that was my friend coming out as gay, was that it triggered a whole cascade of truth and happiness in my life. I am profoundly grateful for that gift.

So, when your teenage child has indicated what their gender or sexual orientation is, why not have a coming out ritual to mark the occasion and assist them to feel comfortable in their new role. The beginnings of sexual feelings of any kind are a huge new thing for a teenager, and they may want to keep them private and tender and fluid and noncommittal; that is fine too, and that privacy and autonomy should be respected. They might prefer it if you just let them throw a party to celebrate.

A transgender coming-out ritual could include welcoming the person to their new gender community (preferably involving both cisgender and transgender people of that gender), crossing a threshold, and perhaps being given a new name, if they have chosen one, and putting on a new set of clothes that they have chosen to express their true gender. They could also make offerings to transgender deities, or symbolically enact the story of a transgender deity.

A genderqueer, non-binary, or agender [129] coming-out ritual could also welcome the person to the genderqueer, non-binary, and agender community, include the conferring of a new name, new genderqueer or agender clothing, and making a connection with genderqueer, non-binary, and agender deities.

A lesbian, gay, or bisexual coming-out ritual could involve a recognition and celebration of the person's sexual orientation, a connection with lesbian goddesses, gay gods, or bisexual deities; the crossing of a threshold (the transition here would be from uncertain identity to certain identity, not from an assumed straight default into a gay identity).

An asexual coming-out ritual could include recognition and validation of the person's asexuality, a connection with asexual deities, the crossing of a threshold, and the conferral of a new name or new clothing, if desired.

There are flags for each sexual identity, so the flag for the identity being celebrated could be included in the ritual.

Many LGBTQIA+ adults will have missed out on having any sort of coming-out ritual, of course, and many of us may have experienced great trauma and sadness if parents and friends rejected us for revealing our sexual orientation or our true gender; so a ritual to celebrate our coming out could be a healing experience for many of us.

Other identities that could be celebrated with a coming-out ritual are polyamory, kink, and bears, but these usually emerge a bit later, and are more likely to be celebrated with a

---

[129] Agender means 'without gender', not preferring or expressing any gender.

community of peers of one's own age. Again, the key features are a period of preparation and contemplation of the new role or identity; some sort of ordeal or crossing of a threshold, and a reintegration into society with a recognition of the new role, with the blessing of the gods, the ancestors, and the community.

Initiation

Several Pagan and other religious traditions have initiation ceremonies, in which the initiate becomes more fully part of the tradition into which they are being initiated, is given a new and sacred name, and has some of the tenets of the tradition imparted to them, usually in the form of ritual drama and ordeal.

There is sometimes controversy among Pagans as to the value of initiation, and whether self-initiation is the same thing as initiation into a coven or other group.

There are several different aspects of initiation, some of which are conferred by either form of initiation (encounter with the gods, inner transformation, encountering the Mysteries), and some of which can only be conferred as part of a group initiation (being given the secrets of the initiating group, joining the group mind of the initiating group; and the joining of the lineage or tradition of which the coven is part).

Wicca and Druidry both have initiation rituals, often based on the initiation rituals of occult orders such as Freemasonry. Isaac Bonewits identified three types of initiation ritual: [130]

---

[130] http://www.neopagan.net/Initiation.html

Initiation as a recognition of a status already gained

Initiation as an ordeal of transformation

Initiation as a method for transferring spiritual knowledge and power

I have identified six aspects of initiation, which may be present in a single ritual, or may be a gradual process. There is the inner process of transformation; the initiation by the gods and goddesses (making contact with the numinous); experiencing the Mysteries (that which cannot be spoken, or Arrheton); being given the secrets of the initiating group (that which must not be spoken, or Aporrheton); joining the group mind of the initiating group; and the joining of the lineage or tradition of which the coven is part.

In Heathenry, initiation is replaced by profession, a ceremony where someone professes a desire to become part of the Asatruar (people who are true to the Aesir, the Heathen deities), and then takes an oath.

Being initiated into the Mysteries is the crossing of a threshold par excellence. The process begins with the initiate waiting in a separate room and meditating on life and death; then they enter the circle, typically with some sort of challenge at the threshold; and then there is an ordeal, followed by being welcomed into the tradition and the community. It is a classic rite of passage, although it does not mark a biological change, but a spiritual one.

At the Wiccan first degree, the initiate steps into the circle, which in some traditions is regarded as being in the realm of the gods, and in others, as being between the world of humans and the world of the gods. The ritual marks an expansion of awareness, and an encounter with the expansive principle of spirit, frequently referred to as the Goddess or the feminine principle.

At second degree, the initiate encounters the principle of contraction and limitation, often referred to as death, or as the Horned God. They realise the cyclical nature of life, death, and rebirth, and that cyclicity and change is what makes life worthwhile. Death gives meaning to life.

At third degree, the initiate synthesises the principle of expansion and the principle of contraction within the self, undergoing the *hieros gamos* or sacred marriage. This inner marriage can be experienced by a person of any gender or sexual orientation.

Some traditions such as Feri witchcraft have only one initiation ritual, and they mark these shifts in consciousness differently. They also use metaphors such as apprentice, journeyman, and master for the stages of the journey through life.

An initiation should represent a profound transformation. It is the commencement of a new phase of the inner work; an encounter with the deities; the experience of an ordeal; becoming part of the group mind of the coven, and the egregore of the lineage; the revelation of the mysteries, the taking of an oath, and the conferring of secret techniques and rituals. The initiate takes on the identity of the witch, a liminal and powerful archetype, and of priest or priestess - a traveller between the seen and unseen realms.

Graduation

Graduation is a rite of passage from student to alumna or alumnus. The preparation - studying for your degree - is long and arduous, and some universities even have small rituals to mark the transition from the first year to the second and third years of the course. There is also a rite of passage in the sense that most students live in rented accommodation in the second year of their course - sent out from the bosom of the university to sojourn in the world of dodgy bedsits and multiple-occupancy housing.

For the graduation ceremony, the student puts on special clothing and a special hat, becoming a graduand (the liminal phase) and undergoes the graduation ceremony, after which they venture forth into the world of graduate employment.

Changing jobs

Even changing jobs has a series of rituals associated with it. There is the moment you hand in your notice; the leaving card and leaving do, with speeches and cake and a good-luck card. Many people like to have a 'breathing space' of a week or so between the old job and the new job.

Then there is the induction process when you arrive at your new job; meeting new colleagues for the first time, easing into the new role; the probationary period, the training sessions, and so on.

Transition

Beginning to live as a different gender than the one you were assigned at birth has many features akin to a rite of passage. Some transgender support groups recommend that the transitioner spends some time apart from their family and friends, getting used to their new gender and name, before returning as a fully-fledged transgender person. This gives them time to 'grow' their new identity. Some families who are supportive of their loved one's transition may find this hurtful, but it is similar to the classic rite of passage in tribal societies, where young people go out into the wilderness to grow into their new adult status.

Even without this time apart from family and friends, the transgender person might benefit from some sort of ceremony or ritual to mark and honour their transition. Many workplaces have a set of protocols in place to welcome people who have transitioned back into the workplace in their new identity. One transitioner reported receiving a marvellous welcome from their colleagues, involving cards and a cake and balloons. A gender transition is, in a way, a rebirth, and should be celebrated and honoured. The steps along the way are important, too, and should also be celebrated. These include the person's first time out in public dressed as their true gender, getting hormones, getting surgery if they have chosen to do so, and getting their gender recognition certificate, official name change, etc. Obviously, it is also important to recognise that not every transgender person wants surgery; that does not make them any less the gender they identify as.[131]

Friends, family, and colleagues of people who have transitioned have reported feelings of loss and confusion about what happened to the old identity of the trans person.

---

[131] Please note that when I use the phrase 'identify as', I don't mean to undermine their true gender. All gender identities, including cisgender, identify as their gender, in my understanding.

Some people feel they need to get to know the trans person all over again. A rite of passage to mark and celebrate the transition and reintegrate the trans person back into the community in their new role would help people to cope with these feelings, too.

Marriage and handfasting

A marriage is the coming together of two people to create a relationship. Whether they are polyamorous or monogamous, a handfasting or marriage ceremony signifies a new level of commitment. Ideally, they should feel some sort of inner connection or transformation - a meeting of minds and souls, hearts and bodies.

A Pagan wedding is called a handfasting and can be contracted for a year and a day, for a lifetime, or for all lifetimes to come (the last of these seems a bit reckless to me). Pagans recognise and perform both same-sex and opposite-sex weddings.

The couple are crossing a threshold into their new life together, and this is often symbolised by jumping over a broomstick. This part of the ceremony is part of African diasporic traditions as well as witchcraft traditions.

In Heathenry, wedding ceremonies are usually hallowed by holding them beneath the hammer of Thor (Mjöllnir), and arm-rings are exchanged. The couple may also hold an oath-ring while exchanging vows.

Pagan weddings have legal validity in the USA and Canada if the celebrant is registered with a recognised religious body, in Scotland if you are a registered celebrant, but not in England

and Wales, where it is the building that is registered and not the celebrant.

The creation of a new connection is represented in the handfasting ceremony by the binding of the couple's clasped hands with ribbons or cords. The act of handfasting was originally part of a formal betrothal ceremony (the precursor to today's engagement) perhaps going as far back as ancient Celtic Scotland and surviving up to the 16th century. During the betrothal ceremony, in which a couple agreed to marry each other in the future, there was a formal handshake to seal the deal. This was called the handfæstung, meaning, a pledge by the giving of the hand. To illustrate the imagery and importance of the handshake, the knotting of cords around the hands was eventually incorporated, possibly by contemporary Pagans.

In some handfasting ceremonies, the couple also exchange rings, which is an important symbol of a pledge or promise. Some also light a fire or a candle to symbolise the hearth and home they will create together (this is often said to be a Native American tradition).

The wedding ceremony is a transition from a state of singleness to being part of a couple. The two members of the couple are still individuals, but they are also in a mystical union of bodies, hearts, and minds. They will grow together over the years, learning to live with each other's foibles, celebrating each other's triumphs, and commiserating with each other's trials and setbacks.

Parenting

Becoming a parent for the first time is a big deal. Suddenly you are no longer responsible only for your own well-being, but for a small person who is utterly dependent on you (at least to begin with). That is why parents should have the support of the whole community, and not be left to cope on their own. The much-quoted Indian saying "it takes a village to bring up a child" is often quoted because it is so wise, and so little heeded in our fragmented culture.

Informal rites of passage for parents include the visits to the hospital, the first scan of the baby, the birth itself, breastfeeding, teething, the first crawl, baby's first word, the first toddle across the room, weaning, potty training, the first tooth, the first adult tooth, and many other landmark moments in a child's development. Some of these are marked by parties and rituals; others are marked by taking a photo or posting about it on social media.

However they are marked, each of these moments is a gradual progress towards independence for the child, until they reach adolescence and can begin their transition to adulthood - which many parents experience as a wrench, after so many years of the child being dependent on them. Now they need to relate to their offspring in a new way, as a fledgling adult, and do something to assuage the feeling of 'empty nest syndrome'. Rituals to mark these transitions and phases would be helpful for parents as well as children. An excellent guide to Pagan parenting is Ashleen O'Gaea's book, *Raising Witches*.

Divorce

Pagans have always been liberal about divorce, and the fact that a handfasting allows a trial marriage shows that Pagans are aware of the possibility that a relationship may change for the worse, and therefore divorce may become necessary. Of course, marriage should provide security and be a commitment to work at the relationship and treat one's partner with integrity - but that does not preclude divorce, as that is sometimes the only way of dealing with a marriage that's not working any more.

The Pagan revival lacks a ritual for divorce, but individual Pagans may have crafted divorce rituals. When I split up from my ex-husband, I got my hair cut, moved into a new flat in a different city, and did other things to mark the transition. As the split was amicable, we carried on running a coven together, which was a bit strange. When I finally got the decree nisi and then the decree absolute, I bought cake for all my work colleagues.

In many ways divorce is a gradual process, as you start to notice cracks appearing in the marriage, and eventually realise it is time to split up and move out and start a new life. Then there is the long separation period followed by the legal recognition that the marriage is at an end.

A significant moment for me was the realisation that seven years had passed since we split up, as seven years is, on average, how long it takes for all the cells in your body to be replaced [132] (except your cornea and the neurons in your cerebral cortex).

---

[132] http://skeptics.stackexchange.com/questions/7837/are-all-cells-of-the-human-body-completely-replaced-every-seven-to-ten-years

Again, some sort of ritual to mark this transition would have helped. I never changed my name to that of my husband, but for many women, changing back to their 'maiden' name can be very liberating.

Aging

Croning is generally a ritual for recognising the menopause when a person with a womb ceases to menstruate and becomes a 'crone'. Pagans have reclaimed the word crone to signify a wise older person. [133]

A croning ceremony usually takes place after the age of fifty and celebrates the achievement of elder status in the community, and the acquisition of wisdom. As the wisdom of older women has been dismissed as "old wives' tales" in the past, this reclaiming of women's wisdom is important. Some people feel that the ceremony does not need to happen until a decade or two after the menopause.

Transgender women should also be able to have a croning ceremony if they so desire.

Equivalent rituals for men are often called saging or wizarding. I had the honour of attending one of these, and it was individually crafted by the individual and the group to reflect his interests and concerns. It was very moving. Transgender men should be able to have a wizarding or saging ceremony if they so desire.

---

[133] Patti Wiginton (2016) *Croning Ceremony: Celebrating Women's Wisdom*

http://paganwiccan.about.com/od/wiccanandpaganrituals/p/Croning_Info.htm

It would be great to have a gender-neutral or non-binary aging ceremony for people who do not identify as either male or female. For those who are gender-fluid, it could combine aspects of both croning and saging. For those who are genderqueer and non-binary, it could focus more on the acquisition of wisdom and the physical aspects of aging.

All of these rituals recognise a change in the role of the individual and prepare them for the changes that will come with aging. They may present all sorts of physical and mental challenges, changes in mobility, perhaps a decrease in sexual activity and urges (though there is nothing wrong with older people having sex, and I am completely baffled by people who take the view that older people having sex is weird and icky and embarrassing).

As with all rites of passage, the aim is to accept the change in circumstances and reintegrate the individual into the community.

Death

Most Pagans believe in reincarnation, and regard death as part of the cycle of life, death, and rebirth. The souls of the dead rest for a while in the Summerlands (the Pagan afterlife) before returning for another reincarnation. There is no doctrine of sin and redemption, rather everyone must evolve spiritually throughout their successive incarnations. Many souls return to Earth again and again, either because they love and cherish the planet, or because they wish to help others.

We fear death because it appears to be the end. The ego cannot face the prospect of its own annihilation, and fears dissolution in the ground of all being. Therefore, we hide death away, and banish the dying to anonymous hospital rooms. The art of dying well has been lost, and with it, the art of living. If we face the prospect of our own death without fear, it becomes possible to live life to the full. But death is a gateway through which we must all pass; the seeds of our death are contained in our life.

One of the names of the Horned God is 'The Lord of Death and Resurrection'. He guides us through the gates of death and into the realms beyond. He is the lord of limitation and endings, just as the Moon Goddess is the lady of expansion and beginnings. Without death there could be no process of change; there could be no ageing, no experience, no birth, and no rebirth. Many witches believe in reincarnation, and there is much emphasis in the Wiccan tradition on returning to a new life with people you have loved before. The Wheel of the Year expresses this process. Samhain is a time for remembering the dead and recognising the transformative powers of Nature. It is balanced by Imbolc, a spring festival of birth, dedicated to Brighid, the goddess of healing, smithcraft, and poetry.

The Tarot card of Death is another way of looking at the different aspects of death. When it appears in a divinatory spread, it does not usually signify the actual physical death of the querent. What it represents is a radical transformation, the end of one phase and the beginning of another. When the Tarot was created (around the fourteenth century), death was a very visible part of life. You could not ignore death in the past: most people would have seen a loved one die, either in battle or of an illness. Traditional cultures have many stories about death and dying. There are ceremonies to ease the transition into the next world, both whilst someone is dying and after they are gone. There is also space for the experience of grieving, and the possibility of giving oneself up to grief completely for a while as a cathartic and healing process. Western society has largely lost these ceremonies. We need to rediscover them, to reclaim them, and to create new ones out of our own response to death and dying.

Pagan funerals generally focus on celebrating the life of the person who has died. There are some beautiful pieces of liturgy for Pagan funerals, and many of them can be found in the excellent book, *A Pagan Book of Living and Dying*[134], by M Macha Nightmare and the Reclaiming collective. The book includes reflections on death through violence and accident and disease; how to prepare for death, how to wash and anoint a corpse, how to build a funeral pyre. It is a beautiful and poignant book, with many helpful reflections and meditations in it.

Grief

Perhaps because of our culture's general unwillingness to face death and dying, the process of grieving is often poorly understood. People are often expected to 'just get over it'. Fortunately, psychotherapists have done a lot of helpful work on grief. Elisabeth Kübler-Ross identified five stages of grief (denial, anger, bargaining, depression, and acceptance). These are helpful as an outline but should not be taken as a one-size-fits-all model. Some people find this model helpful, some do not. Not everyone will experience all these phases, and not necessarily in the same order.

---

[134] http://books.google.co.uk/books?id=eAW48deQdN4C

Other cultures have ritual periods of mourning and ways of sheltering the mourner from the exigencies of everyday life. The gradual departure of the soul of the deceased is important, too. We need to recover our rituals of mourning and saying farewell. The Irish tradition of the wake, where people sit up with the corpse the night before the funeral, and tell stories of the deceased, is a good tradition.

My own experience of grief is that there is an intense period of mourning, when you cannot stop thinking about the loved one, reliving the moment of their death, or the moment you heard of their death; constantly going over 'if only' scenarios if the death was accidental. At this point, it feels as though every aspect of life is sad, and this is the phase during which frequent crying is likely.

Gradually, the immediate trauma of the loss starts to recede, but you still feel their absence intensely. The mourner may experience guilt at this stage that they are no longer mourning as much as before. It is important to reassure the mourner that their love for the departed one is not diminished, only the intensity of the loss.

Eventually, whilst the mourner may not think about the departed loved one all the time, they still carry the memory of them in their heart, and the grief never entirely goes away. I read somewhere that it is not that the grief diminishes, but that the grief stays the same size and the psyche expands to accommodate it. I found this idea comforting.

One thing to bear in mind if you are supporting a grieving person is that they may be comforted by talking about the departed loved one, or by helping others, or by just being held (emotionally or physically). There is no standard way to grieve or to be comforted; there is no standard length of time that the grieving process takes. It is slightly different for everyone. What I found helpful was people who acknowledged my grief and did not try to dismiss it or offer platitudes about it. They held me emotionally and recognised my grief without trying to change it.

Remembering the beloved dead at Samhain is helpful and important and healing, especially for members of communities that have lost many of their kind. Most people do not have the opportunity to talk about their beloved dead very often, and it can bring about a sense of release and healing to be able to talk about them.

The Transgender Day of Remembrance and the Transgender Rite of Elevation are also really important, because the transgender dead were often murdered and their spirits may be traumatised, and the rest of the transgender community may also feel that their lives are valued less by wider society. It is important to show up and honour the transgender dead. (See Chapter 14, Inner aspects of the festivals.)

A rite of passage is a way of managing a change of identity or role. There are three stages: the recognition that a change is occurring; a period of going out into the wilderness to adjust to the new role; and then a reintegration into the community in the new role. A well-managed rite of passage will have all of these stages present and will successfully negotiate the change of status. The bigger the change, the more need for a well-crafted rite of passage. The more that the individual feels secure in their new role, and recognised by the community, the gods, and the ancestors in their new role or identity, the better.

Discussion

What are the key features of a rite of passage?

How can we create meaningful rites of passage for life-changes in contemporary society?

How can we better support people through life's ups and downs?

Exercises

Make a list of the pieces of music and readings that you would like at your funeral and/or your wedding, or another rite of passage.

Make a list of the important moments of transition and change in your life, and write a ritual exploring your journey through myth, symbol, and story.

If you have a witch-name or magical name, write a ritual exploring the symbolism of your name, and why you chose it. If you do not have a magical name, either use your given name, or a name you would like to use as a magical name.

27. Inclusive Wicca

Inclusive Wicca is not for people who want to stay safe and cosy in their heteronormative cisgender worldview, pretending that oppression is not happening and that racism is a thing of the past. Being inclusive means becoming aware of others' pain and working to support the oppressed and the marginalised. It means doing some work to make your rituals inclusive and healing for everyone, and understanding your own privilege - the degree to which your reality, your worldview, is considered 'normal' and 'natural'; the degree to which you are safe from oppression, and the extent to which your right to existence is not constantly questioned and undermined.

What does an inclusive coven look like?

A lot of people seem to think that inclusive means "I've got some gay people in my coven". That is certainly welcoming – but is it inclusive? I think there is a spectrum of inclusivity – so one coven might score 100% and another might score 80% – but I think we have to accept that different people will have different ideas and priorities. However, it would avoid a lot of heartbreak all round if people stated upfront how inclusive their coven is.

An inclusive coven ticks some or all of the following boxes:[135]

Understands that diversity has a place in celebration, theology, and cosmology. This means that rituals, stories, and

---

[135] Thanks to Alder Lyncurium, Anna Hammarlund, Anya Read, Brian Paisley, Francois Schaut, Lirilin Lee, Susan Harper, for suggestions and comments on the first draft of this set of guidelines.

images of deities do not reinforce white, cisgender, heterocentric norms.

Understands that gender, gender expression, sex/gender assigned at birth, and biological characteristics are distinct (when I say distinct, I mean noticeably different, but interpermeable and with fuzzy boundaries).

Understands that you can make energy through polarity (tension of opposites), resonance (two similar people), or synergy (joining the energies of the whole group).

Understands that polarity can be made by two or more people of any gender and sexual orientation, and by two or more people of the same gender, and that polarity exists on a spectrum where Person A may be yang in relation to Person B, but yin in relation to Person C.[136]

Understands that you can make polarity with any pair of opposite qualities (e.g. morning people and evening people, cat lovers and dog lovers, tea drinkers and coffee drinkers, air signs and earth signs, fire signs and water signs).

Understands that fertility is not strictly biological and may refer to creativity (and that you do not need a male body and a female body to produce fertility on a symbolic level – e.g. when blessing crops).

Allows invocation of any gender deity onto any gender human.

Allows gender fluidity in ritual roles and does not make people stand boy/girl/boy/girl in circle.

---

[136] Thanks to Mhairi Strauss for the insight that one can be yin in relation to one person but yang in relation to another.

Does cakes and wine with reference to lover and beloved, or using two cups, or on the understanding that we all contain both 'masculine' and 'feminine' energies, or some other inclusive variation, and can be done by two people of any gender.

Respects members' genders and uses their pronouns.

Accommodates difference (e.g. neurodivergence, dyslexia, left-handedness, aphantasia[137]) and disability.

Embraces the social model of disability: the idea that disability is exacerbated and, in some cases, imposed by society's refusal to accommodate disabled people.

Is open to other cultures and ethnicities and does not insist on a genetic basis for culture (e.g. anyone can worship gods from any culture).

Is aware of the concept of systemic racism, and actively tries to avoid reinforcing racist stereotypes or engaging in microaggressions.

Tries to avoid cultural appropriation.

Is accepting of kink, polyamory, and monogamy.

Promotes consent culture.

Welcomes members of all ages (over 18) and accommodates older members' needs.

Does not automatically exclude people with mental health issues.

---

[137] Aphantasia is the name given to an inability to visualise

Accommodates different theological perspectives (animism, atheism, pantheism, polytheism, duotheism etc).

Body-positive: does not allow fat-shaming or body-shaming.

Is prepared to accommodate coven members who are less well-off (by not organising expensive social activities, or having a massive and expensive reading list, for example).

Does not insist that its members reach a specific educational level or belong to a specific socio-economic class.

Listens to the views of all the members.

Values the contributions and ideas of all the members.

Inclusive Wicca is about being inclusive towards everyone. There is not a competition over who is more oppressed, and there is no queue for liberation. We can work on small issues and large issues at the same time – I am not suggesting that all the categories mentioned in the list receive the same degree of oppression in society – they are included in the list because at some point, they have been excluded from some Wiccan circles for some reason.

Inclusive Wicca is not a new or separate tradition; it is a tendency within existing Wiccan traditions. (Though just to confuse matters, in Australia, there actually is a tradition called Inclusive Wicca, which is unconnected to the inclusive tendency – though it may have similar goals.)

But what is it that you do?

Some people have expressed confusion about what inclusive Wicca does that is different from other Gardnerian and Alexandrian Wiccans (even though there is massive variation among covens and lineages in the rest of Wicca).

But Wicca is not just about the words we use in ritual - many covens within the Gardnerian and Alexandrian communities use different words for casting the circle, calling the quarters, consecrating and so on. The point is that we are orthopraxic - we do the same actions and we use the same techniques.

Gerald Gardner gave different books of shadows to several different priestesses - consequently there is quite a lot of variation between and within the lineages descended from them.

There are also various texts available for creating sacred space. Different covens will use different versions of these within Wicca as a whole. Some covens use words based on the Key of Solomon; some use other words.

What is the same as in the rest of Wicca?

The initiation ceremonies. These are the same as what we were handed by our initiators. You might be surprised about variations between lineages in the rest of Wicca, but the basic core ceremony is the same. Some of us do same-sex initiations, but the actual ritual will be the same.

Casting the circle and calling the quarters. We use the same words and procedures that were given to us by our initiators. We do not tend to say "Lords of the Watchtowers..." but lots of covens do not do that.

Making magic. We use the same methods of making magic that other covens use.

Celebrating festivals. We celebrate the Wheel of the Year, the eight Wiccan Sabbats. (Some covens in the USA use the same words for every Sabbat; most covens in the UK create new rituals for each festival using a combination of words from their Book of Shadows and newly created words. Some covens use a story about the God and Goddess that fits the festivals; some do not.)

What is different from the rest of Wicca?

Polarity. We believe that polarity can be made by any pair of opposites.

Consecration of participants. This can vary - but we do not divide people up by gender.

Invocation: any person of any gender may invoke a deity of any gender onto another person of any gender (other than that, it is the same).

Cakes and wine. We do the same actions, with slightly different words, which emphasise that the symbolism of the chalice and athame encompasses all acts of love and pleasure.

Degree of flexibility. Many covens are prepared to flex things to accommodate differences - but how far they are prepared to flex can vary widely. In inclusive Wicca, we try to accommodate disability, gender variance, sexual orientation, other cultures, and so on.

Given the huge variation between and within lineages in Gardnerian and Alexandrian Wicca, adding a bit more variation to the mix should not be in the slightest bit controversial - but strangely, as soon as you mention including LGBT+ people, disabled people, and people of colour, it becomes controversial. I wonder why that is?

Other witchcraft traditions such as Feri and Reclaiming are often described by their practitioners as inherently queer.

Queerness is placed at the heart of these traditions, in a way that the heterocentrism of much of Wiccan practice simply fails at. Given the long and proud history of queer and gender-variant folk magic, this is a shocking state of affairs, and is part of why Wicca is often seen as playing 'respectability politics'.[138]

The Feri tradition, founded by Victor and Cora Anderson, focuses on ecstasy rather than 'fertility', according to T Thorn Coyle and Willow Moon [139].

Traditions such as the Clan of Tubal Cain, 1734, and other folkloric witchcraft traditions also appear to be much less obsessed with heterocentric practices, and much more queer-friendly, than much of Wicca. Their focus is more on the older, wilder elements of witchcraft, many of which are inherently queer.

It is rather odd that many Wiccans are so heterocentric, since there are queer elements in Wicca. These include the concept of Dryghtyn, who is seen as both male and female; the balance of light and darkness; and an emphasis on wildness; but there needs to be more emphasis on these elements, and on the folkloric roots of Wicca, and perhaps less emphasis on its roots in ceremonial magic and Christian occultism. I am not sure where the heterocentric bias of Wicca came from – unless

---

[138] This is a term originally coined to describe power dynamics in the Black civil rights movement, so I am not sure if it is right to apply it in other contexts where people replace the struggle for rights and justice with courting respectability.

[139] Willow Moon (2015), *Qwyr Magic, Part 1*. Anderson Faery Witchcraft. https://andersonfaery.org/2015/12/30/qwyr-magic-part-1-by-willow-moon/

it was from the notion that 'fertility' is something to do with heterosexual procreation.

Creating inclusive rituals

It is a useful magical and intellectual exercise to examine each segment of your ritual structure and ask yourself why you do it the way that you do. Why do we sweep the circle, consecrate it with water, salt, and incense, cast it with a sword, and so on? What is the function and symbolism of each of these actions? Can they be improved – either in the sense of making them more magically effective, more reflective of reality, or more inclusive?

Sweeping

The circle is swept to prepare the space for ritual. This was also done in mumming plays to prepare the space for the performance. Participants in the ritual should pay attention while the sweeping is happening, because it helps to clear the mind of mundane concerns and get ready for ritual.

I always sweep the circle in the same way that I would sweep the kitchen floor: sweep the whole area, sweeping the dirt into the middle and then out of the door.

The mundane concerns that get left outside the circle are things like worrying whether you got all your shopping done, or what you are going to do at work next week. Core aspects of your being, such as your sexual orientation or your gender, do not get left outside the circle.

Casting the circle

The circle creates a safe space, a filter bubble that excludes malign influences but allows in good energies. It is also a microcosm of the macrocosm, the sacred representation of the cosmos, and a container for the energies we raise within it.

Consecrating the elements

Some groups only consecrate water and salt, and not incense. This is derived from magical traditions where Water and Earth are regarded as 'feminine' elements and therefore in need of more consecration. We consecrate incense as well.

When consecrating the participants in the ritual with water/salt and incense, there are many ways of being more inclusive than having a priest consecrate all the men and a priestess consecrating all the women. You can have a person of any gender consecrating everyone; or you can use a different pair of polarities, such as introvert / extrovert, or morning person / evening person.

Calling the quarters

Some groups and traditions call the "Lords of the Watchtowers". I avoid gendering the four elements and refer to them as 'powers' (e.g. Powers of Fire). I also ask them politely to join us in the circle, rather than summoning them peremptorily to attend. This was suggested by Fred Lamond in his book *Fifty Years of Wicca*.

Raising power

This can be done in many ways – dancing, chanting, visualising, and many more. My personal favourite is making balls of energy and merging them together. Dancing in a circle makes me dizzy. You can raise power using polarity, resonance, or synergy.

Invocation

A person of any gender can invoke a deity of any gender onto another person of any gender. Deities do not necessarily have gender the same way we do; nor do they have biological sex (though we may perceive them as having it). There are many legends of deities changing gender (e.g. Vertumnus) and sex (e.g. Loki), or having more than one gender (e.g. Shiva, Ardhanadishwara).

Cakes and Wine

Cakes and wine can be consecrated by two people of any gender, using the words "as the athame is to the lover, so the cup is to the beloved".

We also use the two chalices ritual, devised by me in 1995, further developed by a group of LGBT ritual participants in 2015, and based on the Temperance card in the Tarot.

Considerations when writing a ritual or workshop

Who will be taking part? Do they have any specific requirements for accessibility or inclusion? These might include sexual orientation, gender, food allergies, disabled access, relationship with alcohol, immunological status.

Does the ritual have somewhere between 3 and 7 symbols? (Most people can hold about 5 ideas in their head at any one time, so more symbolism than that is too much.)

Does the symbolism include everyone? For example, if you are talking about rites of passage, does this include transitioning, coming out, same-sex weddings or handfastings, and the psychological aspects of coming of age ceremonies?

Have you alternated between activities that involve standing up or dancing, and activities that involve sitting or lying down?

Is there an accessible alternative to activities like kneeling or standing that some people find physically difficult?

If your ritual involves extemporising, do the participants have sufficient knowledge of the symbolism to feel comfortable?

Can the participants opt out of anything that makes them feel uncomfortable?

Accessible rituals

There are several activities that happen in Wicca and other Pagan traditions that might make our rituals inaccessible.

That does not mean we can never do those activities: it does mean being aware of the needs of participants, preferably by asking them in advance what their needs are.

The great news is that an activity or resource that is accessible is better for everyone, because everyone has some needs that are not met by inaccessible resources. I am a web developer and I specialize in user experience, which brings together usability and accessibility requirements with what happens offline to create a seamless and satisfying experience.

I am not disabled, but I get really dizzy from circle dancing (partly because I have had labyrinthitis), so it is not a good way for me to raise energy in circle. There are various conditions which might make it difficult for people to circle dance. A great alternative way to raise energy is to make energy balls: draw in energy from your surroundings, direct it down your arms and into your hands, and shape it into a ball, which you can then merge with the energy balls of everyone in the circle, and send off to its intended recipient.

Be careful with hugging and kissing, as some people can experience physical pain from physical contact. Always seek consent before going in for a hug and be prepared to accept no for an answer.

If your ritual involves kneeling, this can cause cramps for a lot of people, and is just impossible for people with reduced mobility (whether this is due to age or other factors). There are other ways to express reverence, such as hand gestures.

If you work out of doors, a ritual site that is deep in the woods may not be accessible to wheelchair users. Check out the route beforehand, especially footbridges and stiles.

If your tradition requires people to copy out your Book of Shadows by hand, consider that this is really difficult for some people, either because of dyslexia (which makes it hard to remember the sentence you have just read on one page in order to copy it onto another), or because of mobility issues. Consider allowing people to make an audio recording of the text instead, or to transcribe the text from an audio version (if they are blind, visually impaired, or severely dyslexic).

Even if you share all your ritual scripts electronically, not everyone can use shared drives online or email, so you may need to find other ways to help them access resources.

If you work skyclad, consider that some people cannot retain heat in their bodies for various reasons and may find working outdoors too difficult without thermal gear. According to some accounts, witches used to rub themselves with grease to keep the cold out (also handy if you were apprehended by the law, as you could literally slip out of their grasp).

Be careful with incense and flowers, as some people are allergic to specific perfumes and flowers. I am allergic to star lilies (they give me a very bad headache). I call them *fleurs du mal*.

Various people have food intolerances and allergies: coeliacs cannot eat gluten, and some people are allergic to peanuts. If someone in your coven has a food allergy, it could be serious. It is no good just asking them to bring stuff they can eat: the aim of a coven feast is to share food together, so if there is something in the feast that is potentially poisonous, that is a bit antisocial.

Recovering alcoholics may need accommodation around alcoholic drinks. If you have alcohol in your chalice, they can just kiss the cup as it passes, or you could use a non-alcoholic alternative. A lot of people use alcohol because it seems somehow alive, but you could use kombucha, kvass (both of which have a very low or zero alcohol content – check the label), or lassi (zero alcohol content) instead.

Standing for long periods of time may be difficult for a lot of people, so it is a good idea to alternate different types of activity in the circle. When doing meditation or visualization, I always invite people to sit, stand, or lie down according to their preference.

In case of difficulty or emergencies, it is a good idea to have a back-up plan. What are you going to do if someone is deeply psychologically distressed by the content of your ritual? What will you do if someone has a sneezing or coughing fit in the middle of your ritual? Do you have antihistamine tablets on hand in case someone is allergic to your cats, flowers, or incense?

Obviously, if someone has a condition that they know about, it behoves them to inform you and make sure they have their inhaler, epi-pen, meds, or whatever with them, and that you know what to do if someone has an epileptic seizure.

Some disabilities are not visible or obvious, and conditions can change over time, so it is always worth checking with people about mobility issues, specific learning difficulties, and other conditions. Not all disabled people use wheelchairs, either.

In our coven, we have a quick round of updates from everyone to say what is happening in their lives, so we all know how everyone feels. This means everyone gets to hear everyone else's news, and it gets the energy moving in a circle. This would also be a good time for people to give updates on their condition, if they wish or need to.

It is also worth mentioning what not to say to disabled people and people with chronic illnesses. Do not post pictures of disabled competitors in the Olympics with the implication that people can "overcome" their condition, or glurge (probably untrue, excessively sentimental stories) about disabled kids, also known as disability porn or inspiration porn. Do not say "oh but your disability means your other senses magically make up for the missing one". Do not say "have you tried turmeric / lemon-juice / meditation / hanging out in Nature?" (or whatever the latest snake-oil is this week). If the thing were effective, they would be using it.

Do not assume that you know better than they do how to manage their condition.

Above all, everyone appreciates having as much autonomy and self-determination as possible, so the more information you can give people about what is going to happen in your ritual, and the more you make getting informed consent a core value of your group, the more autonomy and sovereignty your members will have. If in doubt, ask. It is better to ask than to assume that you know.

Tips for ritual writing

Beginning the process of writing a ritual can be scary. Staring at a blank screen or sheet of paper can be daunting. Here are a few tips to get started.

Get yourself in the mood. If you are writing a ritual for a festival, read and/or listen to stories, songs, podcasts, poems, articles, other rituals about or relating to the festival. If your ritual theme is not festival-related, read around the theme in the same way.

What is the theme of your ritual? Other than the festival itself, what is the main idea you want to get across? For example, Beltane can be about love in all its forms, or it can be about creativity. Imbolc can be about the first intimations of spring (in the UK anyway, where there are snowdrops coming up then); in Canada the land is still very much in the grip of winter, so the ritual could be about maintaining the fire on the hearth, like the perpetual flame of Brighid.

List some key symbols for your ritual. Somewhere between 3 and 7 is about right; more than that, and the ritual will probably be too complicated. How will the symbols be represented in the ritual?

How many speaking parts do you need? Can you double them up or split them up into more parts if you get more or fewer people than you expected?

It does not have to rhyme. Good prose is always better than bad rhyme. If you absolutely have to make it rhyme (and my advice is, don't), then use a decent metre, like iambic pentameter, and don't force the rhymes by changing the word order in the sentences or putting in phrases that don't fit.

For example, try to avoid writing poetry like this:

> 'Twas in the year of 1869, and on the 19th of November,
> Which the people in Southern Germany will long remember,
> The great rain-storm which for twenty hours did pour down,
> That the rivers were overflowed and petty streams all around.
>
> — from *Saving a Train* by William McGonagall

I do, however, tend to put line breaks in where there are natural pauses in the prose, because if people are reading from the script, it makes it easier to read it well.

The one exception to the "don't make it rhyme" rule is spells and energy-raising chants. Because these go straight to the part of your brain that responds to rhythm and symbols and other non-verbal cues, and that's most likely the part of your brain that produces magic, a bit of rhythm and rhyme is a good thing here. It is not necessary – other poetic tools are also useful, like assonance, alliteration, and rhythm – but provided the rhymes are not cheesy or forced, it can be powerful.

Remember to think about practical considerations. If you have your participants holding too many things at a time (like two candles at once, or a candle and a wand), things can get difficult. It is also important to consider health and safety.

Put a list of the props you will need, including ritual tools, candles, incense, etc, at the top of the script. Add a list of the characters who appear in your script.

Make sure there is something for everyone. Make sure that everyone who wants a part in the ritual gets to participate (this mainly applies to small group rituals rather than large public ones). If you have a part of the ritual where someone is giving an oracle to individuals, make sure there's something for the other participants to do, whether it's a chant, or a circle dance, or making something, or drawing mandalas, or whatever: something to keep the energy of the ritual flowing.

Once you have written your ritual, read it aloud. Check for unfamiliar words that people might not know how to pronounce. Make sure you know how to pronounce them (hint: *deosil* is pronounced "jeshl", not "day-o-sil"). Check that you have created something that can be read easily. I once made the mistake of splicing together some 18th and 19th century poems for a ritual. It did not work.

It is good to write the lines for invoking the deity as part of your script; but not so good to write lines for the deity to speak. Let the deity speak through the invoked-on person. If nothing happens, they can just cross their arms to indicate that no words came through.

Allow for extemporization. Encourage people to extemporize rather than scripting the quarter calls. It is a good idea to start and finish your quarter call with the same words each time, to provide a frame and a sense of continuity.

Discussion

Are there any areas of your coven practice that are not inclusive? Can they be modified?

If you are uncomfortable with any aspect of inclusive practice, can you identify the source of your discomfort?

How does your group feel about same-sex initiation?

Explore and discuss the genders of people in your group, and how that relates to the roles they adopt in circle.

Exercises

Invoke a deity of another gender than yourself. How does it feel?

Working in pairs of any gender combination, get one partner to practice sending energy, and the other to practice receiving it. After a few minutes, switch around so that the one sending is now receiving. Get people to identify whether they were more comfortable sending or receiving, or whether they were equally comfortable with both. Does this have anything to do with gender?

Practice making polarity with pairs of opposites such as morning people and evening people, tea drinkers and coffee drinkers, people who like Marmite and people who like chocolate, people who love winter and people who love summer, extroverts and introverts, people of different astrological signs, elements, and triplicities.

Practice making resonance between people who are similar to each other (not necessarily because of gender, but because of any factor). How does the energy produced by resonance differ from energy produced by polarity?

Practice making synergy, with the whole group pooling their energies together. One way to do this is to place a cauldron in the centre of the circle and have everyone pour their energies into it. Another way is to imagine a spindle or bobbin in the centre of the circle and imagine everyone winding a thread of energy onto the bobbin.

Conclusion

Witchcraft is a religion that is rooted in the body and the interface between physical and spiritual reality. It regards the deities and spirits as immanent in Nature, and most witches believe that we can draw magical energy from our surroundings, transmuting them within the alchemical still of our own bodies. As such, both the inner work (what happens in the psyche during ritual, and the processes of visualisation and energy working that are part of ritual and magic) and embodied spirituality are key components of witchcraft.

The practices of ritual and magic in witchcraft are deeply intertwined. It is often hard to say where ritual ends and magic begins. Is the practice of invoking a deity a magical act, a religious act, or both? According to Ronald Hutton, the practices of witchcraft are part of the Western Mystery Tradition, which is ultimately derived from Egyptian magico-religious practices. The Egyptians did not make a distinction between religion and magic. This distinction comes from other religious traditions.[140]

If witchcraft is to survive and flourish, it needs to do several things. It needs to develop a theory of magic, the gods, the universe, and the place of humans and other animals in the cosmos. This theory of magic needs to include an understanding of gender and sexual diversity (including LGBTQIA+ people, kink, polyamory, and how these can produce magical energy). It needs to develop a theology and ethics of the body and relationships. It needs to live up to its promise of being a liberatory and transformative movement

---

[140] Ronald Hutton, talk at Witchfest 2016, Brighton.

for the Earth and all beings who live on this beautiful planet. Without a theory and a theology underpinning our practice, we tend to fall back on biases and assumptions from the surrounding culture, which does not necessarily have our best interests at heart.

The practice of initiatory witchcraft is aimed at the transformation of the psyche, the person, their sense of self-worth, their relationships to other people and to Nature. Most commentators agree that Wicca is about attuning ourselves to Nature. Feri Tradition practitioners often state that theirs is a religion of ecstasy, but it seems also to be a religion of self-transformation and empowerment. Feri and Reclaiming witches are also politically engaged and seek to promote social and environmental justice.

If we are serious about being attuned to Nature and promoting social justice, then focusing on the inner work of ritual, and developing embodied spirituality, will be very useful tools in our magical toolbox.

The inner work will help to deepen our experience of ritual and facilitate the transformation of the psyche. Embodied spirituality will help to heal our dysfunctional relationships with our bodies, our sexuality, other people, and the world around us. The practice of our craft will be enriched by these practices, and our magical understanding will be expanded by having an inclusive theoretical underpinning that does not rely on unrealistic models of gender and sexuality.

The world does not consist of a series of binary dichotomies, but rather of a multiplicity of dyads, triads, spectra, and networks. This complexity cannot be reduced to either/or binaries, and it is dangerous to do so, because we risk othering and excluding large groups of people, either by labelling them as bad, or because they do not fit neatly into a binary worldview.

Ultimately, the inner work of witchcraft consists in making connections with the other, the strange, the preternatural, and the mysterious world of the unconscious. In the process of developing these connections, we move away from a binary worldview, and come to appreciate the glorious complexity of Nature, and the benefits of diversity.

Further Reading

Chapter 1

Christine Hoff Kraemer, *Seeking the Mystery: An Introduction to Pagan Theologies*

Barry Patterson, *The Art of Conversation with the Genius Loci*

Brian Bates, *The Way of Wyrd*

Chapter 5

Victoria Schmidt, *45 Master Characters: Mythic Models for Creating Original Characters*. ISBN: 1582970696

C G Jung, *Four Archetypes: Mother, Rebirth, Spirit, Trickster*. ISBN: 0415304415

Joseph Campbell, *The Hero with a Thousand Faces*. ISBN: 0586085718

John Suler's *Teaching Clinical Psychology: In-class exercises.* http://truecenterpublishing.com/tcp/inclassex.html [accessed 24-11-2015]

Martin Laird (2006), *Into the Silent Land: A Guide to the Christian Practice of Contemplation*, Oxford University Press. https://books.google.co.uk/books?isbn=0199779430

Martin Laird (2011), *A Sunlit Absence: Silence, Awareness, and Contemplation*, Oxford University Press. https://books.google.co.uk/books?isbn=0195378725

Chapter 8

Yvonne Aburrow (2000), *The Magical Lore of Animals*, Capall Bann Publishing.

Yvonne Aburrow (2012), *A little book of serpents*, Birdberry Books.

Yvonne Aburrow (1994), *Auguries and Omens: the magical lore of birds*, Capall Bann Publishing.

Yvonne Aburrow (1994), *The Sacred Grove: mysteries of the forest*, Capall Bann Publishing.

Yvonne Aburrow (1993), *The Enchanted Forest: the magical lore of trees*, Capall Bann Publishing.

Randy P Conner et al, eds. (1997), *Cassell's Encyclopedia of Queer Myth, Symbol and Spirit: Gay, Lesbian, Bisexual and Transgender Lore*, Cassell.

J C Cooper (1979), *An Illustrated Encyclopaedia of Traditional Symbols*, Thames & Hudson.

T Thorn Coyle (2005), *Evolutionary Witchcraft*, Tarcher Perigee.

Katie Gerrard (2009), *Odin's Gateways: A Practical Guide to the Wisdom of the Runes, Through Galdr, Sigils and Casting*, Avalonia Books.

Nigel Pennick (1989), *Practical Magic in the Northern Tradition*, Aquarian Press.

Reclaiming Quarterly, http://www.reclaimingquarterly.org/archives/

Anderson Faery witchcraft, https://andersonfaery.org/

Chapter 10

Deborah Blake (2014), *The Witch's Broom: The Craft, Lore & Magick of Broomsticks* (The Witch's Tools Series), Llewellyn Publications.

Robert Cochrane with Evan John Jones, *The Robert Cochrane Letters*. Edited by Michael Howard. Capall Bann Publishing.

Gemma Gary, *Traditional Witchcraft; A Cornish Book of Ways*. Troy Books Publishing

Evan John Jones and Robert Cochrane, *The Roebuck in the Thicket: An anthology of The Robert Cochrane Tradition* Edited by Michael Howard. Capall Bann Publishing.

Evan John Jones and Doreen Valiente, *Witchcraft; A Tradition Renewed*. Robert Hale Publishing.

Alferian Gwydion MacLir (2015), *The Witch's Wand: The Craft, Lore, and Magick of Wands & Staffs (The Witch's Tools Series)*, Llewellyn Publications.

Jason Mankey (2016), *The Witch's Athame: The Craft, Lore & Magick of Ritual Blades (The Witch's Tools Series)*, Llewellyn Publications

Chapter 12

Further reading on consent

Christine Hoff Kraemer & Yvonne Aburrow, editors (2015), *Pagan Consent Culture: Building Communities of Empathy and Autonomy*. Asphodel Press.

http://www.paganconsentculture.com/ - website of resources to accompany the above book

http://www.consentiseverything.com/ - Consent and Tea

Further reading on groups

Patti Wiginton, *How to find a coven*, http://paganwiccan.about.com/od/howtofindacoven/ht/Find_Coven.htm

Phil Hine (1998), *Approaching groups*, http://www.philhine.org.uk/writings/gp_appgrps.html

Patti Wiginton, *Warning Signs in Prospective Covens*, http://paganwiccan.about.com/od/wiccanandpaganrituals/a/Warning_Signs.htm

Patti Wiginton, *Should I Join a Coven I Found Online?* http://paganwiccan.about.com/od/wiccanandpaganrituals/a/Internet_Safety.htm

Patti Wiginton, *Are you an older newbie Pagan?* http://paganwiccan.about.com/od/PaganCommunity/a/Older-Adults-New-To-Paganism.htm

Léon van Gulik (2012), "Cleanliness is Next to Godliness, But Oaths are for Horses: Antecedents and Consequences of the Institutionalization of Secrecy in Initiatory Wicca", *Pomegranate, 14.1.* [accessed 2020-08-06]. Available from: www.academia.edu/3074898/

Further reading on relationships

Morning Glory Zell (1990), *A Bouquet of Lovers: Strategies for Responsible Open Relationships*, http://www.patheos.com/Resources/Additional-Resources/Bouquet-of-Lovers

Franklin Veaux, Eve Rickert (2014), *More Than Two: A Practical Guide to Ethical Polyamory*. Thorntree Press.

Dossie Easton and Janet Hardy (1997), *The Ethical Slut: A Guide to Infinite Sexual Possibilities*. Greenery Press

Raven Kaldera (2005), Pagan Polyamory: Becoming a Tribe of Hearts

Chapter 14

Lee Harrington (2016), *Sacred Kink: The Eightfold Paths of BDSM and Beyond*, Mystic Productions Press.

Thista Minai (2020), *Suffering For Spirit: Empowerment Through Ordeal*, Ellhorn Press.

Mark Thompson, *LeatherFolk: Radical Sex, People, Politics and Practice*.

Raven Kaldera (2006), *Dark Moon Rising: Pagan BDSM & the Ordeal Path*

Raven Kaldera (2010), *Double Edge: The Intersection of Transgender and BDSM*

Chapter 16

Sabina Magliocco (2001), *Neo-Pagan Sacred Art and Altars: Making Things Whole*. University Press of Mississippi. http://www.upress.state.ms.us/books/521

Sabina Magliocco (2004), *Witching Culture: Folklore and Neopaganism in America*.

Chapter 24

Storytelling Scotland - website with resources and links to traditional storytellers. http://www.tracscotland.org/tracs/storytelling

The Society for Storytelling - promotes storytelling as an art form. http://www.sfs.org.uk/

Robertson Davies (1960), *A Voice from the Attic: Essays on the Art of Reading*.

Three Acres and a Cow, A History of Land Rights and Protest in Folk Song and Story: http://threeacresandacow.co.uk/

Bruno Bettelheim (1991), *The Uses of Enchantment: The Meaning and Importance of Fairy Tales.* Penguin Psychology.

Stephen Fry (2005), *The Ode Less Travelled: Unlocking the Poet Within.*

James Gunn and Matthew Candelaria (eds, 2004), *Speculations on Speculation: Theories of Science Fiction.* Scarecrow Press.

Clarissa Pinkola-Estes (2008), *Women Who Run with the Wolves: Contacting the Power of the Wild Woman.* Rider Books.

Sue Woolley (2016), *Gems for the Journey: one Unitarian Pilgrim's Progress.* UCA.

Jack Zipes (1979), *Breaking the Magic Spell: Radical Theories of Folk and Fairy Tales.*

Jack Zipes (1985), *Fairy Tales and the Art of Subversion: The Classical Genre for Children and the Process of Civilization.*

Jack Zipes (1987 / 1992 / 2002), *The Complete Fairy Tales of Brothers Grimm.*

Jack Zipes (1989), *Beauties, Beasts and Enchantments: Classic French Fairy Tales.*

Jack Zipes (1994), *Fairy Tale As Myth, Myth As Fairy Tale.*

Jack Zipes (1995), *Creative Storytelling: Building Community/Changing Lives.*

Jack Zipes (1997), *Happily Ever After: Fairy Tales, Children and the Culture Industry.*

Jack Zipes (2000), *Sticks and Stones: The Troublesome Success of Children's Literature from Slovenly Peter to Harry Potter.*

Jack Zipes (2002/3), *The Brothers Grimm: From Enchanted Forests to the Modern World.*

Jack Zipes (2004), *Speaking Out: Storytelling and Creative Drama for Children.*

Jack Zipes (2006), *Why Fairy Tales Stick: The Evolution and Relevance of a Genre.*

Jack Zipes (2011), *The Enchanted Screen: The Unknown History of Fairy-Tale Films.*

Jack Zipes (2011), *Literature and Literary Theory: Fairy Tales and the Art of Subversion.*

Jack Zipes (2012), *The Irresistible Fairy Tale: The Cultural and Social History of a Genre.*

Chapter 27

Yvonne Aburrow (2014), *All Acts of Love and Pleasure: inclusive Wicca.* Avalonia Books.

The inclusive Wicca website at www.inclusivewicca.org

Jo Green (2016), *Queer Paganism: a spirituality that embraces all identities.*

Thista Minai (2017), *Casting a Queer Circle: Non-Binary Witchcraft.*

Yvonne Aburrow (2020), *The Night Journey: Witchcraft as Transformation.*

Jenny Blain (2002), *Nine Worlds of Seid-Magic: Ecstasy and Neo-Shamanism in North European Paganism.*

Randy P Conner, *Blossom of Bone – Reclaiming the Connections Between Homoeroticism and the Sacred*

Randy P. Conner, *Cassell's Encyclopedia of Queer Myth, Symbol and Spirit: Gay, Lesbian, Bisexual and Transgendered Lore.*

Christian de la Huerta, *Coming Out Spiritually: The Next Step.*

Misha Magdalene, *Outside the Charmed Circle: exploring gender and sexuality in magical practice.*

Raven Kaldera (2008), *Hermaphrodeities.*

Christopher Penczak, *Gay Witchcraft: Empowering the Tribe*

Gina Pond, *Gender And Transgender In Modern Paganism*

Tomás Prower, *Queer Magic: LGBT+ Spirituality and Culture from Around the World.*

Mark Thomson, *Gay Body: A Journey Through Shadow To Self*

Mark Thompson, *Gay Soul*

Mark Thompson, *Gay Spirit: Myth and Meaning.*

Mark Thompson, *The Fire in Moonlight: Stories from the Radical Faeries.*

Julian Vayne and Steve Dee, *Chaos Craft.*

Thanks

Thanks to everyone whose conversations led me to a deeper understanding of the inner work.

Thanks to my initiators, without whom I would not have embarked on this journey.

Thanks to Julie Belham-Payne and Emlyn Price of the Doreen Valiente Foundation for publishing the new, revised, and expanded edition of these books.

Thanks to Dalia Heiser, Jake Leo, Julie Belham-Payne, Emlyn Price, Darren Jones, Helix, Vernon Marshall, Jim Blair, Sarah Tinker, Sue Woolley, Linda Haggerstone, Alder Lyncurium, Brian Paisley, Kumar Devadasan, Mhairi Strauss, Anna Hammarlund, Anya Read, Brian Paisley, Francois Schaut, Lirilin Lee, Susan Harper, for sharing ideas and techniques.

Thanks to Geraldine Beskin, Tim Landry, Misha Magdalene, Lydia Knox, Sabina Magliocco, Paul Pearson, Julia Phillips, Lucya Starza, and Morgana Sythove for reviews and feedback. Special thanks to Thista Minai for expert, detailed feedback, and their wonderful foreword.

And thanks to my beloved Bob, the members of my coven, and the members of the Inclusive Wicca Discussion Group, for your encouragement and enthusiasm.

Any errors or omissions in the text are mine.

Yvonne Aburrow

Dark Mirror: The Inner Work of Witchcraft

Yvonne Aburrow

www.ingramcontent.com/pod-product-compliance
Lightning Source LLC
Chambersburg PA
CBHW070526090426
42735CB00013B/2874